Supplier Certification II:

Handbook for Achieving Excellence through Continuous Improvement

Supplier Certification II:

Handbook
for Achieving Excellence
through
Continuous Improvement

PETER L. GRIECO, JR.

PT PUBLICATIONS, INC.
4360 NORTH LAKE BLVD.
PALM BEACH GARDENS, FL 33410

First Printing — November 1988
Second Printing — August 1990
Third Printing — July 1992
Fourth Printing — April 1993

Library of Congress Cataloging in Publication Data

Grieco, Peter L., Jr, 1942-
  Supplier Certification II: handbook for achieving excellence
through continuous improvement/Peter L. Grieco, Jr.
    p. cm.
  Includes bibliographical references and index.
  ISBN 0-945456-08-5
  1. Industrial procurement — Quality control — handbooks,
manuals, etc. I. Title.
HD39.5.G75 1992
658.7'2—dc20   92-5830
              CIP

Copyright © 1993 by PT Publications, Inc.

Printed in the United States of America

All rights reserved. This book or any parts thereof
may not be reproduced in any form without permission of the publisher.

TABLE OF CONTENTS

PREFACE

We believe in practicing what we preach at Professionals for Technology (Pro-Tech). In order to constantly update this book which has become an industry standard, we instruct our printer to print on a frequent schedule. Our first two printings sold at a brisk enough pace that it was not necessary to make any significant updates. By the time of our third printing, however, we wanted to add a great deal of timely material. We added so much, in fact, that the book went from approximately 220 pages to over 525 pages. That's more than double the size of the first edition.

With all this significant new material, we decided to call the book **Supplier Certification II** in order to demonstrate that the field was in constant flux. Without the help of Pro-Tech colleagues Mike Termini, Mel Pilachowski and Wayne Douchkoff to help me pull together the case studies, examples and anecdotes published in this edition, I would not have been able to cover the field so thoroughly.

Since the cycle time between the third and fourth printing was so short, there are no significant changes in this fourth printing. We are, however, presently engaged in looking for case studies and successful implementations from World Class companies to include in our next revision—**Supplier Certification III:** *Handbook for Achieving Excellence through Continuous Improvement.*

With almost 20,000 copies sold of our Supplier Certification title and over 500 in-house seminars conducted at companies (small, medium and Fortune 500), we saw that it was necessary to produce a Video Education series to get the word out. The videotapes cover all the essential points of our books and seminars and we are proud to say that many people have found the videotape series to be beneficial when implementing their own Supplier Certification programs.

For those of you who are unfamiliar with Supplier Certification and for those of you who have already been part of a program, let's start with a working definition and some basic principles upon which we can all agree.

Supplier Certification is necessary and it will work if we can remember one simple rule: We are all suppliers. If we fail to recognize that a Supplier Certification program has both external and internal aspects, then we will never be able to meet the challenge of domestic and global competition. We will never be able to eliminate the causes of wasted time, money and labor, nor destroy the "Ubiquitous RE-"—rework, repair, reject, refuse— which erodes productivity and profits.

Traditionally, we think of suppliers as companies which deliver products to our plants. They are vendors; they sell their product to us. But, when we think of a supplier as only a vendor, we see only one part of the supply network. There are many other parts as well which many programs neglect. For example, once the product is in our plant, we ship it from department to department, from work station to work station. All these deliveries are also part of the supply network. Finally, once we have manufactured a final product from the various parts and subassemblies shipped to and within our plant, we then supply our customers. A successful

Supplier Certification program takes all of these shipments and deliveries into account.

A successful program relies upon the just-in-time delivery of zero-defect material, parts, subassemblies and finished products throughout the supply network. This puts a premium on **making it right the first time**. Thus, the emphasis is on defect prevention, rather than routine inspection. Consequently, the burden of proof will not rest upon Inspectors, but on the makers or suppliers of a part. Quality cannot be inspected into a part; it must be there already.

One other piece must also be in place before success can be assured. That piece is top management's commitment to work toward the levels of excellence demanded by Supplier Certification in our own plants. Since many American manufacturers see Supplier Certification as a program only for vendors, top management becomes either surprised or disillusioned by the changes which become necessary in their plants. If we can convince top management to see Supplier Certification as something more than a program imposed upon outside vendors, then there is a real chance to achieve the same levels of quality inside our plants as we demand from our outside suppliers. To accomplish this, however, means that we must also see our outside suppliers not as victims, but as partners in a struggle for excellence which will benefit both.

Creation of Supplier Partnerships

We need to develop a close relationship with suppliers which is based upon trust and communication. Suppliers will become a part of our organization for the life of the part and the life of the company. These are not "feel-good" statements. As we work together in a partnership to improve quality, we will inevitably find that prices and costs go down for both us and our outside suppliers. Both of us will subscribe to the same specific goals:

- Lower the total cost.
- Strive for smaller lots and frequent deliveries.
- Implement a quality control module.

Quality is the number one issue. Without defect-free parts coming into and being moved around our factories, there is no chance for us to achieve higher levels of efficiency and productivity.

The Certification Process

In other words, we are trying to achieve quality at the source. But how do we get that quality? By entering into a partnership with a supplier which is based on trust and cooperation. The next question is: How do we get trust, cooperation, and quality from a supplier? The answer is Supplier Certification. We see this as a program in which you can think of yourself as a scientist. You gather facts, make a hypothesis, run your experiment, and use the results to reformulate your hypothesis. The phases in Supplier Certification are similar. Here, too, you gather facts about a supplier, you design quality improvement processes, you put them into practice, and then you audit and maintain the process based on the results which you are continuously gathering and interpreting.

In this program, then, you can think of yourself as a medical researcher who takes a patient and not only finds a cure, but finds means for the patient's continued well-being. You can think of this process as the compilation of a medical history, the implementation of a nourishing diet and a schedule of exercise, and the institution of regular check-ups. Your goal is to develop a healthy supplier, one which will act according to the regimen of TQC and JIT (Just-In-Time).

Supplier Certification is not easy. It requires effort and time. Once completed, it allows for the smooth flow of material, cooperation, communication and, most of all, increased productivity. Quality is the key word — quality of products, information, delivery and counts. Supplier Certification can put you and your suppliers at the leading edge.

One last word. We often speak of ideal situations as though nothing less than their attainment is satisfactory. We won't back down from that demand which we think all American manufacturing companies should place upon themselves. If you have achieved a 95 percent quality level, strive for 98 percent. When you reach that level, go for 99 percent. Once there, go for 99.8 percent. There is no stopping in Supplier Certification, no resting on your laurels. It is a commitment to the elimination of all waste in your company.

Peter L. Grieco, Jr.

ACKNOWLEDGEMENTS

We have educated over 50,000 people and 200 companies since the first edition of this book. Now in its third edition, it continues to be one of our most important education and training tools for Supplier Certification. And we have all of these people plus our numerous clients to thank for their successful implementations of the Continuous Improvement Process. It is through our association with these professionals in this country and throughout the world that we have been able to witness the achievement of success. Many of their stories are in this book. We would also like to thank all those companies who shared their successes with us, but whose stories we did not have the room or time to include. They are as important to us as those whose stories were used.

We would like to take this opportunity to thank our consulting staff, Mel Pilachowski, Wayne Douchkoff, Tom Petroski, Mike Termini and Joe Becker for their examples, anecdotes and suggestions included in this book.

Another pillar of support has been provided by our capable office staff and by Kevin, Leslie, Samra and Judi. In addition, we would like to thank Dick Maccabe who drew the illustrations which so aptly interpret the text.

As always, we would like to express our appreciation to Steven Marks for his editorial assistance in helping us prepare our fourth printing of a series which covers today's most urgent quality and manufacturing problems. We hope that your reading will be as pleasurable as our efforts in preparing this book.

To Mary

who provides
the strength,
love and peace
which has brought
stability and
happiness
to my life

Peter

WHY SUPPLIER CERTIFICATION?

========== 1

Supplier or Vendor Certification is commonly misperceived as a program in which external suppliers guarantee the on-time delivery of zero-defect parts to your plant. In other words, Supplier Certification is a one-way street where you get to pick the direction the traffic takes and the speed at which it travels. The problem with this perception is that it does not allow your own organization to see the internal routes taken by material within your environment. It is highly probable that if an organization views Supplier Certification as a one-way street, then it will soon find itself in the midst of a colossal traffic jam which could threaten the existence and certainly the company's vitality.

As the introductory videotape in our VideoEducation Series, *Supplier Certification: The Path to Excellence*, shows, Supplier Certification is both an *internal* and *external* program. We view a company with its divisions, plants and departments as part of the supplier base. A single part which moves from one operation to a another has gone through two supply operations. If you demand that a part shipped by an outside supplier to a machining area be free of defects and on-time, then why would you expect any less when it moves from one internal operation to another?

A successful Supplier Certification program demands that the internal flow of material be as orderly as the flow from external suppliers. What is true for the supplier side is also true for the customer side to which you supply finished items. You will be required to view yourself as a certified supplier (on-time delivery of quality products in the quantity needed) to internal departments and customers.

Let's define the supplier/customer as the shipment of product from one function to another. This can best be shown as a diagram:

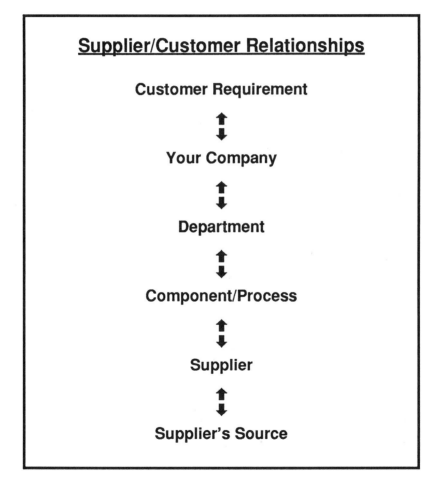

Another view of the supplier/customer relationship looks like this:

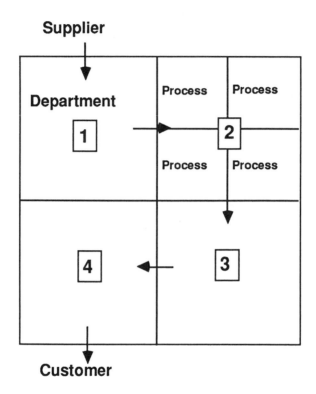

When starting to implement a Supplier Certification program, look at both internal and external sourcing. Internally, this will mean reducing the number of production operations, minimizing queues, reducing set-up times, simplifying product design, evolving toward ship-to-WIP (work-in-process) and working toward lot sizes of one. These improvements eliminate waste and simplify material flow, thus reducing the number and complexity of supply movements.

Externally, a look at sourcing primarily means eliminating the attitude that a large number of suppliers brings security in the form of a consistent flow of material. In reality, that approach is far from the truth. You end up with a supplier network which is out of control and likely to result in logistical nightmares. Shipments from suppliers either come too early or too late and all too often do not adhere to specifications. Since we believe that suppliers won't deliver what we want, we build a system where there are backup suppliers to those who fail for one reason or another. Unfortunately, we perpetuate the problem. Where is the guarantee that the backup suppliers will deliver quality components on time? Now, instead of dealing with one supplier for a particular commodity, we have several, all of whom are equally capable of missing delivery dates, shipping out of specification components or delivering incorrect quantities.

On a recent fact-finding tour of Japan, we asked a production worker what he would do if the single supplier of a part failed to deliver a good product on-time. As politely as possible, he answered: "We aren't allowed to think that way." "Why?" we wanted to know. "Our suppliers are all certified" was his reply.

With a reduced base of certified suppliers, there are no early or late shipments or defective parts. A certified supplier delivers quality products on-time because the operations of the company are under control. The supplier has done for his or her company what you have done for yours. You both have processes under control.

TIMING OF SUPPLIER CERTIFICATION

Supplier Certification is a process which can take years to complete. We recommend that you do not address all your suppliers at one time and tell them to get their processes under control and then start delivering zero-defect products as you need them. First of all, not all suppliers are capable of this level of excellence. Certainly, you will begin to work first with suppliers who show a commitment and capability of working with you as a partner in reaching a level of sustained performance. Second, not every part is equally critical to your company. We suggest using Pareto's law to uncover the 20% of your suppliers which account for 80% of the part numbers. Finding the suppliers who are capable of and committed to working with you in a Supplier Certification program has added value. These suppliers will also quickly demonstrate the effectiveness of the program and have the most visible results. Success with them will induce other suppliers to match their results.

These results, however, are difficult to obtain if we view Supplier Certification as a one-way street. It is a two-way street where information about product design, processes and trust travels in both directions. A two-way street raises suppliers from the level of victim to the level of partner. And partners help each other. They share information, eliminate waste and thus reduce total costs together. Shared information will lead the way to long-term agreements between a supplier and a customer.

QUALITY AND THE COMPETITIVE EDGE

Supplier Certification is built upon the road bed of total quality at each level of the company. The two most important traits you want in a supplier are quality and reliability. Without quality as a way of life, or as a part of the company culture, the two-way street will become riddled with potholes which nobody will be inclined to fix. Quality means never "fixing" or reworking something. It must be built into the product and into all stages of the manufacturing process. Quality focuses on the operator, the process and the product, not on inspection.

Quality is of vital importance to Supplier Certification simply because a defective product or process stops production lines. In a Supplier Certification environment, both process and inventories are brought to a level where "safety" margins are reduced to the lowest possible level. If a shipment arrives in which two out of every 100 are rejected, then a problem exists. Since safety stock doesn't exist, even reworking the parts will affect operations. The time normally spent sorting or reworking components steals time away from operations and throws off the entire production process. Quality is the *oil* which makes the precision components of the Supplier Certification machine function smoothly and in perfect sequence.

Quality means higher profits because it eliminates waste in manufacturing. In short, quality reduces the total cost of a product since it demands that we "do it right the first time" as we pointed out in our book, **MADE IN AMERICA: The Total Business Concept** (PT Publications, Inc., Palm Beach Gardens, FL). Inventory costs money; lack of a preventive maintenance program costs money; late deliveries cost money; engineering costs money; and so on. The point is that when we add up each element of these costs, we will find the sum to be a considerable percentage of product cost. That number is either subtracted from profits or added to the price of a product. Either way, it will make us less competitive.

Quality, then, is the absence of waste. The absence of waste reduces total costs which increases profits as we discussed in our second book, **JUST-IN-TIME PURCHASING: In Pursuit of Excellence** (PT Publications, Inc., Palm Beach Gardens, FL). Over the years, we have looked at the profit equation in the opposite way:

$$\text{Profit} = \text{Price} - \text{Costs}$$

As costs went up, we raised prices to maintain profit levels. From a quality viewpoint (where waste is eliminated), however, the equation looks like this:

$$\text{Price} = \text{Profit} + \text{Costs}$$

In order to maintain profit levels and a competitive price, we need to reduce costs and eliminate waste as defined in all of our books.

Waste is:

Anything other than the absolute minimum level of *material, machines* and *manpower* required to make the product.

Put another way, this definition says that anything or any operation which does not add value to the product is waste. It is obvious that if we eliminate waste, we will increase profits and improve our competitive position. We must streamline our operations in order to exist in a "stockless" environment. To do so, we must first eliminate the problems associated with waste, such as:

Scrap
Supplier Delinquencies
Purchase lead-times
Change Orders — Purchasing and Engineering
Long set-ups
Machine Downtime
Equipment Imbalances
Inspection Backlog
Paperwork Backlog
Absenteeism

How do we tackle these items? They have existed in our companies for a long time. The cost of quality consists of three categories — Appraisal Costs, Failure Costs and Prevention Costs. That, however, is no excuse for failing to begin quantifying the cost in each of these categories. Determine what they cost now.

Cutting costs, however, can be deceptive as this example shows. Until 1984, a food company sold its product in cans with tin-plated tops. In 1985, the company switched to aluminum tops for a one-time cost improvement of $30,000. Prior to 1984, the company had received only 42 complaints about its product. But, in the three years after 1985, complaints rose to 601, most of them about metal shavings. After spending an additional $300,000 to find the cause of the complaints and how to rectify the problem, the company switched back to tin tops. What looked good from a purchasing objective (Purchase Price Variance) was not effective from a cost of quality perspective or from customer requirements.

As we use supplier certification to eliminate failure costs, total costs will go down. Our experience tells us that you can start to have a Supplier Certification program in place in 6 months, but it takes years to implement fully. If that looms as a formidable task, remember that it doesn't get easier if you begin five years from now when you think you will be in a better position to take on the task. In five years, the only thing that will disappear may be you or your company.

THE GOALS OF SUPPLIER CERTIFICATION

Eliminating waste and consistently achieving zero defects are the premier goals of Supplier Certification. Supplier Certification has other important goals which are similar to those of WC (World Class) and TQM (Total Quality Management) philosophies. Both Supplier Certification and WC/TQM address the elimination of waste and both have a win/win mentality. What's good for you is good for your supplier. What you expect from your supplier, you should expect from your own company. Supplier Certification works in concert with WC/TQM. In fact, it is difficult to think of one without the other because the definition of World Class is "the right product in the right place at the right time." Since Supplier Certification demands the same standard as WC/TQM, it is not surprising that they both have similar goals.

SUPPLIER CERTIFICATION	
GOAL	**ACTION**
Total Quality Management	Ensure that the entire manufacturing cycle from design review through customer receipt meets quality standards established by the customer.
Quantity	Process and produce the lowest possible quantity by manufacturing on-time. The smaller the quantity, the easier it is to control.
Supplier Partnership	Establish a relationship based on a win/win philosophy.
Logistics	Simplify the control and movement of material between functions and activities. Incorporate standard objectives.

WORLD CLASS
AND TOTAL QUALITY MANAGEMENT

Unfortunately, many of us believe JIT (Just-In-Time) to be something it isn't. This is why its connection to Supplier Certification is not emphasized nearly enough.

JIT is <u>not</u>:

An Inventory Control or Reduction Program.
A Scheduling Technique.
A Materials Management Project.

JIT is a concept which integrates the activities between a supplier and your plant, between department and department, and between you and the customer. The three items above are a byproduct of employing the problem-solving philosophy of JIT and allow all of us to function as World Class companies.

JIT is <u>not</u>:

A Program for Suppliers Alone.

It is for you and the customer.

JIT is <u>not</u>:

A new fad.

It has a long history. Henry Ford used it when he first began to mass produce automobiles. Deming and Juran taught its principles to the Japanese in the 1950's. JIT is a return to the basic fundamentals of sound manufacturing management.

JIT is <u>not</u>:

A cultural phenomenon.

If it was, then why are the Japanese building plants which employ the JIT and Supplier Certification philosophies in America using our workers? We have proven it can be done anywhere.

WORLD CLASS THEN, WORLD CLASS NOW

JIT is <u>not</u>:

A Program which displaces planning.

It evolves out of planning material requirements. JIT coordinates these requirements with the rest of the manufacturing process and suppliers.

JIT is <u>not</u>:

A panacea for poor management.

It is a way of doing business, a management mind-set based on the *Total Business Concept* (TBC) as stated in our book, **MADE IN AMERICA** (PT Publications, Inc., Palm Beach Gardens, FL).

ISSUES, CONCERNS AND OPPORTUNITIES

When we wrote the first edition of this book, everybody was thinking and talking about JIT manufacturing and Total Quality Control, while we continued to address the total business, or company, and not just a few parts. The Total Business Concept says that we must squarely face issues and concerns as an integrated team and turn them into opportunities. Many people in this country believe that work ethics preclude any attempt to function as an integrated team. We believe that the integration of all levels of management with workers (union and nonunion) as well as with suppliers is necessary to a successful implementation. What it really requires is a change in mind-set, in the way we approach problem-solving.

This means that we need to involve everybody in problem-solving from the shipping clerk to design engineering. We must find out what the customer requires and the most efficient way to procure the material needed to build the product. Furthermore, top management must be committed and involved. They must provide focus and direction to the various teams attacking problems in the business. We tend to forget that our people want to contribute their ideas when they feel they will be heard and appreciated.

Companies think of themselves as unique. We are, in terms of having proprietary processes and unique products, but at the most basic level we are all very similar. We procure material, move it, process it and then ship it to customers. Every time we conduct seminars either in the USA or other countries around the world, the same questions come up, whatever the national culture or industry. The most frequently asked questions comes in the form of a negative statement: "Our workers don't have that level of commitment." Our response is that neither did many companies in this country when they embarked upon a Supplier Certification program. Harley-Davidson, for example, was slipping badly before they decided to change their company's mind-set and commitment. They went out and looked at companies who were succeeding. They came back and dedicated themselves to attacking the problems of waste. They were so successful that they asked for government import controls to be removed before they were scheduled to run out.

Another key issue is flexibility. While visiting the Brothers manufacturing plant in Japan on a fact-finding tour, we were amazed to see various sewing machines, both industrial and commercial, coming down the production line. How was this possible? First, suppliers shipped the right product to the right place at the right time. Second, set-up times for machines were drastically reduced from the levels we see today in industry. At this plant, it was possible to change an entire line in a matter of minutes. Third, lot sizes were much smaller than those in most companies. This was possible because it was so easy to set up a machine for another operation. When you take these three improvements into account, the mystique disappears and commitment becomes easier since there are visible results. For additional readings on set-up reduction, we would suggest **SET-UP RE-DUCTION: Saving Dollars with Common Sense** (PT Publications, Inc., Palm Beach Gardens, FL), **SMED II: Practical Applications** by Shigeo Shingo and **Quick Die Change** by David A. Smith and also available from PT Publications, Inc.

ARE WE KEEPING PACE?

The relationships which exist between companies and their internal and external suppliers has improved since we first wrote this book, but there is still a great deal of room for improvement. A recent article in *Manufacturing Engineering* about the pace of change indicates that concerns about supplier quality, selection and relations rank low. For example, while "partner-like manu-facturer/supplier relations" is rated at 40% by the big three automakers, only 35% of their suppliers rate their pace in this area as rapid. For "more OEM functions involved in supplier selection," the Big Three gives a 30% rapid rate, while their suppliers come up with 26%. While "increased supplier engineering contribution" does get a much higher rating (67% by the Big Three and 51% by their suppliers), it still ranks behind five other categories of change being instituted at a rapid rate by American companies.

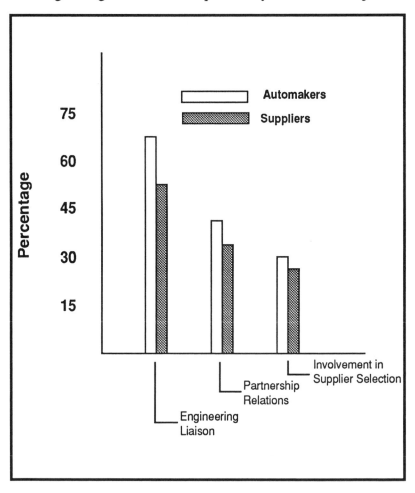

Some may say that the pace is slow because it costs so much money and time to make Supplier Certification work, but they are wrong. It costs far more *not* to implement such a program. A report in *Electronic Business* shows that companies which buy from suppliers with no quality program can expect costs up to four times greater than companies with a Total Quality Management (TQM) program. Texas Instruments, who came up with the figures in this report, estimates that a company buying from a supplier with no program will pay $0.20 more for Incoming Inspection, $0.24 more for Inventory, $0.48 more for System Manufacturing, $1.06 more for Warranty and $2.12 more for User Maintenance for each dollar of purchased goods. That compares to $0.00 more for Incoming Inspection, $0.00 more for Inventory, $0.02 more for System Manufacturing, $0.10 more for Warranty and $0.20 more for User Maintenance from a company with a TQM program. We think these numbers speak for themselves.

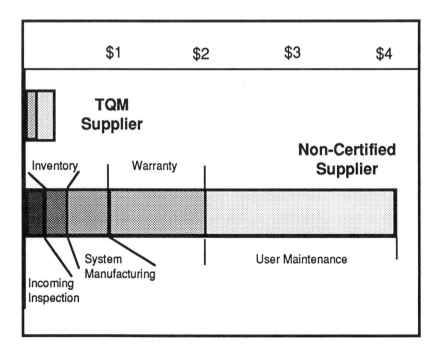

WORLD CLASS TRANSPORTATION

Supplier Certification, then, is the management of material and quality both internally and externally. This may present a major logistical problem. You will need to coordinate the activities of a great number of movements of material.

One way to control this movement would be to hire a number of transportation experts to police the movements. This is a superficial solution, however, much like hiring more inspectors in order to improve quality. You need to look at the flow of material. You will find that this in-depth look at the underlying causes of material flow and quality will dictate the need to reduce your supplier base. It is far easier to control internal and external supply movements if there are frequent moves being made from fewer sources.

Smaller lot sizes also affect the issue of transportation. Obviously, it is much easier for the supplier to deliver 10 parts on time than 1,000 parts. Supplier Certification works toward lowering the quantities of components and increasing the frequencies of deliveries. There are a number of ways to coordinate the consolidation of deliveries and shipments. You may elect a single consolidation point for a common carrier, send your trucks to a geographical area every day or take advantage of back-haul rates. Standardization of shipping containers can reduce costs and improve accuracy dramatically.

Accuracy of count, by the way, is often a hidden cost put into the cost of the material. These efforts will reduce the total cost. Every time you accept a 2% AQL (Acceptable Quality Level or A Quick Look), you're paying for 2 bad parts out of 100. To add insult to injury, you're also paying to have them shipped to you.

A frequent criticism of both JIT and Supplier Certification is that it won't work if your supplier isn't geographically close. Certainly it would be convenient if your suppliers were all next door. It would be like knocking on your neighbor's door to borrow a cup of sugar or gallon of gasoline for your lawnmower.

We aren't saying that proximity is not a factor, but that it is a factor you can deal with. At the Apple Macintosh plant in Fremont, CA, for example, we were able to receive products transported by ship from the Orient, 100% on-time, all the time. At Kawasaki, their experience was the same. Deliveries from Japan were always on-time, 100% acceptable and in correct quantities. How? By bringing everybody involved—customs, shipping, receiving—together to discuss how to insure timely and frequent delivery. We suggest that at some point you invite customs, the freight forwarder, your supplier and the local trucking company to a meeting to discuss requirements. Standardizing rates, tariffs and routing is an extremely important part of the process.

ZERO BREAKDOWN MAINTENANCE

A frequently overlooked Supplier Certification issue is preventive maintenance and its effects on manufacturing. In order for Supplier Certification to work, both you and the supplier must have a zero breakdown maintenance program in effect. Furthermore, it must be a scheduled one, not one in which maintenance is done after the fact, when the process is already out of tolerance or the work center is down. Also overlooked is the interfacing between a Quality Management system and maintenance activities. Such aspects of Quality Management as repair reporting, failure analysis and statistical data accumulation must also be built into the process. This is a function of knowing the characteristics of a machine (bearings, bolts, hoses, etc.) and stopping the process on time for maintenance.

EDUCATION AND TRAINING

Let's review the issue of education and training. There are two questions with which we should be concerned:

- **Are time and funding available to educate personnel?**

- **How much would it cost if education and training were not implemented?**

These costs are often not considered until it's too late. Education and training also require top management commitment. At one of our clients, for example, we conducted a seminar on Supplier Certification which all managers were required to attend.

On the first day, the president states, "I'm 100% behind this program. It's great. It's just what we need, but I can't be here all day. I'll be in and out."

What's the message the managers were receiving? Is this president truly behind the project? This program won't work if management doesn't show everybody in the room that they are committed. Leaving a seminar throughout the day for meetings does not demonstrate commitment.

IMPACT OF ENGINEERING DESIGN

In traditional manufacturing environments, engineering's impact is usually limited to product design. In an environment employing supplier certification, engineering's responsibility extends to the process and producibility. It also extends outside the company to the development of suppliers and customers. Engineering is involved in determining customer requirements and designing to that specification. This involvement also includes integrating your company's manufacturing process. The objective is to simplify and reduce the costs of product through design.

There are several reasons why we fail to successfully integrate engineering into a Supplier Certification program. The main reason is the presence of excessive Bill of Material and process changes. The more changes there are, the more difficult it is to implement Supplier Certification. Changes to a drawing should occur when either product reliability causes a problem in the field or when a change lowers the total cost of the product. That means no more "nice-to-have" changes.

DISCIPLINE

Another reason companies fail is they lack the discipline to make changes in a timely fashion. These changes are not limited to product design, but include process and organizational changes. Nor are they limited to your plant, but include the supplier's as well. Lack of discipline is the absence of a system and methodology to control and support the needs of the organization. This system absence and lack of control results in people not forming a clear picture of their responsibilities and a management that cannot clearly articulate them.

PRODUCT LIFE CYCLES

We also fail when product life cycles are not considered in the planning of various manufacturing activities, such as length of production runs, integration with existing products or supplier availability. When you design a product, producibility is one of the first questions which needs answering. The second question to ask is whether your suppliers can produce the parts you need. You won't find out if they are able to or not by looking at samples provided by suppliers. These samples are always good. We don't know of any companies that send out bad ones. Therefore, you should be looking at your supplier's factory, not its product. Determine for yourself if the supplier has the discipline and levels of productivity to work with you on this product?

At a recent Design for Producibility program that Pete Grieco was teaching in Finland, he got a firsthand look at the importance of including suppliers in product design. The vice president, Jouko Karvinen, of the sponsor company, ABB Power System Group, stated that the life cycle for some of their products was shorter than the development cycle. Jouko and John Gossman, vice president of materials at ABB, said that they wanted to commit their company to supplier based management and early supplier involvement in the design of all products. As a result of this commitment, ABB invited six key suppliers to participate in the seminar so that they all could share concerns, issues and opportunities for a partnership relationship. Supplier Certification is an international phenomenon.

DESIGN INTEGRATION

Supplier Certification programs often encounter difficulties because Design has not integrated the following functional groups in the product life cycle:

Marketing	**Manufacturing**
Quality Assurance	**Engineering**
Purchasing/Materials Management	
Supplier	**Finance**
Customer	

The Macintosh computer is one example of a product that came in under the Design to Cost (DTC) target. They succeeded because everyone was involved in the design right from the beginning. We had a team which developed and selected suppliers based on specific criteria.

PRODUCT TESTING

Many companies also fail to adequately define how a product is to be tested either in the product requirements or the design specifications. The result is that manufacturing does not know how to test a product to achieve the desired results. Instead, we end up establishing test criteria after the product is already in the marketplace. Testing has to be part of the design process. Otherwise, how can we demand zero-defect material from a supplier if we don't know how to test for quality ourselves?

COORDINATION OF ACTIVITIES

One final reason companies fail is because there is a lack of coordination and trust between the supplier and manufacturer. At a Connecticut tool and die manufacturer, we saw an excellent example of this lack of coordination and trust. The company was asked by a customer to build a prototype. After producing one small lot, the company sent the parts to the customer to see if they were acceptable before they produced the remaining 300 parts.

"We can't tell you if the part is acceptable or not," the customer answered back. "The part is in process. Besides, we're not sure if the design we gave you is correct. We're testing the parts, but we can't tell you how."

This way of business has to stop. As we mentioned before, Supplier Certification is a two-way street. If you don't tell your suppliers how to test a part, how can you expect them to build a good one? This is especially true if you don't know whether your prints are correct, which is all too often the case.

RESOURCES REQUIRED

The environment for Supplier Certification requires a *culture change*, a new set of attitudes which reflects a partnership with each supplier. This is accomplished by implementing program requirements at the supplier as well as at your own plant. Attaining mutual trust will be difficult for American industries whose supplier relations in the past have been decidedly one-sided, but it is not an impossible task. Certainly the best argument for changing your company's attitudes toward suppliers is the program's ability to create a "win/win" situation for both sides.

One electronics company in this country sees its Supplier Certification program as "a long-term, mutually rewarding business partnership ... in which material quality is assured through open communication, cooperation, design for producibility and functionality, quality planning and effective process control." With this kind of attitude, you can expect to receive high quality parts which could eliminate incoming inspection, lower inventory levels, permit integration of Design and Manufacturing and lessen paperwork. Suppliers, on the other hand, can expect to speed up their cash flow since certified material is accepted upon receipt, to improve their quality levels and to receive more orders since their quality and costs are under control.

With culture change comes the adoption of a **Total Cost Approach**. As mentioned earlier, a supplier's quoted price is not the true cost of material. Quality and delivery must also be taken into account, but this will mean getting Finance to see beyond the traditional cost systems based on Purchase Price Variance (PPV),

Economic Order Quantity (EOQ), machine utilization and the solicitation of three quotes. These systems are outdated. They were derived from the railroad industry in the early years of this century and, as the authors, H. Thomas Johnson and Robert S. Kaplan, point out in **Relevance Lost: The Rise and Fall of Management Accounting,** bear little resemblance to current methods of production. We can no longer be dependent upon price analysis as major criterion for determining product costs. Cost analysis will have to augment, and even replace, price analysis. This is because cost analysis examines all the costs involved in the manufacturing process, whereas price analysis uses the seller's price without examining the costs and profit which make up the price. A total cost approach is based on the following formula:

Total Cost =
Variable Costs + Fixed Costs + Semivariable Costs

The goal is to eliminate overhead allocations as much as possible. A system based on the total cost approach is much more realistic and accountable than traditional approaches for two interrelated reasons. First, the newer approach is based on the Theory of One which says that an operator on a production line only uses as much material as is needed to build to the demand set by the operation in front. Consequently, there isn't any excess material in the plant since only material for which there is a demand is present on the factory floor. Second, what material there is in the plant contributes directly to the production of a finished good, not to inventory carrying costs, not to time lost in receiving areas, not to expediting and not to late materials. Control of material flow is the equivalent of financial control.

LOT SIZING

The control of material is made easier with a *lot-for-lot rule.* We should make only what is sold, produce only the quantity scheduled, store only one container of material on the floor, and so on. Lot-sizing goes hand-in-hand with set-up reduction. On the ideal shop floor, set-ups are so fast that lot sizes of one can be run. To attain levels approaching that ideal requires a persistent effort within your company and with suppliers. A Supplier Certification program has to work toward ensuring the delivery of the right material in the right quantity at the right time. This means frequent, small deliveries directly to the production line in order to reduce inventories. To do so, however, is of no value until the factory floor is weaned from long production runs and large lot sizes in favor of a more *flexible* method of manufacturing.

HUMAN RESOURCES

Another resource required for a successful Supplier Certification program is the cultivation of *generalists*, not specialists. A generalist is better able to see the entire picture, a quality which is almost mandatory in an environment employing the company-wide perspective of Supplier Certification. We are strong advocates of moving people from one department to another as many of the best-run companies in America do. If you have a good person in Quality, but he or she doesn't know Purchasing, then teach them. Give your people at least one week of training per year in an area they are not familiar with. Good people are hard to find; good people with an awareness of the entire company are even rarer, but necessary to the most successful implementation of Supplier Certification.

CONTROL AND APPLICATION TECHNIQUES

True awareness of an entire company's policies, procedures and operations is not possible without a movement toward *simple control techniques*. The easier it is to explain something, the better the chance of success. The trend toward computerization is somewhat at odds with this requirement. You will have to pay particular attention to the tendency to say that if a computer can't do it, we can't do it. Remember: the Far East has accomplished much of its astonishing gains in quality and productivity without sophisticated computer systems. Many Manufacturing Resource Planning (MRP II) programs, for example, have poor Shop Floor Control (SFC) modules which people can't use effectively. Company routings and bills of material are poorly designed. We often complicate the problem by putting these structures on a computer. Now we have computerized chaos instead of control over the basics. The simplest approach is generally the one that works the best.

The same reasoning for selecting simplicity over complexity also applies to the creation of *small work cells*. Whether we call them cells, teams, families, or groups, these units are most effective at problem-solving when they are kept to 6-8 people. Despite the small size, however, they should be given all the tools to make a project happen and should be given profit-and-loss responsibility. This authority and responsibility is instrumental in generating the commitment to drive a Supplier Certification program.

WILL IT WORK?

Success begins with the commitment of your top management and your suppliers' top management to the process of continuous improvement. Top management must be committed to the creation of a company culture which fosters responsibility, authority, vision (company-wide) and accountability. Anything short of this commitment will doom a Supplier Certification program to failure. Middle and lower management as well as direct labor are not about to embark upon a difficult voyage unless they see that their leaders are on board as well. The people who work in our companies will not strive for continuous improvement unless top management has created an environment in which they feel that they can contribute to the company's success and profit.

SUPPLIER CERTIFICATION at DYNACHEM ELECTRONIC MATERIALS MORTON INTERNATIONAL

The LeAnn Zunich Story

The Dynachem story is one of our favorites because we had to work hard to convince LeAnn Zunich that Pro-Tech was as good as people were telling her. LeAnn is also one of those rare people who fully documents what she and the members of her Supplier Certification team have done. We will be sharing Dynachem's success story throughout this book. So that their story is easier to follow, we have decided to begin with an overview. And so, as LeAnn says:

"In the beginning ...

we had a Supplier Quality Team."

This initial team met twice a month to work on problems of mutual interest to both the Quality and Purchasing departments. All the team members worked at the company's headquarters in Tustin, CA, and the team consisted of the following members:

2   Production Buyers — Juanita Lloyd and Gene Collins
1   Non-Production Buyer — MaryAnne Weatherwax
1   Staff to the Director of Quality — Cassandra Rice

1   Quality Manager — Nick Segro
1   Director of Quality — Jeff Hecht
1   Purchasing Manager — LeAnn Zunich

According to LeAnn, the Supplier Quality Team had been talking for awhile about certifying suppliers. No headway had been made until one day all the team members show up with a flier (except for LeAnn who says she threw hers out) from a company named Professionals for Technology Associates, Inc. describing a class on Supplier Certification. A good portion of the meeting is then spent discussing what the flier says and everybody agrees that the advertised training would be a great help to the company. Jeff, the Director of Quality who has already named the institution of Supplier Certification as one of his "Goals and Objectives" for the year, thinks that Pro-Tech's program sounds wonderful.

LeAnn, who takes a dim view of most seminars advertised on fliers, suggests that the team contact the references cited on the flier. After some discussion, it turns out that LeAnn herself is assigned the task of calling the references. She makes the calls and is somewhat surprised, she admits, that the references "were uniformly enthusiastic about the training." The consensus of the past attendees is that "your company will be able to implement a Supplier Certification program if you attend this seminar."

At the next meeting, LeAnn dutifully reported what she had heard. Based on these excellent references, the team decides that somebody should attend Pro-Tech's seminar. The natural choice is Jeff since he has been championing such a program for a long time, but Jeff says that he has to be out of town on the day that the seminar meets. LeAnn says that she will attend. And in March 1990, she shows up at Pro-Tech's Supplier Certification program in Irvine, CA, which was conducted by Pete Grieco. By the time she leaves, she says, "it had changed the way I looked at my job."

So great is her enthusiasm that she volunteers to put together an implementation plan for Supplier Certification at Dynachem while giving her report about Pro-Tech's seminar to the Supplier Quality team. LeAnn says she will base the plan on what she has learned at the seminar and tailor it to Dynachem.

A TEAM IS FORMED

Jeff suggests that they implement certification at just the company headquarters in Tustin, CA, to "see how it goes." If it works, he continues, then they can take the idea and implement programs in the rest of the company. LeAnn thinks that all company locations should be involved so that no time is lost in gaining the benefits of Supplier Certification. Eventually, the team agrees with her and the Supplier Quality team grows in members and gets a new name — the Supplier Certification team. Below is the makeup of the new team:

Woburn, MA   Administrative Clerk — Gerri Jackson
                      Materials Supervisor — Rich Crowley
                      Quality Supervisor — Tom McNamara

Moss Point, MS   Senior Buyer —Henry Loper
                      Quality Supervisor — Grady Bunkley
                      Materials Supervisor — Betty Stone

Elmhurst, IL   Regional Operations Manager (Sales)
                      — Fred Lester

Tustin, CA   Quality Administrator — Donna
                      McHaney
                      Transportation Specialist — Kathy
                      Parham
                      Planning Specialist — Sara Simpkins

> 2 Buyer Specialists — Gene Collins and
> Ray Linthicum
> Senior Buyer — Lou Boffardi
> 2 Buyers — Mary Bennett and Sid Bloom
> R&D Administrator — Phil Lofty
> (ex-Quality)
> Purchasing Manager — LeAnn Zunich
> (Chair)

Now that Dynachem has a team, the members draw up an outline of steps which they will take as they implement their Supplier Certification program. (A more complete description of Dynachem's program appears in Chapter 8.) Below is the outline which the team developed:

STEP 1: Goals of Supplier Certification

STEP 2: Developing Supplier Selection Criteria

STEP 3: The Supplier and Customer Symposium

STEP 4: Certification Candidate Selection

STEP 5: The Certification Program
  a. Documentation History
  b. Performance History
  c. Program Review and Process Evaluation
  d. Finalize Compliance Documentation

STEP 6: Supplier Audits

STEP 7: Tracking for Certification

STEP 8: Certification

STEP 9: Audit and Maintenance

STEP 10: Identifying Partners

STEP 11: Continuous Improvement

THE TEAM TAKES ITS FIRST STEPS

For Step 1, Dynachem draws its goals from Pro-Tech's workbook and Supplier Certification book. LeAnn says that these goals were then organized in a way which was significant to her company. Step 2 isn't quite as easy. LeAnn reports that the team spends two weeks brainstorming, organizing, categorizing and listing (in order of importance) their criteria for selecting and measuring suppliers. Even though the team thought they had covered every possible criteria, they decided (at Pro-Tech's recommendation) to get input from the rest of the company. A memo is sent out to every manager and supervisor in the entire company. Unfortunately, the initial response is not good, so Jeff convinces the Supplier Certification team to divide up the list amongst themselves and start calling everybody in order to get a valid response. Their instructions are to ask the manager or supervisor to fax or send the memo if they lost it. If the person being called said it was "some place on their desk," the team member waited while the form was filled out. The final result: a 90+% response rate and the discovery of some criteria which the team had forgotten.

At last, the Supplier Certification team develops a list of 10 major criteria which the company would use to select and measure its suppliers. They are as follows:

- **Product that meets Dynachem specifications, providing batch-to-batch consistency.**

- **Least Total Cost.**

- **A program of Statistical Process Control.**

- **On-time complete delivery.**

- Technical and commercial assistance with new and existing products.

- A commitment to Dynachem's certification process.

- Consistent, complete quality documentation.

- Lot continuity with a minimum number of lots per shipment.

- Integrity.

- Regulatory and Environmental compliance.

The list completed, it was now the team's task to define what each criterion meant. This was accomplished by assigning a criterion to each team member who then had the responsibility of writing a definition.

PROBLEMS UNCOVERED

Even after all of the work described above, not everybody is pleased with the list of supplier selection criteria. Both the transportation and non-production people insist that a single list of criteria wouldn't meet the requirements of measuring all of the company's suppliers. They also point out that the measurement criteria worksheet, which has also been developed at the same time, will not apply to their suppliers. Although LeAnn is opposed to multiple lists, the team members prevail and develop four lists of supplier selection criteria for the following areas of the company (listed on the next page):

- Production. (Green)
- Non-Production. (Blue)
- Transportation. (Beige)
- Warehousing. (Gray)

In order to avoid confusion, the team color codes the program for each area as noted above. The complete Supplier Selection and Measurement Criteria Worksheets can be found in Chapter 4.

Meanwhile, the team defines four levels for a supplier to achieve in their Supplier Certification program:

- *CERTIFIED SUPPLIERS* **must receive a rating of 90% or more on the Supplier Selection and Measurement Criteria Worksheet and meet other criteria.**

- *QUALIFIED SUPPLIERS* **receive a rating of 70% to 89%.**

- *RESTRICTED SUPPLIERS* **receive a rating of less than 70%.**

- *NEW SUPPLIERS* **have not yet been rated.**

Here, at Pro-Tech, we like to think this company's response is indicative of what is good for all companies today. We hear so much about how lazy we are, but here was solid evidence that this is not entirely true. The truly innovative companies are moving ahead with their own Supplier Certification process. Let's now turn to Chapter 2 — the development of supplier selection criteria. Where does a company start? What is important? What isn't? These are some of the questions we address in the next chapter.

SUPPLIER SELECTION CRITERIA

2

The actual criteria you choose to select suppliers will vary according to the size and nature of your business. However, there are criteria which are common to every industry. Therefore, the checklist we have included in this chapter should be used as a guideline. Each company will have to tailor and develop its own checklist. The process of development is extremely important. It is an exercise in creating an integrated approach within your company. Our *Supplier Certification* VideoEducation Series illustrates how companies develop their own supplier selection criteria using the guidelines laid down in this chapter. With this in mind, let's look in more detail at some of the criteria you will want to consider. The following list is in no particular order of importance.

SUPPLIER SELECTION CRITERIA

Specifications	Market Involvement
Producibility	Capability
Geographical Location	Capacity
Quality History	Financial Condition
Environmental Programs	Quantity
Facilities and Equipment	Labor Conditions
Education and Training	Cost Control
Process and Quality Control	Customer Base
Competitive Pricing	On-time Delivery
Prior and Post Sales Support	Tool Tracking
Knowledgeable Sales Force	Smoking Policy
Organization	Ethics
Preventive Maintenance	Housekeeping
Policies and Procedures	Percent of Business
Subcontractor Policy	Multiple Plants
Research and Development	Calibration History
Self Assessment	Six Sigma Program

Supplier's Management Commitment

ISO 9000

Manufacturing to Specifications — We don't want to send specifications to suppliers for their interpretation. We want them to build the product we specify. To see how well a supplier conforms, look at the number of rejects and the corrective action taken when there are problems. A supplier should be able to answer the following questions:

- When was the last time a corrective action was received from a customer?
- What was done with it?
- How was the corrective action instituted in the supplier's plant?
- How does information about the action get fed back to the customer?

Producibility — Can the supplier make the part to specification? And, in the quantities needed? Can the supplier take a design and produce the part consistently in a cost-effective manner?

Financial Condition — Be careful about what information is used to make judgments in this category. We recommend using a "10K" because it goes into more detail than other financial reports. If the supplier is a private company, it may be difficult obtaining financial information unless the Chief Financial Officer is willing to share it. A supplier willing to share information demonstrates openness and an ability to be a partner.

Geographical Location — Our rule is that we should make every effort to do business with companies (approved by the team) who are within 60 minutes of our plant, whether that's by truck, rail, airplane or boat. There will be exceptions, of course, but this rule should be in place to limit the areas in which we should search for suppliers. This brings procurement under the umbrella of a Supplier Certification program. Furthermore, we recommend that any supplier outside the 60-minute radius be accepted by a certification team. This is to avoid other functional areas developing their own sources without looking at local suppliers.

Quality History — Besides checking with previous customers of suppliers, it is also important to check for quantitative data which substantiates quality. Don't rely on vague statements that the supplier is committed to quality. Look for evidence of quality throughout the supplier's facility.

Customer Base — Know the supplier's customer base for two reasons:

- To check for references.
- To see if they are doing business as partners with other corporations.

Education and Training — A supplier who has an extensive education and training program is one already committed to continuous improvement. These are the companies we want to buy from because our own Supplier Certification program will fit neatly into their plans. The basic question we want answered is how many hours per week of training do workers and management get in areas such as Statistical Process Control (SPC), material management, purchasing, set-up reduction, etc.? A supplier with well-rounded employees, who have a complete picture of their company, is one who will help the most. Another question we might ask to determine the extent of their education and training is what does the supplier do when it hires a new worker. Are they thrown right into their job? Or, as in the early stages of the Macintosh plant in Fremont, CA, does the company orient all new hirees (management and production) to the product by having them spend a week on a mock production line building the product? The rationale is that when it comes time to make a decision, an employee is better equipped to decide correctly having undergone hands-on experience. In such an environment, for example, a buyer would not be ignorant to the quality tests performed on the product he or she is buying.

Process and Quality Control — Another label for this category is Statistical Process Control (SPC). As noted before, process and quality control is critical. We want to select suppliers who will allow us to look at their process routing sheets and documentation. Does the company make the product as the sheet indicates? If it does, then we can be more sure that the process is under control. If the route sheet is inaccurate, then we should begin to question the degree of process control. Certification is difficult without process control.

Competitive Pricing — Quite simply, are the supplier's prices competitive with those of its competition? Competitive pricing is not the answer, however, if it is based on a "three-bid" mentality.

Prior and Post Sales Support — Besides the presence of warranties, guarantees and replacement parts, we should also look for suppliers who are committed to solving problems before and after a sale is made. Obviously we want to avoid the fly-by-night companies which disappear after a delivery is made. Here, too, we can look at the history of a supplier's performance with other customers.

Organization — Although the emphasis here is on the presence of well-organized quality and material departments, the same criteria apply to the company as a whole. Basically, we should be looking for the difference between organization and bureaucracy. We can determine which state exists by observing how many levels of management the supplier has; whether information flows as it is designated or whether an informal grapevine exists; or, by questioning all levels about their understanding of quality. A well-organized company is a well-informed company whose operations are streamlined to eliminate waste.

Preventive Maintenance—Look for three particular conditions:

- Preventive maintenance on a regular, standard schedule.
- Service while machines are running.
- Scheduled stops in the process for maintenance.

The Good, the Bad and the Ugly

Ethics — Suppliers should subscribe to and follow all Good Manufacturing Practices (GMP) and obey all laws and regulations they are subject to. Our philosophy is that you can't teach ethics; employees must be ethical.

Subcontractor Policy — Suppliers should divulge whether or not they use subcontractors. Obviously, such subcontractors must be able to produce to your specification if they are shipping parts to a company which will supply you in turn. If your supplier does use subcontractors, you should know how they source these companies and how much control they have over their process. One weak link in the chain of the suppliers can weaken the entire Supplier Certification program. Subcontractors should be avoided, if at all possible.

Research and Development — Suppliers who have aggressive and innovative R&D departments, as evidenced by the number of patents they have, are most desirable. They are the companies that will grow with you, that are open to new ideas and new ways to cut costs. This same innovative attitude should extend beyond the research department and should be a consequence of management commitment to continuous improvement.

Tool Tracking — Part of process control is tool tracking since bad tools make bad parts. A supplier should know how many parts have been produced off of any tool and what is the life of that tool. Tools should also be on a regular maintenance schedule and be replaced before they begin making bad parts. Suppliers who eke out a few more strokes from a tool to cut costs are being penny wise and pound foolish. These are not the suppliers we want for our program. If the tool life exceeds what was planned, that is acceptable; if the tool is used beyond its life limits, that's not acceptable. This criteria is used in Phase One of the Supplier Certification process.

Market Involvement — Here we look to buy from suppliers who view the material we procure as their main line of business. As a participant at one of our seminars put it: "If you want to print a hardcover book, you don't go to a printer who specializes in spiral-bound covers." Ideally, we would like to do business with an industry leader who is at the forefront of any technological advances. These are the suppliers who can advise us best about the producibility of the product we want to build. In effect, this category directs us to the experts.

Capability — Is the supplier adequately and correctly staffed for machines and manpower? Does it have the methods in place to be capable to produce parts to specifications?

Supplier's Management Commitment — This category is a consequence of all the other categories. It is likely that the presence of process and quality control means that management is committed. A truly committed management assigns responsibility and authority to all levels of the company and expects them to be accountable for their areas.

Capacity — We don't want a supplier that runs its machines 100% of the time. Nor do we want a supplier who puts on extra shifts during peak periods. We want a steady state: 80% capacity with time for preventive maintenance and problem-solving. We can't implement Supplier Certification with a supplier who does not allow an operator to shut down a machine until it finally breaks down. One way to see whether this happens or not is to ask the operator. Let the operator show you how the machine gets calibrated and maintained and how frequently. While we are on the subject of machine maintenance, we don't advocate having a special shift just for preventive maintenance workers. Operators should do some maintenance themselves and it should be scheduled by the Planning department as a work order. The problem with a special shift is that the maintenance workers don't talk with the operators who know the most about the machines.

Facilities and Equipment —We should not look only for new equipment and facilities. What will the equipment and facility look like six months from now, or one year? This is the question we want answered. A good supplier manages and maintains all its equipment whether they are old or new. In fact, well-maintained older equipment could be a sign of a better managed company than brand new equipment.

Labor Conditions —Whether the supplier has a union or non-union shop, the company should have good relations with its people. We have worked with both types of companies and we have found that when employees are treated with respect and listened to, they will build quality parts. Not only that, but they will help their company continuously improve to build still better parts at more cost-effective prices. Supplier Certification relies on this type of participation to be effective itself.

Cost Control — Under this category, we should look for suppliers who are willing to work with us in breaking down the components of cost: material, labor, overhead, profit, transportation, etc. This is a prelude to a whole program of total cost measurement and subsequent waste elimination undertaken by both you and the supplier.

Knowledgeable Sales Force — Knowing prices is not enough. A supplier's sales force should know the answers to questions you have about the process, machine capability and methods. Avoid suppliers who use their sales force as merely order-takers.

On-Time Delivery — Look for a record of timely delivery by checking references and other customers. Remember that on-time delivery does not mean delivering early. That is just as detrimental to a Supplier Certification program as is late delivery. On-time delivery means 100% on-time, every time.

Environmental Programs — When a supplier is regulated by environmental agencies, be sure that it has control over any methods and procedures used for getting rid of hazardous wastes, etc. Failure to comply with government regulations is a violation of the law and we should avoid companies who practice bad business.

Policies and Procedures — In a way, this is the crux of supplier certification. There is one simple question to ask here: Are policies and procedures being followed at the supplier's plant? Or, do they just sit on a shelf?

**A Place
for Everything,
and
Everything
in its Place**

Housekeeping — An example from one of our fact-finding tours of the Far East best demonstrates what we mean here. At a factory we visited in Japan, the floors were so clean you could eat off of them. The management at this company told us this was because they wanted to see when a machine started to leak oil. Then, they would know that it needed immediate attention. Housekeeping in Japan is part of Preventive Maintenance. This is not usually the practice here in America. When a machine leaks, we put a drying compound on the floor to soak up the oil. We don't see it as a sign of a problem. We tend to live with it and don't fix the machine until it finally breaks down. Housekeeping also means everything has a place and everything is in its place.

Percent of Business — An objective of the program is never to be more than 35-40% of a particular supplier's business in terms of dollars or parts because that could put the company out of business if we were to cut our orders or end them. We had a client who initially shipped almost 100% of its products to the computer industry. We warned him that if this industry slumped, his company might fail. Since the company was in the plastic injection molding business, we suggested they develop a business plan in which it would sell 20% of its products to the automotive industry, 40% to the computer industry, 20% to the toy industry and 20% to the cosmetic industry. Now, even if the company were to lose a third of their business, it would not fail. It may not make a profit in the interim, but at least it would be around to find more business. When selecting suppliers to be certified, find ones who will not fall over if one leg of their business is pulled out from beneath them.

Multiple Plants — If a supplier has more than one plant, then they really are more than one supplier. This means that we must certify each of the plants if they all participate in supplying material to us. Otherwise, we run the danger of getting parts from the plant which does not have its process under control.

Calibration History — This area is similar to tool tracking. We need to look for evidence that gauges and fixtures are maintained and calibrated on a regular schedule. We don't want to see calibration done only when bad parts are produced.

Quantity — Does the supplier deliver in the quantities ordered? We cannot allow the established tolerances of +/- 10%. We only want what we need; no more, no less.

Smoking Policy — We mention this policy, since one of our clients, Brown & Williamson Tobacco Corporation, has a firm policy of working with suppliers who support the right to smoke. Other companies will take a different approach in this area.

ISO 9000 — The ISO 9000 is a set of international standards for quality management and quality assurance. The American version is the ANSI/ASQC Q90 Series. Although these standards are not the same as certification, any supplier which meets these standards should be a very eligible candidate for certification.

Self Assessment — A supplier using a self assessment program for evaluating its quality management systems is also a very eligible candidate for certification. Certainly, you will need to evaluate their assessment program, but it could make your job easier if they are already measuring criteria important to your company.

Six Sigma Program — A company which is working toward Six Sigma is setting a very ambitious target. Six Sigma is a statistical term which designates the achievement of only 3.4 defective components for every 1,000,000 components produced. Such a supplier is undoubtedly using state-of-the-art techniques and tools. This is almost definitely a supplier you want to use.

MULTIPLE SUPPLIER SELECTION LISTS

As we discussed in Chapter 1, there is often a need for different lists of supplier selection criteria for different types of suppliers. Each list must reflect the unique requirements of the respective customers. Non-Production, for example, may not require their suppliers to have a program of Statistical Process Control. On the other hand, Transportation and Warehousing have many areas not in common with Production or Non-Production materials. The criteria for these two areas should reflect the special interests and conditions present when dealing with their suppliers. We think a company would be making the correct choice in using their creativity when employing our guidelines for selecting and developing specific criteria which are truly meaningful and useful to their respective areas.

HOW TO USE THE CRITERIA

The highlights above indicate the creative ways we can assess a supplier. Although there are almost 40 categories listed, most companies look at less than half when they select a supplier. Traditionally, companies give a small order to a new supplier and look at their performance before deciding whether to issue more purchase orders. But since first orders are almost always perfect, companies start to depend on more subjective criteria. For example: "I feel good about this supplier" or "I think he'll do a good job."

We must move away from this "feel-good" process of selecting suppliers. Once we have drawn up a list of criteria, our next step is to clean up the categories so there is no duplication and write a self-explanatory paragraph which describes what we are seeking. Then, assign a point value to each so that the categories add up to a total of 100 points. Now, we can determine where to draw the line for those suppliers who qualify. The qualifying score can vary, but it should be 70 or better. Note that if a supplier ships two different classes of material, it must qualify for each commodity.

Scoring suppliers requires an on-site survey, but you can't do that without an objective checklist of criteria. Determining that criteria is the most important part of the Supplier Selection process, only just ahead of involving a multi-disciplined team.

In the past, companies have selected suppliers haphazardly. Typically, buyers are hurried in the task of finding suppliers. They base their decision on a sample first order or by allowing Engineering to sidestep the procurement process and select suppliers without input from other members of the selection team. A goal of Supplier Selection is to shrink the supplier base. Allowing departments to use any method not based on objective criteria will have the opposite effect. We know of one semiconductor company which set a goal of shrinking their supplier base from 1,000 to 750. But, since they failed to bring the program together under a team given the task of drawing up selection criteria, the supplier base had grown to 1,340 by the year's end!

We must have a team to select suppliers. This team should consist of representatives from Purchasing, Engineering, Manufacturing, Finance, Quality Assurance, etc. They should gather information from as many sources as possible in order to make their selection decision. These sources can be professional societies, marketing contacts, the Thomas Register and past experience. Then, the team sits down and votes on which suppliers are potentially certifiable. This decision depends upon how many suppliers we need for each product and commodity. It may be that we need two suppliers for sheet metal and two for injection molding when we start the program. We may be able to lower this figure as the program gets underway. We don't want to move too quickly, however. We don't want to set a goal of dropping from 500 suppliers to 100 if that endangers our comfort level.

WHO SHOULD YOU SELECT FIRST?

Frequently, clients ask us "Which suppliers should we work with first?" We always tell the story of our personal friend, Tom Melohn, at North American Tool and Die Company who was highlighted in Tom Peter's book, **Thriving on Chaos**. When Tom Melohn started his company, he targeted 25 companies he wanted to do business with. One of these companies was Digital Equipment Corporation where one of us, Peter Grieco, was working at the time as the Materials Director. Melohn calls up Digital one day and states, "I'm not looking for any orders. I would like a half-hour of your time so you can define what you want from a supplier."

We make an appointment to list what Digital wants from a supplier. A month later, we receive a follow-up call.

"I recently completed a business plan. Will you take an hour to critique it?"

I tell him I would be glad to look it over and make some comments for him. A month later, he calls again.

"I wrote a final draft of my business plan. Will you take a look at it?"

By now, I can't refuse. I'm interested in what he's doing. I look at it, make some comments and send it back. Two weeks later, it's Tom Melohn on the phone again.

"Can I have an order to see if my plans work?"

I can't say "no." I'm hooked. We've worked together for the past two-and-a-half months and developed a relationship. That's the type of supplier you want to work with first: one who is concerned with doing it right the first time.

In selecting suppliers, we can choose among several options or alternative factors:

---

1. Best Supplier/Products
2. Worst Supplier/Products
3. Highest Dollar/Volume Items
4. Lowest Dollar/Volume Items
5. Pareto's Law
6. Bulky Items/Large Space Concerns
7. Frequent Delivery

APPROVED, QUALIFIED AND CERTIFIED SUPPLIER LISTS

There are a limited number of suppliers who have Tom Melohn's qualities at the outset of the certification process. We must work with potential suppliers to raise them to the level of partnership. Companies generally have supplier lists which identify those suppliers which meet certain criteria. These lists are known today as the Approved Supplier List (ASL), Qualified Supplier List (QSL) and Certified Supplier List (CSL).

The ASL is the list of suppliers that a company can buy from now or has bought from in the past. Being on the list does not mean that the supplier ships material which meets all engineering requirements. In fact, the material can range from good to poor. The criteria today for getting on the ASL is very simple: the supplier has previously been given a purchase order and now has an account number on our records. This alone makes them eligible to buy from.

The QSL is the list of suppliers who meet specifications which were established earlier. Their material is rarely rejected and they perform satisfactorily in a high percentage of the areas in the supplier selection criteria. They are the cream of the crop, the suppliers we want to work with and the ones we think can end up on the Certified Supplier List.

Good, Better and Best

All too often, however, the QSL is not what it should be. Let's say Purchasing needs to buy a new product. One of the suppliers on the ASL manufactures the needed part, but they have not been qualified for it. They are not on the QSL. Normally, Purchasing would need authorization from Quality before it could buy the part. Quality would do a survey to see if the parts conform to requirements, but it often doesn't because there isn't enough staff and the company needs the part right away. So what happens is that the supplier gets put on the QSL without a survey.

Such fuzzy definitions of the ASL and QSL make it easy for a supplier to move up a notch. A QSL rating should be the result of an objective process, one in which the supplier meets at least 60-70% of the supplier selection criteria. This is as true for medium or low technology companies as it is for hi-tech ones. The item that will shut down a production line is the bracket bought from a supplier who moved from the ASL to QSL without a rigorous appraisal.

The decision to be put on the QSL must be made by the same team responsible for the selection process. Including somebody on the QSL must be a conscious, not an unconscious, process. We need to go through the whole supplier list and separate the non-inventory items. Then, let the buyers break down the supplier list into the ASL and QSL categories. When a supplier of a certain part makes the QSL, then stop buying that part from suppliers on the ASL. The QSL supplier is the candidate for a long-term partnership and eventual certification.

STARTING THE PROCESS OF DEVELOPING SUPPLIER SELECTION CRITERIA

One of the most important issues in developing supplier selection criteria is to involve as much of the company as possible in order to assure the overall success of the program. This is a sample memo that a Supplier Certification team can send to representatives of different functions in their company to elicit that support:

```
TO:  Plant Staff, Managers and Supervisors
FM:  Supplier Certification Team
RE:  SELECTION CRITERIA FOR NEW SUPPLIERS
```

The Supplier Certification Steering Group is seeking your input to develop criteria which can be applied when selecting new suppliers. We would like you to represent your function in reviewing the attached draft of selection criteria and by adding any other elements which you think are important to the process.

If you disagree with any criteria we've listed, please cross it off and provide your explanation of its non-applicability. When completed, please check the three elements you deem most important when selecting a new supplier.

Please return the form to the attention of
_____ by _____.

Selecting criteria is the first step in our journey toward implementing a successful Supplier Certification program.

(List your first pass criteria below.)

As we learned in Chapter 1, the response rate to this type of memo is not always as good as you may hope. In fact, the survey may not be valid unless you obtain high levels of response. It may be necessary for the team to divide up the representatives who did not respond and personally contact them in order to collect the balance of the surveys. When Dynachem did this, they were able to tabulate the list below which shows all the criteria and their ranking:

1. Material Meets Specs
2. On-Time Delivery
3. Technical Assistance
4. Competitive Price
5. Batch-to-Batch Consistency
6. Service
7. Responsiveness
8. Statistical Process Control
9. Integrity
10. Complete Documentation
11. Certificate of Analysis Compliance
12. Total Quality Management
13. Lead-times
14. Technical Interaction
15. Innovation

All of the remaining criteria received one "vote" each

Continuing Lots
Minimum Lots/Shipment
Returns
Understand Theory of Constraints
Environmentally Conscious
Equal Opportunity Employer
Buy American
Supplier Relationship
Understand Dynachem's Specs and Requirements
Requirements within Supplier's Capabilities
Financially Sound
Favorable Terms
Apply for Baldrige

Discount Terms
Communications
Maintaining Inventory
Continuous Improvement Program
JIT Deliveries
Warehousing Location of Products
Willing to meet custom specs we develop
Work with us to establish quality or performance level
Quality Program for raw materials
Agreement to participate in Certification Program
Clear commitment to product lines we buy
Generally well managed
Length of time product has been on the market
Total number of customers using product
Toxicity data (TOSCA)
Packaging
Stocking arrangements
Supplier's sources and quality partnerships in place with their
    suppliers
Audit of supplier facilities and process
Recycling programs
Flexibility

Your next task is to make some order out of this list of criteria. The team must develop a set of criteria by which the company could measure suppliers. Dynachem's first pass at the process of making order from this list was as follows:

QUALITY

Management Committed to Total Quality Management and
    Continuous Process Improvement
A Commitment to the Certification Program
A Program of Statistical Process Control

Product that Consistently Meets Company Specifications, providing Batch-to-Batch Consistency

Consistent, Complete Quality Documentation

Minimum Number of Lots per Shipment with Lot Continuity

Willingness to Meet Custom Specifications

A Quality Program for Raw Material Suppliers

Supplier Quality Audit of Facilities and Processes

SERVICE

On-Time, Complete Delivery

Technical and Commercial Assistance

Accurate Lead-Times, and Updated Regularly

Lot Continuity with a Minimum Number of Lots per Shipment

Open, Honest Communications

Willingness to Inventory and Stock; Warehouse Locations

Packaging

Flexibility

TECHNICAL

Innovation and Creativity

Availability of Technical Interface and Assistance

Complete Technical Documentation

Willing to Help Us Establish Quality and Performance Levels

BUSINESS CONSIDERATIONS

Least Total Cost

Integrity

Complete Documentation

Financially Sound and Generally Well-Managed
Attractive Payment Terms

OTHER

Understand the Theory of Constraints
Environmentally Aware Including Recycling Programs
Equal Opportunity Employer

CASE STUDIES

As you will notice in the numerous examples and case studies that
we have added to the third printing of this book, companies take
different approaches in the development of supplier selection
criteria. What is most important is that the criteria you develop
work for you and that they are quantified. That way you can
always work toward improving the base line. Supplier Certification is, after all, a Continuous Improvement Process.

INTERNATIONAL TOTALIZATOR SYSTEMS, INC.

International Totalizator Systems, Inc., a manufacturer of
parimutuel ticket issuing machines located in Carlsbad, CA,
prepared a six-phase Supplier Qualification Process while Pro-
Tech was providing education and assistance to the company. We
would like to thank the ITS Supplier Certification Team for
sharing the program shown on the next two pages with our
readers.

The twenty-eight action items in this qualification process are
further outlined and defined by six more pages of documentation.
Many companies think that this is too much time to spend on
laying a foundation, but we think it is more costly in terms of time

ITS SUPPLIER QUALIFICATION PROCESS

PHASE A

PRE-QUALIFICATION
1. Analyze Supplier
2. Visit Supplier's Facility
3. Decide to Survey

PHASE B

SURVEY
1. Select Survey Participants
2. Set up Survey and Confirm Date
3. Perform Survey and Present Booklet
4. Discuss Survey and Compile Results
5. Send Results with Letter to Supplier
6. Receive Response from Supplier

PHASE C

ESTABLISH PARAMETERS
1. Establish Review Period for Supplier
2. Review Design and Documentation of Parts
3. Collect QC Incoming Inspection Data
4. Record Supplier's Performance

and money to do a job half right. Then, you spend all the rest of your time correcting mistakes, rather than eliminating waste. Do it right the first time!

Now, let's take a look at one area in more detail — the classifications of suppliers and their definitions. ITS came up with five supplier classifications. Note that they are similar to the classifications that we have addressed. In fact, any classifications your company develops will be similar to what follows:

ITS SUPPLIER QUALIFICATION PROCESS

PHASE D

EVALUATION & MONITORING
(Quality Engineer)
1. Evaluate Supplier's Performance
2. Meet with Supplier to Review Evaluation
3. Implement Corrective Action Plan, if Needed

PHASE E

RESURVEY (only as required)
1. Submit Request to Resurvey Supplier
2. Set Survey Date and Confirm
3. Perform Survey
4. Evaluate Survey Results
5. Discuss Survey and Compile Results
6. Send Results with Letter to Supplier
7. Receive Response from Supplier

PHASE F

QUALIFICATION
1. Set Up Team Review of Supplier
2. Analyze Supplier's Performance
3. Poll Supplier Qualification Team
4. Arrange Annual Award Luncheon
5. Present Framed Certificate to Suppliers

SUPPLIER CLASSIFICATIONS

It is the intent of the Supplier Qualification Team that, eventually, all ITS suppliers will be rated as one of the following five classifications. Purchasing will then place orders with suppliers based on their current rating. Using this system, suppliers rated as Qualified will be ITS preferred suppliers.

I.   LIMITED-SOURCE SUPPLIER: A supplier that...

- ITS must buy from because they are a sole, or one of two, source of supply for the specified part(s).

II.   NEW SUPPLIER: A supplier that...
- has not provided parts for ITS in the past or has provided an insufficient amount to be used as a basis for rating.

- has not been surveyed by the team.

- ITS can buy from now, provided no Approved or Qualified Supplier is available to supply the part and/or meet delivery requirements.

III.   APPROVED SUPPLIER: A supplier that...
- ITS has purchased parts from in the past and has been a reliable source.

- has been surveyed by ITS.

- during the preceding review period has

  - averaged a 90% on-time delivery performance.
  - averaged a quality level of 90% acceptance.

- ITS can buy from now, provided no Qualified Supplier is able to supply the part and/or delivery required.

IV.   QUALIFIED SUPPLIER: A supplier that ...
- the team has surveyed and has achieved a rating of 70 or better.

- during the preceding review period has

  • averaged a 98% on-time delivery performance.
  • averaged a quality level of 98% acceptance.

- has demonstrated a willingness to work with ITS on a partnership basis in the continuing improvement of supplier performance and product quality.

- is a preferred supplier of ITS parts.

V. **SUSPENDED SUPPLIER:** A supplier that …
- has been removed from the Approved or Qualified Suppliers List for lack of performance.

The ITS program described above provides a vehicle for the qualification step only. Their intent is to move toward Supplier Certification, based on their present volume and sales.

WAUKESHA ENGINE

Michael J. Termini, Pro-Tech's executive vice president, helped the team at this company develop their supplier selection criteria. Termini says that the company wanted to put its emphasis "on selecting suppliers who have both the CAPABILITY and the INTEREST to become certified suppliers." To the people at Waukesha, this meant that the supplier was also "dedicated to the principle of CONTINUOUS QUALITY IMPROVEMENT." The capital letters are theirs and we think the words they chose deserve to be capitalized. These principles will be the foundation of our country's ability to prosper in the global marketplace. The criteria on the following pages is what Waukesha uses to select suppliers:

WAUKESHA SUPPLIER SELECTION CRITERIA

CAPABILITIES

1. Type, age, condition and suitability of equipment to Waukesha products.
2. Available capacity vs. booked business.
3. Long-term vs. short-term interest in Waukesha business.
4. Industries and customers currently served ... References.
5. Source of supply of raw materials and under what terms.
6. Process controls (SPC?) for parts and tooling.
7. Inspection equipment and procedures (documented).
8. Material handling equipment and methods.
9. Packaging equipment and methods.

FINANCIALS

1. Length of time company has been in business.
2. Financial stability ... Asset ratio, debt ratio (long and short term), cash flow, profitability.

MANAGEMENT COMMITMENT

1. Preventive maintenance program in place (documented).
2. Quality program in place (documented).
3. Company quality statement.
4. Employee involvement programs.
5. Business plan (one to five years).
6. SPC program ... Active/documented/understood by employees.
7. Cost reduction programs/value analysis.
8. Subcontracting policy and environmental policy/controls (i.e.: EPA compliance, hazardous waste disposal, etc.).
9. ETHICS.

LABOR CONDITIONS

1. Union or nonunion operation.
2. Contract expiration date.
3. History of labor disputes.

4. Employee training programs used.
5. Management's philosophy regarding employees.

DEDICATION TO QUALITY

1. Formal quality system in place (documented).
2. Employees aware of company's position regarding quality.
3. Experience as a certified supplier for other customers.
4. Existence of company's Supplier Certification program.

PRICING

1. Delivered cost compared to other supplier's pricing.
2. Supplier's previous pricing history/policy.
3. Commitment to price reductions/value analysis/cost savings over a defined period.
4. Supplier's position relative to long-term price agreements/consignment programs/JIT deliveries/quantity pricing.

LOGISTICS

1. Ready access to primary transportation arteries.
2. Availability of an in-house fleet.
3. Typical mode of delivery and typical timing.

SUPPORT

1. Knowledge of supplier's sales representatives relative to Waukesha-type products and requirements.
2. Competency of supplier's technical staff and availability to assist Waukesha manufacturing.
3. Supplier's responsiveness to requests for information and/or assistance (at all levels within the operation).

AFTERMARKET PHILOSOPHY

1. Receptiveness to a non-compete contract which guarantees Waukesha Engine's exclusive right to market its products to aftermarket customers and distribution channels.

We would like to thank the team at Waukesha for allowing us to share their criteria with you. You have probably noticed already the openness shown by companies willingly displaying their reference material in order to share information which will shorten the implementation cycle time for other companies. We, at Pro-Tech, believe in this philosophy as well. The more information we make available, the faster we will all cross the finish line.

ARCHIVE

The following is a condensed version of an eight-page document shared with us by the Supplier Certification team at Archive. The first page and a half of the document emphasizes the importance of developing a win/win relationship with suppliers. Although noting that quality, low price and delivery are still the main criteria that go into supplier selection, the report comes to the conclusion that today's business world requires more from a supplier. For example, quality must be expanded to include goals such as parts per million (PPM). Price needs to include such items as service after the sale and cost improvement activities. We fully support the move toward Total Cost or Activity Based Costing.

In order to reach the levels required by the world marketplace, Archive has committed itself to the following responsibilities:

1   Evaluate the capability of suppliers to deliver parts that meet our quality requirements. This is done jointly with the help of the Quality department.

2   Assure that the terms and conditions in the procurement contract establish supplier responsibilities for compliance to quality requirements.

3   Provide the supplier with all the necessary information required to assure that the delivery and quality requirements can be met.

Archive has listed the following methods as a means to "accomplish these responsibilities," according to the supplier selection document. These methods are:

1   Supplier surveys.

2   Past performance.

3   Product evaluation (qualification tests of the supplier design).

4   Industry reputation.

5   Information from other buyers.

6   Financial reports (Solvency? Resources to meet our expanding requirements).

7   Resources and personnel available to help with technical problems.

8   Willingness to participate in JIT and Supplier Certification.

9   Plant easily accessible to Archive engineers and buyers.

10   Ability to perform special processing or provide special services.
     A Plating/Coating.
     B Die Casting.

11   Willingness to participate in part certification programs.

These methods will, of course, form the basis for Archive's supplier selection criteria. All of the case studies in this chapter are solid examples of what a company should do to develop their own criteria. In fact, being able to adapt our guidelines to your particular circumstances is what we advocate.

WHAT ABOUT DISTRIBUTORS?

Before we conclude this chapter, we want to say a few words about distributors. Many of us, of course, don't buy directly from manufacturers, but from distributors. How can we control the selection of suppliers in this situation? If we're a high volume buyer, we can exert control over the distributor's choice of suppliers. If we aren't a high volume buyer, then we should make every effort to find distributors who are selective and who have a good reputation. Perhaps the best idea, however, is to show our Supplier Certification program to your distributors so that they can select better suppliers themselves. The rewards are self-evident. If they buy from better suppliers, they will get better parts and thus get more business. In essence, this is the same evidence of mutual benefits that we showed to our own suppliers. Our objective is to work only with suppliers who can be certified at some point in the future.

In conclusion, we want to tell you that it's acceptable to use Pro-Tech ideas and the ideas you may have picked up from the examples we provided, but they will not be fully successful unless you mold them to fit your individual requirements. In the next chapter, we will show you how to survey your suppliers to find out which ones can meet your minimum criteria.

SUPPLIER SELECTION PROCESS

3

Changing the one-way street of supplier relations to a two-way street means there will be new directions in the way we select suppliers. The one-way street of the fifties, sixties and early seventies was marked by a signpost which looked like this:

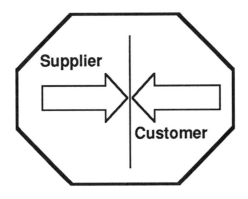

"Adversary" Supplier Relations

This was the era of adversarial relations in which customers made demands upon suppliers without extensive consultation in order to build an understanding between the two parties. By the late seventies, however, customers began to notice that this relationship had serious shortcomings. It was never entirely clear who was supposed to do what and when, so a new era was ushered in marked by this new signpost:

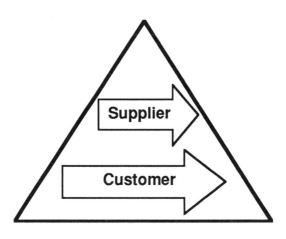

"Contract" Supplier Relations

The contract era of supplier relations lasted well into the eighties and, as the sign shows, did point both parties in the same direction. Contract administrators, or lawyers, were hired in procurement functions to review contracts so there would be no ambiguity about how customers would work with suppliers. What this era still left out was continual contact with the supplier to work on building a partnership. This is the work of the new era of supplier relations which will be marked by a transition to a signpost which looks like the one on the following page.

The partnership era shows both arrows side by side and pointing upwards as the supplier and manufacturer work together to

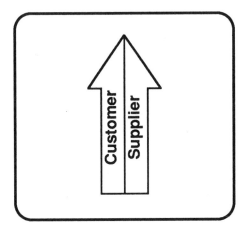

"Partnership" Supplier Relations

improve quality, delivery, performance and cost. Thus, the first question we should ask suppliers today is: Are you willing to become our partner in eliminating waste and embarking upon a continuous improvement process? All of these supplier relationships and the supplier selection process are covered as well in our videotape series, *Supplier Certification: The Path to Excellence.*

THE SIGNS OF PARTNERSHIP

Along the "partnership" highway, there will be several other signs which indicate the general direction taken in your own company and in your supplier's operation.

The first sign will be a clear *commitment* to quality by management at all levels of the organization.

The second sign will state the need for *visible/measurable* quality programs available to all personnel in both internal and external companies about to enter into a partnership. These types of programs mean that achieved results are plotted against the objectives and goals to track performance of the program.

The third sign will mark embracing a *zero-defect* philosophy which states "do it right the first time" and that a company does not accept continued rejects at any point in the process.

The fourth sign, *on-time delivery*, demands the arrival of material when it is required and not before or after. The objective is to use material as soon as it hits the receiving dock (Ship-To-Stock) and eventually to have material shipped directly to the line (Ship-To-WIP). This will be greatly helped, of course, by the adoption of standard packaging which will eliminate the need for counts.

THE SUPPLIER SELECTION TEAM

The task of a manufacturer is to develop an open and trusting relationship with the supplier. The first step in selecting partners is **not** to designate one department as being solely responsible for selection. You will have difficulty entering into a partnership with a supplier if you haven't established a partnership between the existing departments within your company.

The supplier selection team should be composed of representatives from at least the following departments:

Engineering — design, manufacturing, industrial, etc.
Manufacturing — operations, process
Purchasing — international, domestic, commodity
Finance — cost accounting
Quality — supplier quality engineer, manager

There are various techniques available in starting this type of program. For new start-up programs, selection is a far easier process. When developing a new factory, there is an excellent opportunity to select suppliers for a new plant and product from their inception. Most companies, however, need to first review their existing supplier base and then rank them in an order which distinguishes between good and bad performers. When reviewing the supplier base to determine a reasonable number that we can work with in an efficient and productive manner, we can apply Pareto's law to the existing supplier base. Pareto's law says that 20% of your suppliers account for 80% of your procurement costs.

Commodity	SKU	Present # of Suppliers	Required # of Suppliers	Supplier Meeting Req't	Required New Suppliers
Plastics					
Sheet Metal					
Molded					
Cables					
Electronics					
Totals					

Commodity Code and Product Type Chart

Another approach is to determine, by commodity codes and product types, how many suppliers are required by category and in aggregate as shown in the chart on the preceding page. In this manner, we can determine from the chart how much of our existing supplier base we will retain and how many new suppliers we need. The selection team will have to address this issue as a first step in the selection process.

Let's now take a look at how one company, International Totalizator Systems, Inc. (ITS) went about breaking down its suppliers by commodity and product type as shown in the chart on the opposite page. When ITS began its Supplier Certification program, there were approximately 172 suppliers. A mere six months later that number had been cut to 112 (see graph below) simply by applying the supplier selection criteria they had developed to their supplier base. As you can see from the Commodity and Product Type chart, ITS also determined early in the program

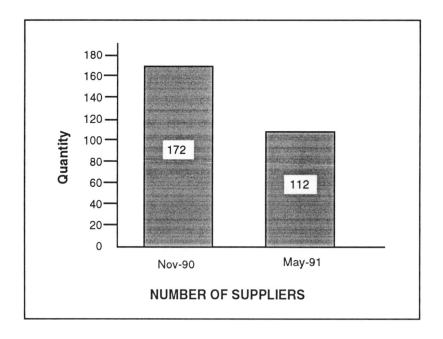

NUMBER OF SUPPLIERS

Commodity	Present # of Suppliers	Required # of Suppliers	Supplier Meeting Req't	Required New Suppliers
CRT's	2	2	2	0
Printheads	3	3	3	0
Elec. Dist.	35	5	5	0
Machine shop	18	3	3	0
Motors	7	4	4	0
Power supply	5	4	4	0
Rollers	4	2	2	0
Assembly	8	3	3	0
PCB's	9	2	2	0
Keypads/boards	3	3	3	0
Sheet metal	9	3	2	1
Gears	2	2	2	0
Hardware	20	10	10	0
Springs	6	2	2	0
Magnetics	2	2	2	0
Glass	2	2	2	0
Extrusion	1	1	1	0
Vacuum/injection	10	7	7	0
Packing mat'l	2	1	1	0
Bearings	1	1	1	0
Labels/logos	5	2	2	0
Plastics	4	1	1	0
Cable/wire	4	2	2	0
Magnets	1	1	1	0
Solenoid/clutch	2	2	2	0
Ribbons	1	2	1	1
Locks	2	2	2	0
Dust covers	1	1	1	0
Power cords	1	1	1	0
Batteries	1	1	1	0
Keycaps	1	1	1	0
TOTALS	172	78	76	2

that it did not need 35 electronic distributors or 20 hardware suppliers, if the suppliers they kept were eventually going to end up being certified. Being certified means, of course, that ITS will have a true partner relationship with its suppliers and that means there will be no problems getting defect-free product on-time.

A supplier selection team's next task, now that the supplier base is reduced, is to establish supplier selection criteria. Each member of the team brings expertise to the task which together adds up to a whole greater than the sum of its parts. *Engineering*, for example, is responsible for product design and whether the design for an existing product can be simplified. In conjunction with *Manufacturing*, they should also be determining whether the product is being efficiently produced. Manufacturing, along with *Quality*, is responsible for process control both at their plant and the supplier's. Remember that we cannot inspect for quality, it must be built into the product through the effective control of both design and the manufacturing process. *Purchasing*, of course, smooths the way for good supplier relations in which zero-defect parts are always delivered on time. Lastly, *Finance* needs to be on the team to insure that outdated purchasing measurements and practices like Purchasing Price Variance (PPV) and Economic Order Quantity (EOQ) are replaced by new procedures reflecting company-wide measurements and a Total Cost approach. In addition, they supply the required financial data about the supplier to the team.

REQUIREMENTS OF A CERTIFIED SUPPLIER

The supplier selection team's next task is to determine what are the basic requirements to become a certified supplier and the key questions to ask when selecting a supplier. A high technology electronics company recently defined their requirements as:

1. Average reject rate less than 5%.
2. Average delinquency rate less than 10%.
3. Willingness to produce parts to *center* of specification range as demonstrated by statistical process control charts.

These are certainly good goals although they aim too low and don't place an emphasis on continuous improvement. Without a WC/TQM philosophy, there is little assurance that the goals above can be attained or maintained.

WHAT ARE THE GOALS?

The first requirement a potential certified supplier must meet is that its philosophy agrees with yours and that you share similar goals. You can detect this by exploring a potential supplier's relationships with its own suppliers. A supplier must have a quality management system in place which subscribes to the same zero-defect goals and process controls as your company does. This does not exclude suppliers who fail to meet these requirements initially, but to exclude them from the first forays into a Supplier Certification program. We can't afford to waste time and money on suppliers who accept poor quality or who don't want to enter into a partnership.

Another key requirement is a satisfactory answer from suppliers to the question of dedicated capacity. We advocate that a supplier schedule capacity at only 80% in order to leave time for preventive maintenance, emergency situations, flexibility and problem-solving. Given that, an objective is to "regularize" the production schedule so that it can be expressed as a daily requirement. We want suppliers who are flexible enough to make what we want when we want it. If you need 10 parts today and eight parts tomorrow, then you receive 10 parts today and eight tomorrow.

Another criterion is suppliers who are capable of entering into long-term agreements for 3-5 years or the life of a product. In these agreements, it is stipulated that both you and the supplier will work together on:

Product Cost Reduction
Quality and Specifications
Value Engineering
Total Cost Reduction

These agreements can be executed as a system contract or blanket order as long as several criteria are established:

---

1. **The production forecast will fluctuate based on customer demand.**
2. **Criteria will be in place indicating how to add or subtract from capacity in order to "regularize" the production schedule as a daily requirement.**
3. **A ceiling on how much material we are responsible for if the criteria is not met.**

Such a system may work like this:

Every month, you call the supplier with a rolling one-year forecast for that item. You can then change the quantity for one day's production as the following chart shows:

FLEXIBILITY WINDOW		
Days	**% Change**	**Responsiblity**
0-30	**+/-20%**	Raw 30 days WIP 14 days Fin 0 days
31-60	**+/-50%**	Raw 14 days WIP 0 days Fin 0 days
61>	**+/-100%**	Raw 0 days WIP 0 days Fin 0 days

In this system, you are only responsible if the production schedule changes beyond the parameters for 30 days of raw material, 14 days of work-in-process and 0 days of finished goods. This insures that the supplier is producing just-in-time and not filling up warehouses with products we may not need. The example in the Flexibility Window above has a lead-time of six weeks.

Another key requirement is the synchronization of daily production and deliveries with the production schedule. The biggest obstacle to achieving this is long lead-time. Of the five elements of lead-time (queue, set-up, run, wait and move), queue time accounts for 80-90% of the total time. Thus, we have immediate control over a major portion of lead-time by reducing lot sizes and employing a pull system in which both we and the suppliers only build a product when there is a demand for it.

We have been lulled into thinking a supplier's lead-time is unchangeable. A few years ago, we remember that suppliers of ball bearings announced that their lead-time would double from 4-8 weeks to 8-16 weeks. The planners and buyers at manufacturing companies doubled their orders then so they would not run out of bearings. Faced with this sudden surge in demand, the suppliers doubled their lead-time again within a relatively short period of time. The buyers then doubled their orders again. Before we knew it, the lead-time had grown to 82 weeks. In order to bring some order back to this chaotic development, we decided to offer one of the suppliers a total dollar per month purchase order. We didn't know what we wanted next week, let alone next year, but we informed the supplier that we would tell him our forecast at the beginning of each month. Only under this agreement were we able to shrink lead-time.

We often complicate supplier relations more than necessary. In part, this is because we do not truly listen to what customers want. At one of our seminars, a participant asked us what he could do about lead-time when the paper he needed was only produced twice a year in quantities of 200,000 pounds. It may have been possible to arrange delivery with an agreement just described, but we had an easier solution.

"Why does it have to be this stock of paper?" we asked. "Why can't you use a stock that is produced more often and in smaller quantities?"

He hemmed and hawed for awhile and then told us that they had to use that particular paper "because that's what the graphic artists said we needed."

"What does the customer want?" we asked. "Do they need this paper? Do they really care whether the paper is the fancy French vanilla variety or just the plain vanilla?"

It turned out that once the specifications were reviewed, the customers didn't care one way or another. Another example is the use of environentally-safe plain brown cartons by Apple Computer instead of the usual white ones. This was not possible in Steve Jobs' days.

A Supplier Certification program is a long-term commitment. Too many company executives are trying to turn their programs into 3-6 month projects. They don't understand that continuous improvement takes time. They also forget that the programs and buying practices of the past have not worked. A culture change is required at all levels of the supplier's and customer's plants.

Others think that it is possible to develop the program in one plant at a time. We advocate a Total Business Approach. In order to do this, all plants must be treated as suppliers which should meet the same criteria as external suppliers. If sister plants don't meet a specific guideline, then the use of their material is unacceptable. Such a condition requires complete corporate commitment to quality and supplier certification.

The last key requirement for becoming a certified supplier is the existence of a complete process and quality control system. The supplier quality standards of Baxter Travenol Laboratories, Inc. require that "statistical process control should be an integral part of the supplier's operation." Such a system, the standards say, is "necessary during manufacturing operations to monitor and control processes, prevent the manufacture of large quantities of defective parts, provide uniformity, and to identify when corrective action is necessary." We promote their emphasis on process acceptance rather than product acceptance. The goal of Supplier Certification is to eliminate Incoming Inspection and to ship material directly to the line precisely when and where it is needed.

This is only possible when you can be sure that the supplier not only has quality and process controls in place, but a system which maintains those controls.

PRESENTING THE PROGRAM TO THE SUPPLIER

Up to this point, we have discussed the basic requirements of a certified supplier. Now let's look at how to involve suppliers in the certification process. Obviously, we can't start making demands on companies, otherwise suppliers will see themselves as "victims" of your program. An approach is to plan a supplier symposium in which the benefits of Supplier Certification are presented to suppliers who were selected based on how many are needed.

SUPPLIER SYMPOSIUM

We find that the majority of Pro-Tech clients introduce certification to their suppliers via a Supplier Symposium. It is important to make the event geographically convenient for the company's suppliers to attend and to allow all team members to be involved in at least one symposium. As you may remember from an earlier example, one company had members from each of its plants on the team and often utilized telephone meetings in order to overcome logistical problems.

At the suggestion of the sales force at this same company, representatives decided to make the symposium a two-part event. The morning would be devoted to *suppliers* and the late afternoon to *customers* with their salespeople. Below are two sample letters that can be sent out to each of your company's suppliers. The second letter confirms a positive response and announces the agenda. We include both letters since they are excellent examples of how you can get the ball rolling.

INVITATION LETTER

Dear **(Supplier's President)**:

(Your company's name) is developing a process of Supplier Certification to ensure the consistent quantity, quality and delivery of products and services from our suppliers that conform to our specifications.

We have adopted the process developed by Professionals for Technology Associates, Inc., which is being utilized by companies around the world.

The first step in this process will be conducting a Supplier Symposium on **(fill in the date)**, from 8:00 am to 4:30 pm at **(fill in place)**.

As a valued supplier to **(your company's name)**, we cordially invite you and your Quality Manager to join us for our kick-off to the Supplier Certification process.

Please RSVP to **(put in name and telephone number)**.

We look forward to meeting with you and sharing information about our Supplier Certification Program and to establish a long-term relationship which will be profitable to both of us.

Sincerely,

(Name of President)
President

ACKNOWLEDGMENT LETTER

Dear **(Supplier's President)**:

We are pleased you accepted our invitation to attend our Supplier Symposium on **(fill in date)**.

Due to the enthusiastic response of our suppliers, we believe the day will be both beneficial and rewarding. Our meeting will be held at the Marriott Hotel in **(fill in place)**. A block of rooms has been reserved for those of you who are attending.

Our symposium agenda for the day will include:

Registration

Welcome
Introduction to (Your Company)
President

World Class Manufacturing
Vice President, Manufacturing

Total Quality Management
Vice President of Quality

Supplier Partnership
Director of Purchasing

Supplier Certification — Successful Programs
Peter L. Grieco, Jr., President and CEO
Professionals for Technology Associates, Inc.

The Certification Program
Supplier Certification Team Members

Plant Tour

The program starts at 8:00 am and will conclude at 4:30 pm. Breakfast and lunch will be included.

If you have any questions, please call (**put in name and telephone number**).

Sincerely,

(**Chairperson's Name**)
Supplier Certification Chairperson

You should note the tone of partnership in these letters. Nobody said Supplier Certification *had* to be painful. Be sure to send a thank-you letter (see below) after the symposium as well. This friendly persuasion really does work. This follow-up letter should also contain a critique for the supplier to fill out and remind them to contact their representative buyer if they have questions. Including a stamped, self-addressed envelope for the supplier's convenience is a nice touch. Again, Supplier Certification doesn't have to be difficult for your company or for your suppliers.

THANK YOU LETTER

Dear **(Supplier's Name)**:

Thank you for contributing your valuable time at our Supplier Symposium last week. Supplier Certification can only be successful with your involvement.

We are extremely pleased with the excitement expressed by all the participants and we are looking forward to starting the certification process with your help.

We have enclosed a critique form for your comments (see below). This will help us improve our performance. A stamped, self-addressed envelope is also enclosed for your convenience. We encourage your frank comments. Please return your completed comments by **(fill in date)**.

If you have any comments or questions, please contact your Supplier Certification Team representative: **(fill in name)**.

Thank you again.

　　　　　　　　　　Sincerely,

　　　　　　　　　　Chairperson
　　　　　　　　　　Supplier Certification Team

The critique and comments form shown on the opposite page would accompany the thank you letter shown on this page. It is a good idea to have these letters and forms prepared so that you can send them out immediately after the symposium. That way, the event and information is fresh in each of the participant's mind.

SUPPLIER SYMPOSIUM
CRITIQUE AND COMMENTS

1. Were the objectives and goals of Supplier Certification made clear by the speakers? _____

_____

2. How would you rate the brochures and other literature?
   Clear and informative _____
   Needed explanation _____
   Not clear _____

3. Do you think Supplier Certification will have an effect on your business? How? _____

_____

4. Has your company begun a Supplier Certification program? If not, do you plan to? _____

_____

5. Do you think that your company can achieve Supplier Certification?

_____

_____

6. Is your company willing to enter into a win/win partnership? What do you see as your responsibilities? Ours?

_____

_____

7. Please make any additional comments in this space or on the other side if necessary.

_____

_____

_____

Thank you for your cooperation.

Chairperson, Supplier Certification Team

Now that we have seen the overall process for a supplier symposium, let's look at some sample agendas in more detail.

AGENDA
PROGRESSIVE TECHNOLOGY
SUPPLIER SYMPOSIUM

LOCATION: Corporate Offices, Plantsville, CT
DATE: January 15, 1989

9:00 - 9:30	Arrival of Suppliers — Coffee and Pastries
9:30 - 9:45	Introductory Remarks — Supplier Interfaces with Design, Purchasing, Quality, Production and Finance
9:45 - 10:00	Opening Remarks and Review of Objectives by President
10:00 - 10:30	Ship-to-Stock vs. Ship-to-WIP — the Role of Inspection
10:30 - 11:00	Non-Conforming Product and Corrective Action System
11:00 - 11:30	How to Attain 100% Accuracy
11:30 - 12:00	Process Control of Manufacturing Operations
12:00 - 1:00	Lunch
1:00 - 2:00	Do It Right the First Time — Design and Suppliers
2:00 - 2:30	Quality Control
2:30 - 2:45	Coffee Break
2:45 - 3:00	Preventive Maintenance
3:00 - 3:30	Total Cost Approach to Supplier Certification
3:30 - 4:00	Management Issues and Concluding Remarks

Each member of the supplier certification team is required to present a portion of the program. This should be done in an integrated manner so that the presentation demonstrates what Supplier Certification means to your business and theirs. The president of your company should talk about competition and how it is forcing us to develop less adversarial relationships with suppliers. Indeed, the president will want to stress that a partnership is the most sensible and mutually beneficial approach to take.

The Quality team member will talk about what that department expects from suppliers. Purchasing would then discuss the criteria the company will use to select suppliers and the process of how it intends to certify them. The presentation may conclude with Manufacturing announcing that your company will practice what it is preaching by starting an internal program addressing the very same requirements.

Here is the outline of one orientation agenda developed by a client company which supplies auto parts to the Big Three and the Japanese automakers. These are the topics which our client wanted to cover. We think that their outline could be very useful in developing your own discussions at your company's supplier symposium.

SYMPOSIUM AGENDA

POTENTIAL BENEFITS

- Increased Market Share
- Reduced Cost of Quality
- Long Term Agreements
- On-Time Payments
- Process Achievable Specifications
- On-Site Assistance

REDUCED SUPPLIER BASE

- You've Been Selected Based on Our Desire to Help You Succeed
- Cooperative Effort
- Ownership

QUALIFICATION PROCESS OVERVIEW

- Business Focused
- Presurvey
- Survey — Map for the Future
- Continuous Improvement Process
- Strategic Business Initiative
- Yearly Health Check

CERTIFICATION PROCESS OVERVIEW

- Set Expectations at the Part Level
- Key Characteristics Flowdown
- Process Validation
- Manufacturing Process Change Control on Key Elements
- 100% On-Time — 100% Quality

EXECUTIVE PRESENTATION

- Quality Manager
- Purchasing Manager
- Mfg. Engineering Manager
- Vice President Operations
- Director Quality Assurance
- VP Sales & Marketing

QUALIFICATION SURVEY REVIEW

- Management Commitment
- Financial Condition/Cost Control
- Production Control
- Manufacturing Capability & Capacity
- Facilities & Equipment
- Statistical Process Control
- Tool & Gage Control
- Control of Sub-tier Suppliers
- Supplier Internal Measurements
- Configuration Management

CERTIFICATION PROCESS REVIEW

- Phase 1
  Selection of Part Numbers for Certification Process
- Phase 2
  History, Status, Documentation
- Phase 3
  Process Validation at Supplier Facility
- Phase 4
  Finalization
- Phase 5
  Certification
- Phase 6
  On-Going Audit and Maintenance

PLANT TOUR

A supplier's salespeople are not the intended guests of these symposia. We are looking for people who have the authority to buy into the process, people such as the company president, general manager, engineering department head and quality department head.

The principal message of the symposium is that we are going to work together. Therefore, once your company's speakers give this message throughout the day-long meeting, you're committed to following through. The worst thing to do is stir the pot and then let it sit on the back burner. What supplier would ever trust you again. You must demonstrate a commitment to the program before you can expect suppliers to buy in.

In the final analysis, a symposium not only describes the supplier certification program to potential participants, but acts as another step in the winnowing process. At the end of the symposium, there should be some time set aside to sign up those who are interested in joining the effort. Once you have shown your commitment to the program, it is time for the suppliers to show theirs.

One of our most recent clients, Playtex Apparel, Inc., showed its total commitment to Supplier Certification by sponsoring a first-class symposium which included breakfast, luncheon and dinner and even engraved invitations as shown on the next page. Allan W. Hall, director of purchasing, worked with Pro-Tech in putting together a dynamic program of speakers for the attendees and continues to work with Pro-Tech executive vice president Mike Termini in the continuation of that program. Attendees knew, by the careful attention given to this symposium, that Playtex was going to work hard to make Supplier Certification into a way of life. Consider showing this level of commitment when planning your symposium. It is your first chance to influence your suppliers and their first chance to judge you.

Supplier Certification Program

Playtex Apparel, Inc.

cordially invites you
to the
Inaugural Playtex Supplier Certification Symposium

date: April 2, 1992
time: 8:00 a.m. - 2:00 p.m.
place: Peachtree City Conference Center
Peachtree City, Georgia

RSVP by March 23, 1992

Pro-Tech Case Studies

WAUKESHA'S
SUPPLIER CERTIFICATION PROGRAM

What follows is an agenda, a description of Waukesha's supplier selection criteria with some charts showing what Waukesha expects from their certified suppliers and an application form for suppliers who want to participate in Waukesha's Supplier Certification program. All of this material was discussed and made available at a supplier symposium attended by 90 suppliers. First, let's look at the agenda for the two-day combined meeting and plant tour:

WAUKESHA SUPPLIER ROUNDTABLE '91
AGENDA

Monday, February 25

8:00 - 8:30 AM	Registration/Continental Breakfast
8:30 - 8:45	Director of Materials WELCOME & SCHEDULE OF EVENTS
8:45 - 9:15	John Harrison, Purchasing Manager INTRODUCTIONS
9:15 - 9:45	Peter Trombley, President WAUKESHA'S COMMITMENT TO TOTAL QUALITY MANAGEMENT
9:45 - 10:00	BREAK

10:00 - 10:30	Mike Short, Manager — Marketing & New Products WAUKESHA PRODUCTS AND MARKETS
10:30 - 11:00	Chuck Hoefflin, Director — TQM WAUKESHA'S TOTAL QUALITY INITIATIVE
11:00 - 11:30	Bob Morrison, VP — Manufacturing QUALITY IN MANUFACTURING
11:30 - 12:00	Waukesha Management QUESTIONS & ANSWERS FROM THE SUPPLIERS
12:00 - 1:15 PM	LUNCH
1:15 - 2:30	Peter Grieco, President and CEO Professionals for Technology Associates SUPPLIER CERTIFICATION ... WHAT'S IN IT FOR THE SUPPLIER?
2:30 - 2:45	BREAK
2:45 - 4:00	Peter Grieco SUPPLIER CERTIFICATION ... continued
4:00 - 4:15	Director of Materials CLOSING COMMENTS
5:45 - 7:00	RECEPTION/COCKTAILS
7:00 - 9:00	DINNER KEYNOTE SPEAKER ... Al McGuire

	TUESDAY, FEBRUARY 26
8:00 - 9:00 AM	CONTINENTAL BREAKFAST
9:00 - 9:20	BUS TRIP TO MAIN PLANT
9:20 - 11:30	TOUR OF MAIN PLANT & ENGINEERING LABS
11:30 - 11:50	BUS TRIP TO COUNTRY INN
12:00 - 1:00 PM	LUNCH
1:00	ADJOURNMENT

All of the participants at the supplier roundtable received material about Waukesha's Supplier Certification program. One of the pamphlets handed out contained an introduction to the rationale behind Waukesha's supplier selection criteria with definitions of critical points. These particular areas were accompanied by some charts showing what Waukesha expects from their certified suppliers. Above all else, Waukesha expects to "achieve a level of Total Quality consistent with the criteria established for the much coveted Malcolm Baldrige Award for world class quality... Zero defects, 100 percent, on-time delivery, and 100 percent count accuracy." That lofty goal set forth, the pamphlet goes on to say that "attainment of that objective will require a program of continuous improvement from our employees and our suppliers." The introduction concludes by announcing that it is "only through such a program that we can assure our competitive edge in a global market, today and in the future."

The Waukesha pamphlet then defines **quality** as the primary criterion in the selection and certification of suppliers. "Without quality," the pamphlet reports, "there is no market for the products we sell." Two charts accompany this section about Waukesha's quality expectations from suppliers. The first chart shows how the reject rate for a particular part will be graphed in comparison to other suppliers of the same part.

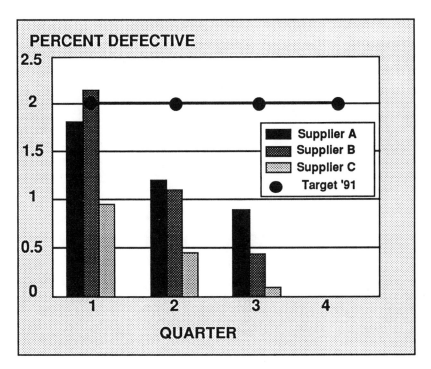

**REJECT RATE BY QUARTER —
EXAMPLE CHART**

The second graph on the next page shows the quality acceptance levels that Waukesha suppliers must maintain in order to become and remain certified. Note that by 1995, Waukesha expects zero defects.

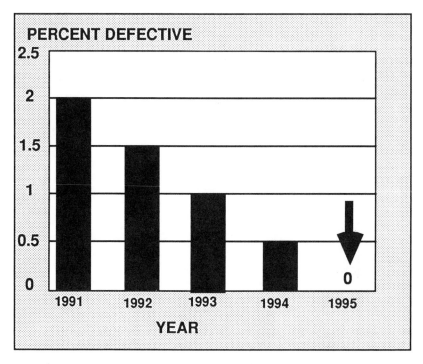

**QUALITY ACCEPTANCE LEVEL
REQUIRED FOR CERTIFICATION**

Next in importance on Waukesha's list of supplier criteria is **delivery**. The first chart on the opposite page shows how Waukesha tabulates on-time performance for each supplier. The second chart (on Page 99) illustrates the on-time delivery performance a supplier is expected to meet in the coming years in order to become and remain certified. Note that 100% compliance is expected by 1995.

Lastly, we want to show you the application form (on Page 98) which Waukesha handed out at the supplier roundtable. As you can see, it asks for a commitment on the part of the supplier to work in a partnership with Waukesha in attaining a certified status.

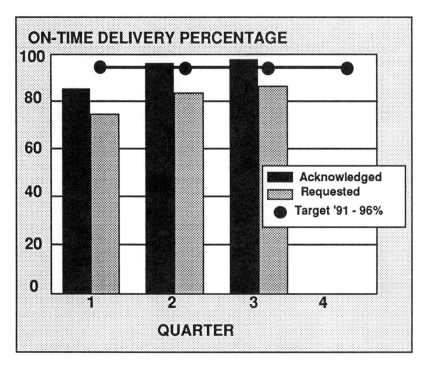

DELIVERY PERFORMANCE —
EXAMPLE CHART

DYNACHEM SUPPLIER CERTIFICATION

<u>RANKING SUPPLIERS</u>
In a previous chapter, we told you that Dynachem began ranking its suppliers by applying their selection criteria and evaluating the existing base. The aim was first to see which suppliers would make a list of Qualified Suppliers. In order to do so, they had to score 70% or above and get at least half the points allocated in the first three categories. Another list of plain Suppliers scored below 70%. Just to give you some idea what such lists look like, look at the lines we have listed on Page 99:

Waukesha ⟨*DRESSER*⟩

SUPPLIER APPLICATION FORM
WAUKESHA-DRESSER CERTIFICATION PROCESS

Applicant

Company Name _____

Address _____

City / State _____

Highest - Ranking Official

Name _____

Title _____

Description of Product

_____

_____

_____

_____

Statement

We understand that this application will be reviewed by the WED Supplier Certification Board for eligibility for certification and will be kept in strict confidence. Should our company be selected for a site survey we agree to host the visit and provide the resources necessary to examine machine capabilities, quality control plans, process flow charts and inspection records. We have read the Partnership for Excellence booklet and understand the commitment required for certification.

Signature, Authorizing Official

X _____   Date _____

Name _____

Title _____

Telephone _____

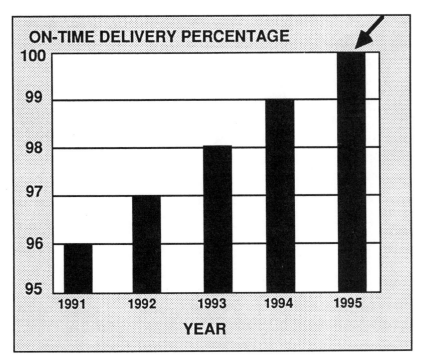

DELIVERY PERFORMANCE —
Criterion for Certification

Dynachem — Ranking Suppliers continued

SUPPLIER NAME	RATING
Company A1	66%
Company A2	64%
Company A3	56%
Company A4	43%
...	
Company B1	69%
Company B2	68%
...	
Company W8	50%
Company Y1	62%

As the company was finding out how good (or bad) their supplier base was, they were also beginning to figure out what kind of supplier base they wanted. The Supplier Certification team started by estimating how many types of suppliers (based on commodities) were needed and how many of each kind. The process they used is virtually the same as the steps described in the preceding case study by Waukesha. Here, for example, is a partial list of categories and items for Production:

CATEGORIES OF PURCHASED ITEMS
Production Items

# of Recommended Suppliers Required	PART NUMBER	DESCRIPTION	SUPPLIER NAME
	FILLER		(Fill in your
		Aerosil R-972	suppliers'
		Aluminum Oxide	names
1		Antimony pentoxide	here.)
		Bentone	
		Micro talc	
		Cab-O-Sil M5	
		Magnesol	
1		Syloid 72	
	INORGANIC CHEMICAL		
		BF-3	

The team also devised a supplier evaluation schedule which placed ownership on each member of the team for each supplier they were responsible for rating in that month. The list below shows how the task of supplier selection was divided up in September 1990:

SUPPLIER EVALUATION SCHEDULE — 1990

Buyer #1:   ABC Advertising
                DEF Cyrogenics
                GHI Co.
                JKL Pipe

Buyer #2:   MNO Science
                PQ and RS Co.
                T&U Glass
                V Glass
                WXY Co.

Buyer #3:   Z Trailer Sales
                AA Paving Co.
                BB Co., Inc.
                CC Instruments
                DD Electric

The final two charts illustrate what the Supplier Certification team decided were the number of required suppliers for two areas of the company. First, the requirements for non-inventory suppliers and then the required number of suppliers for traffic services:

NON-INVENTORY SUPPLIERS TOTAL NUMBER OF SUPPLIERS REQUIRED BY LOCATION					
	Tustin	Moss Pt.	Woburn	Regional	Total
1. ADVERTISING	6	0	0	0	6
2. COMPUTERS					
Hardware	2	2	0	0	4
Software	2	2	2	5	11
Supplies	2	2	2	5	11
Maintenance					
Lab	4	6	0	0	10
Office	1	1	1	5	7
3. CONSTRUCTION					
New	0	3	6	0	3
Remodeling	0	2	6	0	2
4. FILTERS					
Maintenance	6	3	1	5	14
Lab	3	3	0	0	6
Production	2	1	0	0	3
5. LAB					
General	8	0	2	0	8
Chemicals	8	3	2	0	13
Maintenance	2	2	3	0	4
Equip/Instr	8	0	1	0	9
Gases	3	1	0	0	4
Cln Rm Supp	3	3	0	0	6
Repairs (out)	6	5	0	0	11
Silicon Waf	2	0	0	0	2

6. MAINTENANCE				
Electrical	3	N/A	2	0	5
Plumbing	6	N/A	3	0	9
Janitorial	4	N/A	1	5	10
Motors/Bearings	3	N/A	3	0	6
A/C Supplies	3	N/A	1	5	9
Metal	2	N/A	0	0	2
Forklift					
Parts/Svce	2	N/A	2	5	9
Tools	7	N/A	2	5	14
Plastics	3	N/A	1	0	4
Hoses/Gaskets	0	N/A	4	0	4

The traffic area is normally missed by companies in the implementation stage since this department often doesn't report to the same functions as other areas involved in the process. The benefits which can be obtained in on-time delivery in this area make the effort worthwhile.

TRAFFIC SERVICES PURCHASED

Type

Names	**Number Needed**
1. Domestic Air	**2**
Emery	
Federal Express	
Burlington	
Airbourne	
2. International Air	**4**
Expeditors	
Kuegne and Nagel	
Dateline	
Nippon	
Kintetsu	

3. Courier   2
   TNT Skypack
   Federal Express

4. Mail   2
   Skypack Mailfast
   The Courier Company

5. Bulk   7
   Chemical Leaman
   Groendyke
   Matlack
   Miller Transport
   Trimac Bulk Transportation
   DSI Transport
   Ryder Bulk Tran

6. Customs — Brokerage   4
   Barnhart and Associates
   Intercontinental
   CH Powell
   RW Smith

7. Ocean Freight   5
   (APL) American President Lines
   Direct Container Lines
   NLS (Nippon Liners)
   NYK
   Maersk

8. Household Goods   2
   Schick
   Sunset

As you have probably already noticed, the company did not follow a strict rule of one source for each item or service which was purchased.

In the next chapter, we are going to look in more detail at how to do a supplier survey or audit using the criteria your Supplier Certification team has selected.

SUPPLIER
SURVEYS
AND
AUDITS

$$\overline{\underline{}} \quad 4$$

If the first part of the Supplier Certification journey is learning the Total Quality Management (TQM) mind-set and preparing a list of supplier selection criteria, then the second part is surveying suppliers to determine whether they meet a quantitated level of acceptance. The criteria developed in the last chapter forms the basis of surveys.

In general, the criteria looks for two things — the presence of a sound total business process and a manufacturing process which is under control. In particular, we judge suppliers in the major areas shown on the next page.

SURVEY CRITERIA

Quality Management
Design Information
Procurement
Material Control
Manufacturing Control
Final Inspection
Calibration
Quality Information

The above also forms the basis for supplier audits. One of the more frequent questions asked is: "What is the difference between a supplier survey and a supplier audit?" In its simplest terms, a survey of a supplier is conducted before it manufactures a product. The survey determines what is happening at the supplier's plant. An audit, on the other hand, is conducted after a supplier begins making a product. Its purpose is to assure us that what we want to happen is, indeed, happening at the supplier's plant. A survey is used to find a supplier capable of producing zero-defect parts which will be shipped on-time. An audit can be thought of as a maintenance tool, whereby we check to see that the supplier's quality and manufacturing processes remain under control. An audit can also be used as a method to improve a supplier's performance by pointing out weaknesses. It can point out areas where more education and training is needed. For a more thorough discussion of surveys and audits, we recommend that you view Tape #4 in our VideoEducation Series, *"Supplier Certification: The Path to Excellence."*

MANAGEMENT MATURITY LEVELS

The first indicators of a supplier's potential to be certified are company-wide in nature — management commitment and organizational status. These elements, of course, can also be used to determine your own management maturity levels. Let's look first at the levels of understanding and attitude.

At the first level, a company's management has no comprehension whatever of supplier certification, Just-In-Time or Total Quality Management. At the second level, management is aware of what must be done, but have committed no dollars to the program. As money is added, management rises to the third level in which they are willing to learn and support expansion of Supplier Certification programs.

At the fourth level, management is actively participating in quality and manufacturing control programs. The suppliers of level four companies are actively involved with quality in this process. The fifth level is the goal that both we and our suppliers want to attain. At this level, management sees supplier certification as an integral part of their company.

Both the status of the company as a whole and the status of its quality organization go hand-in-hand with management maturity levels. The chart at the top of the next page shows the characteristics of a company at each of the five levels.

We should be looking for suppliers who rank in Level 3 to Level 5 on all three scales. As you can see, there is some measure of management commitment at this level and this commitment is essential to the success of a Supplier Certification program.

Levels	Management Traits	Quality Organization	Company Status
1	Lack of understanding	No inspector present	Unaware of what causes poor quality
2	Sees value of change, but no commitment of money	Firefighting mode; symptoms treated, not causes	Constant quality problems are present
3	Willing to change, support and learn	Management becomes involved in prevention	Commitment to continuous improvement
4	Management is participating	Quality effectively controls process	Shift to defect prevention
5	Management is part of improve-ment team	Zero-defects is the only acceptable method	Supplier certification is a way of life

EVALUATION METHODS

Evaluating suppliers must be quantified with no subjectivity entering into the evaluation. We do this by assigning a point value to each criterion. That is what companies do when they use a Supplier Certification program to determine which suppliers are World Class and which ones will not be able to make the grade. Surveys and audits using quantifiable questions are of extreme importance. *Do not* take a short cut for this step. And don't use fuzzy questions like this:

DON'T ASK: Do I feel like this supplier can make the product?

Instead, we must let this question be our guide:

ASK: Does the supplier have his plant processes under control and the capability to make the product?

The first question elicits fuzzy answers. The answers to the second question can be objectively quantified, using the point values listed below as we record responses and gather evidence for the selection criteria:

Evaluation Criteria Point Value

Points	Statement
5	**DEMONSTRATES HIGH CAPABILITY, CONTINUOUS IMPROVEMENT PROGRAMS ARE IN PLACE** (A) Problem has been identified (B) A solution has been developed to ELIMINATE the problem (C) System has been in place for an adequate period of time and cause HAS BEEN (virtually) eliminated • Documented Continuous Improvement Process is in place
4	**MINOR IMPROVEMENT CAN RESULT IN PERFORMANCE IMPROVEMENTS, EFFECTIVE PLANNING AND IMPLEMENTATION DEMONSTRATED** (A) Problem has been identified (B) A solution has been developed to ELIMINATE the problem (C) System has been in place too short a time to determine if cause will be eliminated • No documented Continuous Improvement Process in place

Evaluation Criteria Point Value

Points	Statement
3	**CORRECTIVE ACTION IS REQUIRED, IMPROVEMENTS EXPECTED IN SYSTEM OR IMPLEMENTATION** (A) Problem has been identified (B) A solution is being developed to eliminate the cause (system has not yet been implemented) • Improvements in the system or its implementation are necessary to meet the expectations • A documented Continuous Improvement Process is required
2	**MAJOR IMPROVEMENTS EXPECTED, COMMITMENT TO IMPROVEMENT DEMONSTRATED AND DOCUMENTED** (A) Problem has been identified (B) No solution has been developed
1	**CRITICAL DEFICIENCIES OBSERVED, LACK OF COMMITMENT TO IMPROVE** (A) Problem HAS NOT BEEN identified • No commitment to improvement with documented corrective action plan
N/A	**NOT APPLICABLE**

One further word about objectivity. There are two schools of thought about how to conduct surveys. One school says to send a survey out to suppliers and ask for their input, then to read the results and conduct the on-site surveys. The second school of thought advocates going directly to the supplier first to conduct surveys. Which method you choose is subject to many variables, but we hold with the second school. We want to avoid a company responding in a positive way, then having us determine if the survey was completed correctly.

There is some material that can be obtained before conducting a survey. Information like annual financial reports, 10K's, and supplier quality manuals are acceptable presurvey material since they are more objective. Other areas, however, need to be explored at the supplier's plant in dialogue with workers and managers so that we can make objective judgments based on the evidence.

Before conducting a survey, we should also be prepared to have the appropriate members of our team pose the right questions to the supplier's representatives. Know in advance who will talk to the supplier's finance, engineering, manufacturing and quality departments. The team is drawn from the people involved in developing the supplier selection criteria. Their questions should start as broad ones which will progressively focus in on an area of detail.

PRESURVEY QUESTIONNAIRE

One of our clients is very thorough about its Supplier Certification Program. Before it does a supplier survey, the team issues a Presurvey Questionnaire (see next page). This survey is for informational purposes only and not all the questions are applicable to all companies who are asked to fill it out. Besides company ownership and type of business, the questionnaire attempts to ascertain how sophisticated the supplier's current quality practices are and whether the supplier is moving toward

Statistical Process Control (SPC) and Total Quality Management (TQM). Its purpose is also to find out if the supplier is already certified by another company. As mentioned before, this makes the certification process at your company go much faster for a pre-certified supplier. A number of categories are indicated in this survey. Most simply ask whether a process or testing procedure is in place and what types of machines are currently being used.

PRESURVEY QUESTIONNAIRE

GENERAL:

Company Name _____   Supplier SIC _____
Street _____
City _____
State, Zip Code _____
Phone _____   Fax _____
Owner _____   Years in Business ___

STATUS OF OWNERSHIP:

Corporation ___
Partnership ___
Sole Proprietorship ___
Who is your parent company? _____

BUSINESS STATUS:

Small ___
Minority Owned ___
Woman Owned ___
Foreign ___
Large ___

CONTACTS:

Sales _____   Quality _____
General Manager _____   Delivery _____
Production Control Manager _____

TYPE OF BUSINESS:

Manufacturing ___   Assembly ___
Service ___   Raw material ___
Distributor ___

Are you presently certified by any other customers? Yes __ No __
List your top three customers and what percentage of your business
they represent.

_____

_____

_____

Do you have (check those that apply):
___ EDI (Electronic Data Interface)?
___ Statistical Process Control?
___ Total Quality Management Program?
___ Computerized Planning System?

List your sub-tier special processing suppliers (Please attach form if
necessary)

_____

_____

_____

FACILITIES:

Plant Size (sq. ft.) _____
Plant condition _____ Equipment condition _____
Number of production shifts _____
Total number of employees _____
    Manufacturing _____ Administration _____ Engineering ____
List all your facilities by location _____

_____

_____

TOOL CONTROL:

Do you have a formal tool control system?
        Yes ___ No ___ N/A ___

FINANCIAL:

Are your records available for audit by appointment?
   Yes ___   No ___   N/A ___
What are your annual shipments (average 2 years)? _____
What percentage of your annual shipments are procured by our
company? _____
What is your total past due committed shipments (in dollars)? _____

PROCESS CONTROL:

Record the elements that apply to the process control systems
applicable to your manufacturing operations.

	Yes	No
SPC used	___	___
Process routing	___	___
Process routing controlled	___	___
Routing ID by customer number	___	___
Tooling controlled	___	___
Special handling explained	___	___
Dimension requirements shown	___	___
Revised procedure	___	___
Geometric requirements shown	___	___
Revision recorded	___	___
In-process revision system	___	___
Sketches/drawing	___	___
Material control on routing	___	___
In-process inspection	___	___
Time standards used	___	___

COMMENTS:
_____
_____
_____

QUALITY CONTROL SYSTEM:

Record the elements that apply to the quality control systems
applicable to your manufacturing operations.

	Yes	No
Vision systems	___	___
Coordinating measuring machine	___	___
Fluorescent penetrant inspection	___	___
Magnetic particle inspection	___	___
Radiographic inspection	___	___
Ultrasonic inspection	___	___
Optical comparator	___	___
Air gauges	___	___
In-process inspection	___	___
Pressure test	___	___
Gear inspection	___	___
Other	___	___

COMMENTS:

_____

_____

_____

_____

PARTS:

What is the maximum part size able to be processed at your facility?
    ___ 6"   ___ 12"   ___ 18"   ___ 24"   ___ other

What is the minimum part size able to be processed at your
facility? _____

Which minimum linear position tolerance is most comfortable for your
manufacturing operation?
    ___ below .001   ___ .002   ___ .003

Which minimum diametric tolerance is most comfortable for your
manufacturing operation?
    ___ below .005   ___ .0005   ___ .001   ___ .002

Which form of raw material is routinely processed in your facility?
    Bar ___%   Sheet ___%   Forging ___%
    Casting ___%   Other ___%

Which of the following most accurately describes the scope of your manufacturing operations?

___ Research and Development
___ Small production (1-50)
___ Medium production (50-500)
___ Large production (500-2500)
___ Other _____

How does your facility handle the following tooling requirements?

Dies?	___ Design	___ Build
Gages?	___ Design	___ Build
Fixtures?	___ Design	___ Build
Special machines?	___ Design	___ Build

Which of the following materials does you facility routinely work with?

___ Titanium   ___ Non-metallic
___ Stainless   ___ Light alloy
___ High temperature   ___ Composites
___ Steel   ___ Hazardous materials
___ Iron   ___ All
___ Plastics   ___ Other

Which of the following test procedures are used at your facility?

___ Pressure   ___ Leak
___ Flow   ___ Other

What percentage of your products are for the military? _____
For commercial? _____

Please record your Franchise Distributor List below:

_____
_____
_____
_____

What control system is presently used for the control of raw stock?

_____
_____
_____
_____

What system is presently used for tool control within your facility?

_____

_____

_____

_____

MANUFACTURING EQUIPMENT:

	QUANTITY		Index or "C" Axis Capability
TURNING	Man.	CNC	Y N
A. Horizontal B. Vertical C. Turret D. Engine E. Chucker F. Micro G. Screw machine			
MILL			
A. Horizontal B. Vertical C. Multi-axis D. Machining center E. Precision boring F. Jig bore G. Profile			

JOINING	QUANTITY		
	Man.	CNC	
A. Arc weld			
B. TIG weld			
C. MIG weld			
D. E-beam			
E. Atmosphere			
F. Spot weld			
G. Laser weld			
H. Roll weld			
I. Seam weld			
J. Planishing			
K. Torch braze			
L. Furnace braze			
M. Dip braze			
N. Induction braze			
O. Riveter			
P. Pre-assembly			
Q. Bi-alloy weld			
FORM	QUANTITY		
	Man.	CNC	
A. Hydro			
B. Drop hammer			
C. Punch press			
D. Bulge			
E. Elec. Mag.			
F. Hot			
G. Super plastic			
H. Hydra			
I. Expand			
J. Mechanical			
K. E-shape			
L. Spinning			
M. Roll			
N. Tube bending			

GRIND	QUANTITY		
	Man.	CNC	
A. I.D. Horizontal			
B. I.D. Vertical			
C. O.D.			
D. Surface			
E. Creep feed			
F. Centerless			
G. Hone			
H. Angle head			
I. Lap			
J. Thread			
K. Jig			
L. Gear			
M. Fir trees			
N. Crush			

NON-TRADITIONAL MACHINING	QUANTITY		
	Man.	CNC	
A. E.D.M.			
B. Wire E.D.M.			
C. E.C.M.			
D. E.C.G.			
E. Laser cutting			
F. Balance			
G. Water jet			
H. Abrasive flow			
I. Chem mill			
J. Plasma cutting			
K. Composites			
L. Wrap-up			
M. Composite fibre			

BROACH	QUANTITY		
	Man.	CNC	
A. Vertical B. Horizontal C. Splines D. Fir trees E. Disc F. Hobs G. Shapers			
DRILL	QUANTITY		
	Man.	CNC	
A. Multi-drill B. Gun drill C. Small hole D. Radial E. Laser			

CASTING/MOLDING:

What are your primary manufacturing processes?

___ Investment   ___ Sand
___ Perm. Molding   ___ Plastic
___ Die casting   ___ Other _____

With what raw materials are you most familiar?

___ Valve bodies   ___ Manifolds
___ Structural   ___ Stators
___ Other _____

What is your maximum pour weight?

Air melt _____ lbs.
Vacuum melt _____ lbs.
Aluminum _____ lbs.
Other _____

What is your Min. and Max. shot capacity?

_____ - _____   2 -10 ton
_____ - _____   2 -30 ton
_____ - _____   2 -90 ton
_____ - _____   2 -150 ton
_____ - _____   2 - _____ ton

What is your ferrous shrink factor?

____ 0 - 1.4%   ____ 2-3%   ____ Other _____

What is your aluminum shrink factor?

____ 0 - 1%   ____ 1.1 - 1.5%   ____ Other _____

What binders and stuccoes do you use?

___ Ethyl silicate   ___ Colloidal silica
___ Raw silica   ___ Fused silica
___ Pepset   ___ Solid mold
___ Dry sand   ___ Green sand
___ Thermoset   ___ CO2
___ SO2

What wax injection machines do you have?

                      Quantity
___ to 35 ton
___ 36 to 50 ton
___ 51 to 100 ton
___ 101 to 150 ton
___ over 150 ton

What molding stations do you have?

                      Quantity
___ Green sand
___ Jolt and squeeze
___ Jolt, squeeze and
     roll over
___ Other _____

What die casting machines do you have?

Quantity

___ to 50 ton
___ to 100 ton
___ to 300 ton
___ to 600 ton
___ over 600 ton

What perm. molding machines do you have?

Quantity

___ None
___ 1 - 5
___ 6 - 10
___ 11 - 20
___ over 20

What plastic injection machines do you have?

Quantity

___ to 50 ton
___ to 100 ton
___ to 300 ton
___ to 600 ton
___ over 600 ton

Record the equipment available within your facility to accommodate the following processes:

	Yes	No
Anodic	___	___
Chem film	___	___
Paint	___	___
Plating	___	___
Metal spray	___	___
Plasma spray	___	___
T.B.C. coatings	___	___
Clean	___	___
Degrease	___	___
Grit blast	___	___
Glass bead	___	___

	Yes	No
Shot peen	___	___
Stress rel.	___	___
High temp heat treat	___	___
Vac. furnace heat treat	___	___
Alum. heat treat	___	___
Carburize	___	___
Nitride	___	___

What military or commercial specification are used as compliance criteria within your facility?

1. _____
2. _____
3. _____
4. _____
5. _____

COMMENTS:

_____
_____
_____
_____

SUPPLIER SURVEY CHECKLIST

At the beginning of this chapter, we identified several major areas of criteria used when surveying suppliers. The survey which follows contains nine critical areas. In the next chapter, you will find several more examples of supplier surveys. We would like to thank all of our clients and associates who allowed us to share this data with you. Our intent is for you to pick the topics that fit your requirements so that you do not have to reinvent the wheel. What is most important is that you begin this process *now*.

SUPPLIER SURVEY FORM

Table of Contents and Score Summary

Section	Supplier Score	Avail. Points
1. Raw Materials: Receiving,Testing, Storage and Release to Manufacturer	_____	21
2. Manufacturing: Record Retention and Control	_____	6
3. Manufacturing: Operation	_____	7
4. Process Control/Capability	_____	21
5. Nonconforming Product and Corrective Action System	_____	12
6. Total Quality Management	_____	13
7. Packing and Shipping	_____	17
8. Safety and Housekeeping	_____	3
9. Management		
Total Available Points in Survey		100
Total Points Earned in Survey	_____	

SECTION 1
Raw Materials: Receiving, Testing, Storage and Release to Manufacturer

The customer's quality requirements should be the same as those of the manufacturer's suppliers. The goal is to verify that procurement procedures are in place which guarantee consistent quality, delivery and quantity. The right material must not only be procured and verified, but identified and controlled to assure that it gets to the right place at the right time. Companies need to control material flow from the time it reaches the receiving dock to the time it is shipped.

	Yes	No	Value
1. Is a supplier selection and evaluation program in progress for new and existing raw materials and suppliers?	—	—	2
2. Is a supplier certification program in existence for the supplier's suppliers?	—	—	3
A. Are audits performed on at least an annual basis?	—	—	1
3. Receiving			
A. Is there a written procedure for receiving raw materials?	—	—	.5
B. Are proper identification labels used for each container of a shipment?	—	—	.5
C. Are records kept describing shipment amounts and arrival dates?	—	—	.5
4. Raw Material Testing			
A. Are supplier-supplied test results of raw materials monitored?	—	—	1
B. Are test results of suppliers correlated to the plant's test results by statistical methods?	—	—	1

C.   Are the same test procedures and
standards shared by supplier and plant?   __   __   __.5__

D.   Is control reference testing
done on a weekly or monthly
basis? Are the results of the
testing monitored and control
charted?   __   __   __1__

E.   Are test procedures reviewed
and audited on a regular basis?   __   __   __.5__

F.   Are written procedures used
for sampling all raw materials
which are tested?   __   __   __.5__

5. Release to Manufacturing
Is there a written plan to make
sure that the raw materials
supplied to the manufacturing
process:

A.   Have passed approved tests?   __   __   __1__

B.   Are the quantities correct?   __   __   __1__

C.   Are they delivered on-time?   __   __   __1__

6. Storage

A.   Is appropriate segregation
and identification provided
for qualified, non-conforming
and untested raw materials?   __   __   __2__

B.   Are written instructions used
for the handling and storage of
raw materials to prevent
degradation or contamination?   __   __   __1__

C.   Are there requirements for
marking containers?   __   __   __.5__

D.   Are storage and retrieval
practices based on control
for shelf life, manufacture
date and correct identification?   __   __   __1__

E.   Do storage practices include
control for correct location
in area, bin or shelf?   __   __   __.5__

F.   Is storage and retrieval of raw
     materials restricted to
     authorized personnel?   __ __ __1__

Total Points for Section 1   _____

SECTION 2

Manufacturing: Record Retention and Control

Unused or unusable data is evidence of poor management. The goal is to
ensure that quality data is used to improve the operations on a continuous
basis.

			<u>Yes</u>	<u>No</u>	<u>Value</u>

1. Manufacturing Documentation
    A.   Is there a person designated
         to control and authorize
         revisions to work instructions?   __ __ __1__
    B.   Is there a list of documents
         to be controlled?   __ __ __1__
    List of documents:

    _____

    _____

    _____

    C.   Is there a written procedure
         and distribution list for
         communicating changes to
         documents?   __ __ __1__

2. Record Control
    A.   Is the retention time for
         records defined?   __ __ __.5__
    B.   If computers are used, is a
         back-up system in place?   __ __ __1__
    C.   Is there a designated place
         for storage of records?   __ __ __.5__

    D.   Are obsolete drawings and
         specifications removed from use?   ___   ___   __1__

Total Points for Section 2   _____

SECTION 3

Manufacturing: Operation

Inaccurate calibration and inadequate preventive maintenance of fixtures and equipment can result in either the rejection of good material or the acceptance of defective material. The goal is to maintain calibration standards which are consistent and conform to national or industry standards as well as good manufacturing practices.

		<u>Yes</u>	<u>No</u>	<u>Value</u>
1 Calibration				
A.	Does the calibration system comply with MIL-STD?	___	___	__1__
B.	Is the calibration function performed by a designated and adequately trained individual group?	___	___	__1__
C.	Are dates of next and last calibration marked on or near the items to be periodically calibrated?	___	___	__.5__
2.	Do operators make frequent gaging checks on their work?	___	___	__.5__
3. Preventive Maintenance				
A.	Is there a computer system or written schedule for triggering periodic preventive maintenance on manufacturing equipment?	___	___	__1__
B.	Is there a written procedure for performing preventive maintenance on manufacturing equipment?	___	___	__.5__

C.   Is preventive maintenance
work documented and are
records maintained for the
life of each piece of equipment?   ___ ___ ___.5___

4. Tooling and Equipment
A.   Is maximum tool life determined
by the supplier and communi-
cated to the employees?   ___ ___ ___.5___
B.   Does the process sheet indicate
the appropriate machine or work
center for certain materials
or processes?   ___ ___ ___.5___

5. Are process instruction, procedure
sheets, batch sheets and travelers
used during manufacture? Do they
contain requirements of each
operation for manufacturing
and process control?   ___ ___ ___.5___

6. Are manufactured lots kept intact
and traceable throughout the
process? How?   ___ ___ ___.5___

Total Points for Section 3   _____

SECTION 4

Process Control

Quality characteristics can best be verified during the production process.
The goal is to institute procedures which guarantee that quality control is
conducted in-process and that process control resides at the operator level.

	Yes	No	Value
1. Is Statistical Process Control used?	___	___	___1___
A. What is the method?	___	___	___1___
B. Is there a plan for SPC?	___	___	___1___

2. Is there a written procedure for
   process control?   — — __1__
   A. Does it define methods of
       reporting?   — — __.5__
   B. Does it outline frequency and
       timing?   — — __.5__
   C. Does it include the maintenance
       of statistically based control
       charts?   — — __.5__

3. Is there a written procedure for
   process audits?   — — __1__
   A. Does it specify methods for
       reporting findings and
       recommendations?   — — __.5__
   B. Does it define methods for
       recording corrective action
       items and responsibilities?   — — __.5__

4. Are process controls set up
   at all critical points in the
   process?   — — __4__

5. Is process control data prepared
   and distributed often enough to
   give early warning of developing
   problems?   — — __1__
   A. Does the data show when the
       process is in control?   — — __1__
   B. Does the data show when the
       process is improving?   — — __1__

6. Does the process control system
   trigger corrective action when the
   process is not within control
   limits?   — — __2__

7. Are process changes controlled,
   authorized and documented?   — — __1__

8. Is SPC at operator level?   ___ ___ ___1.5___

9. Are there training programs
   for SPC at management, mid-
   management and operator level?
   What is it?   ___ ___ ___1___

10. Is there evidence of a set-up
    reduction program to allow for
    quick change?   ___ ___ ___1___

11. Does the supplier use the tools
    of statistically designed experiments
    to solve quality problems and
    optimize process conditions for
    continual quality improvement?   ___ ___ ___1___

Total Points for Section 4   _____

SECTION 5

Nonconforming Product and Corrective Action System

Corrective action is necessary during manufacturing operations to monitor
and control processes, prevent the manufacture of large quantities of
defective parts and to provide uniformity. Corrective action should follow
up the results of fallout and document the follow-up.

                                                <u>Yes</u> <u>No</u> <u>Value</u>

1. Is all nonconforming product
   segregated and physically identified
   to prevent its use as acceptable
   product?   ___ ___ ___2___

2. Is there a corrective action and
   improvement process for nonconforming product to prevent
   and control recurring defects?
   A. Is there a time element for
       response?   ___ ___ ___2___

3. Is there a functioning written
    procedure that outlines the
    process for receiving, testing,
    and processing any returned
    product?   ___ ___ ___2___

4. Do written records include
    reasons for return?   ___ ___ ___2___

5. Do written records include
    reasons for return, defect found
    and corrective action taken?   ___ ___ ___2___

6. Is Pareto analysis of complaints,
    returns and losses performed?   ___ ___ ___2___

Total Points for Section 5   _____

SECTION 6

Quality Management

The key to the management of quality comes from the supplier's philosophy, objectives and organizational structure. The goal is to determine whether management is integrally involved in quality and whether responsibility and authority for quality extends to the operator level.

	Yes	**No**	**Value**

1. Is there a written corporate
    quality policy?   ___ ___ ___1___

2. Quality Control (QC) Manuals
    A.   Are QC manuals and QC
         procedures in use?   ___ ___ ___.5___
    B.   Are all levels of the plant
         trained in QC?   ___ ___ ___.5___
    C.   Are the QC manuals reviewed
         regularly and updated as
         needed?   ___ ___ ___.5___

3. Are written inspection procedures
   used for in-process product and
   final product inspection?   ___ ___ ___1___

4. Are inspection records on file and
   up-to-date?   ___ ___ ___1___

5. Do inspection records show when
   reworked material is submitted
   for reinspection?   ___ ___ ___1___

6. Do inspectors use statistically based
   sampling plans that provide valid
   confidence and quality needs?   ___ ___ ___2___

7. Is there a segregated QC lab or
   inspection area?   ___ ___ ___1___

8. Is there sample retention?   ___ ___ ___1___

9. Is quality data used as a basis for
   corrective action?   ___ ___ ___2___

10. Does the operator have the authority
    to stop the production line?   ___ ___ ___1.5___

Total Points for Section 6   _____

SECTION 7

Packing and Shipping

Proper packing procedures are critical to the elimination of waste and to the guarantee of on-time delivery, 100% of the time. Companies need to put procedures into written form so that customer requirements can be met.

                                        <u>Yes</u> <u>No</u> <u>Value</u>

1. Where are packaging specifications
   maintained and how?   ___ ___ ___2___

2. Are there written procedures for
   packaging product?   ___ ___ __2__

3. Are there written procedures which
   outline the details of shipping the
   product (schedules, logbooks, etc.)?   ___ ___ __2__

   A. Are customer traffic and routing
       instructions visible in the
       shipping area?   ___ ___ __1__

4. Are there written procedures for
   including proper enclosures with
   each shipment?   ___ ___ __1__

   A. Are there written procedures
       for marking containers for
       shipping legally and as
       requested by the customer?   ___ ___ __1__
   B. Are the methods for
       shipping hazardous material
       documented and understood?   ___ ___ __1__
   C. Is a certificate of compliance to
       specifications and test results
       enclosed and signed by an
       authorized person?   ___ ___ __1__
   D. Who has the responsibility?   ___ ___ __1__

5. Is on-time delivery measured?   ___ ___ __4__

6. Is there Bar Coding capability?   ___ ___ __1__

Total Points for Section 7   _____

SECTION 8

Safety and Housekeeping

Housekeeping should be part of preventive maintenance. It means that everything has a place and everything is in its place. This makes for a safer working environment.

	Yes	No	Value
1. Does the supplier understand or use Good Manufacturing Practices (GMP)?	___	___	___1___
2. Is there a written safety program?	___	___	___.5___
3. Are all areas of the plant kept clean and free of non-essential items?	___	___	___.5___
4. Is the supplier in compliance with the right-to-know law for employees?	___	___	___.5___
5. Has the supplier been cited by any agency for any violations?	___	___	___.5___

Total Points for Section 8   _____

SECTION 9

Management

This section provides an overview of each responsibility of management in their relationship with suppliers. You will notice that we place no point values in this section. Without management commitment, a supplier cannot qualify.

	Yes	**No**
1. Management Support		
A. Is area performance communicated to management on a regular basis? (Customer service, accuracy, inventory control, process control, etc.)	___	___

B.   Is quality data utilized by management for corrective action? How?   ___ ___

C.   Is management receptive to new ideas, change for continual quality improvement?   ___ ___
   Examples:

   _____

   _____

   _____

   _____

D.   Does management support a partnership relationship with customers and suppliers?   ___ ___

E.   Are employee education/involvement programs in progress?   ___ ___

F.   Is the organizational structure documented? (Obtain a copy.)   ___ ___

G.   Has management identified and made timely provisions for the special controls, processes, tools and skills required for assuring the product's quality and continual quality improvement?   ___ ___

2. Plant Functioning and Planning

   A.   Are capacity utilization rules in place?   ___ ___
      What is the percentage? _____
      What is the current load? _____
      What percentage is for our company? _____

   B.   Is a production plan in place?   ___ ___
      Is work in process tracked?   ___ ___
      How is it done? _____

   C.   Is the facility capable of frequent deliveries of small lots?   ___ ___

   D.   What is the manufacturing lead time? _____

3. Financial Situation
   Obtain a copy of annual report from supplier.
   Obtain Standard and Poor's index ratings from our company.

If you would like to add more questions to this survey, we suggest that you review the ISO 9000, Q90's and Malcolm Baldrige

Quality Award criteria. For more information on these programs, see Chapter 12.

POST-SURVEY ACTIVITY

Once a survey has been conducted and evaluated, the next job is to write a final report which recommends whether or not a supplier is capable of being first qualified and then certified. Here is an example of a post-survey summary:

QUALIFICATION SURVEY SUMMARY

Company Name		Surveyed by	
Address		Accompanied by	
City, State, Zip		Initial Survey	Resurvey
Phone		Survey Date	
Supplier Code		Contact	

RECOMMENDATIONS

ACTION PLAN IS DUE BY: _____

SUPPLIER ACKNOWLEDGMENT:

_____   _____
Signature   Date

A copy of the completed survey with the final report should be sent to the supplier, whatever the recommendation. We have seen many instances of suppliers who have taken areas of weakness and turned them into positive programs of improvement. Many of these suppliers have eventually gone on to become certified. In a certain sense, the final report is free consulting. Companies that want to improve their performance will use it to their advantage. Companies who ignore it will most likely become extinct.

As for the recommendation, there are three categories. Each requires a different set of post-survey activities.

1. NOT RECOMMENDED:

The supplier, in this case, has no evidence or documentation of a control system; major defects in its control system; or, cannot demonstrate an acceptable process. The deficiency in the control system and/or process will require in excess of 60 days to correct.

A "Supplier Corrective Action" report will be issued requesting correction of these discrepancies. Upon receipt of satisfactory answers, a resurvey will be required. At that time, the supplier may be moved to a conditional status.

The example at the top of the next page is of a letter that can be used to notify suppliers who were not recommended for entry into the company's Supplier Certification program.

2. CONDITIONALLY RECOMMENDED TO THE QSL LIST:

The supplier has inadequacies in its control system documenta-

Date

Supplier Name
Street Address
City/State/Zip

Dear _____:

We have completed our evaluation of your company
and its operations on **(date)** with **(names of company
representatives)** and **(supplier representative)** in
attendance.

This letter is to inform you that your company has <u>not</u>
<u>been</u> <u>recommended</u> to enter into the Supplier Certifica-
tion Process due to the findings recorded during the
evaluation survey.

Should you have further questions, please contact me at
(phone).

Thank you,
(signature)

---

tion, but the process or processes appear to be working satisfactorily. A "Supplier Corrective Action" report will be issued
requesting the supplier to submit an improvement plan for each of
the discrepancies. If the plan is not submitted within 60 days, the

rating will be changed to "Not Recommended." For suppliers in this category, we should sign a conditional agreement with the supplier like the one below:

CONDITIONAL AGREEMENT

THE DISCREPANCY AND/OR DEFICIENCIES DE-
SCRIBED IN THIS REPORT ARE VERIFIED AND
WILL BE CORRECTED BY THE DATE DESIGNATED
IN OUR ENCLOSED ACTION PLAN:

_____   _____
DATE   COMPANY NAME

SUPPLIER STATUS WILL BE UPGRADED TO "REC-
OMMENDED" WHEN PURCHASING RECEIVES
WRITTEN EVIDENCE OF THE PROMISED CORREC-
TIVE ACTION ON OR BEFORE THE AGREED DATES
AND DETERMINES THAT IT MEETS THE SURVEY'S
MINIMUM REQUIREMENTS.

_____   _____
DATE   SUPPLIER SIGNATURE

                              _____
                                          TITLE

---

3. RECOMMENDED TO THE QSL LIST:

The supplier has adequate document evidence of compliance and meets the minimum point value. In addition, the supplier's demonstrated process appears to be working satisfactorily. Within this category are suppliers who are ready and willing to undergo the certification process. The next step, then, is to develop a supplier partnership as described in the following chapters. Below is an example of what an acceptance letter looks like:

Date

Supplier Name
Street Address
City/State/Zip

Dear _____:

On behalf of the Supplier Certification team, we would like to congratulate your company for successfully achieving the status of "QUALIFIED SUPPLIER." Your commitment to the Continuous Improvement Process has resulted in our confidence that your company will supply us with the highest quality products and service complying with every aspect of the specifications. Our Supplier Certification Team will be contacting you to start Phase I in the implementation of the certification program.

Thank you for your efforts in meeting this milestone and for your continued participation in the process.

Sincerely,
(signature)

The next chapter provides you with some real life examples of how some of our clients developed their survey form and process. We think Chapter 5 will be of genuine value to your organization. The work and effort put into these examples should significantly cut your own cycle time in preparing a survey. The surveys should and can be used as benchmarks for your company.

UTILIZING
SUPPLIER
SURVEYS

================ 5

In this chapter's case studies, we will be presenting actual client examples of supplier surveys with additional information which helps in their development. The last example shows a survey form which displays the actual scores earned by a supplier evaluated by International Totalizator Systems. It lets you see exactly how things add up and gives you some idea of how different items get rated. As you look through these surveys, you will note many differences in terms of categories and questions, but the overall design is the same for everyone of them. It is this common ground upon which you will build your own survey.

Pro-Tech Case Studies

KRAFT-GENERAL FOODS
Buena Park, California

This survey was supplied to us by Ken Hollon, C.P.M., Asset Manager, of Kraft-General Foods. It is an excellent example of a survey used by a food products manufacturer for raw material and packaging suppliers. Many companies, it should be noted, develop more than one survey. We suggest that you develop different surveys for various areas of purchasing. Note how it emphasizes sanitation and other areas of importance to the food industry:

SUPPLIER CERTIFICATION TEAM
CRITICAL ITEM CHECKLIST
KRAFT-GENERAL FOODS RAW MATERIAL

SUPPLIER: _____
DATE: _____

                                              COMMENTS

1. BUILDING AND FACILITIES
A. Outer Grounds   _____
B. Building Exterior   _____
C. Building Interior   _____
D. Employee Facilities   _____
E. Utilities   _____

2. PROCESS AREA AND EQUIPMENT
A. Extraneous Matter Potential   _____
B. Maintenance and Sanitary Design   _____
C. Housekeeping   _____
D. Sanitation Programs   _____
E. Sanitation Effectiveness   _____
F. Employees' G.M.P.'s   _____

3. RAW MATERIAL CONTROL
A. List of Raw Material
B. Purchased and Tested per Specification   _____
C. Purchased per Pure Food Guarantee   _____
D. Receiving Inspection Program   _____
E. Receiving Sampling Program   _____
F. Raw Material Testing Program   _____
G. Storage (Proximity to Contaminants)   _____
H. Out of Standard Raw Material (Disposition)   _____

4. IN-PROCESS CONTROLS
A. Written Formula and Procedures   _____
B. Process Control Records   _____
C. Additive usage   _____
D. Rework usage   _____
E. Raw Material Traceability (Lot #'s)   _____
F. In-Line Testing   _____
G. In-Line Testing Points   _____
H. Extraneous Matter Control   _____

5. FINISHED PRODUCT CONTROL
A. Finished Product Testing   _____
B. Finished Product Weight Control   _____
C. Container Testing or Inspection   _____
D. Product Identification   _____
E. Code or Lot Number Breakdown   _____
F. Size of Lot   _____
G. Storage Conditions — In-House   _____
H. Storage Conditions — Outside   _____
I. Age of Inventory (Slow Movers)   _____
J. Recall Procedure   _____
K. Out of Standard Product (Disposition)   _____

6. QUALITY CONTROL PROGRAMS
A. Check Programs   _____
B. Pest Control — Internal   _____
C. Pest Control — Outside   _____
D. Use of Fumigants (Type)   _____
E. Inspection Programs   _____
F. Record Retention (How Long)   _____

7. SPECIAL INFORMATION
A. Management Quality Policy Statement _____
B. Quality Control Reporting Function   _____
C. Following GMP's per FDA Orders   _____
D. Type and Date of Last Government Inspection _____
E. Any Unusual Product Problems   _____
F. Co-Packers Used   _____
G. Date of Kraft Specification   _____
H. Kraft Purchasing Contact   _____
I. Process Flow Chart   _____

ADDITIONAL COMMENTS:

_____

_____

_____

_____

_____

**SUPPLIER CERTIFICATION TEAM
CRITICAL ITEM CHECKLIST
KRAFT-GENERAL FOODS PACKAGING SUPPLIES**

The survey below is used to evaluate packaging suppliers. It differs in many ways from raw materials for obvious reasons.

SUPPLIER: _____
DATE: _____

                                        COMMENTS
1. BUILDING AND FACILITIES
A. Outer Grounds   _____
B. Building Exterior   _____
C. Building Interior   _____
D. Employee Facilities   _____
E. Utilities   _____

2. PROCESS AREA AND EQUIPMENT
A. Potential for Contamination   _____
B. Housekeeping   _____
C. Employee's G.M.P.'s   _____
D. Production Records   _____
E. Production Procedures & Job Description _____
F. In-Process Testing (Frequency & Test Points) _____

3. FINISHED GOODS CONTROL
A. Proper Label Identification   _____
B. Proper Code Date and/or Lot No.   _____
C. Code or Lot No. Breakdown   _____
D. Size of Lot   _____
E. Storage Conditions — Inside   _____
F. Storage Conditions — Outside   _____
G. Age of Inventory (Slow Movers)   _____
H. S/B Career Inspection Program   _____
I. Recall Procedure (Traceability)   _____

4. QUALITY CONTROL PROGRAMS
A. Raw Material Testing (Toxicity, Bacteriological, etc.)   _____
B. Finished Goods Testing (Toxicity, Bacte., Physical etc.) _____
C. Pest Control — Internal (Freq., Records, FIFRA, etc.)   _____
D. Pest Control — Outside (Firm, Freq., Records, etc.)   _____
E. Inspection Programs (G.M.P., Housekeeping, etc.)   _____

5. SPECIAL INFORMATION
A. Management Quality Policy Statement   _____
B. Quality Control Reporting Function   _____
C. Date of Kraft Inspection   _____
D. Kraft Purchasing Contact   _____
E. Process Flow Chart   _____
F. Type and Date of Last Government Inspection   _____

ADDITIONAL COMMENTS

_____

_____

_____

_____

DYNACHEM
Tustin, California

At this point in Dynachem's Supplier Certification Program, the team had thought of every criteria they thought possible. They then sent a memo to every manager and supervisor in the company asking for their input. With a little convincing, the team got a 90 percent response and a number of new criteria to consider. Eventually, all the criteria were categorized into ten areas and weighted by different members of the team and ratified by the whole team. The weighting factors used by Dyanchem are as follows:

Section	Category	Weighted Value
1.0	Product that meets Dynachem specifications, providing batch-to-batch consistency.	30
2.0	Least Total Cost	13
3.0	A program of Statistical Process Control	12
4.0	On-time, complete delivery	10
5.0	Technical and commercial assistance with new and existing products	10
6.0	Commitment to Dynachem's Certification Program	9
7.0	Consistent, complete Quality documentation	5
8.0	Lot continuity with a minimum number of lots per shipment	5
9.0	Integrity	3
10.0	Regulatory and environmental compliance	3
	Total Value	100

Using these criteria as headings, the team then drafted a detailed Supplier Survey and Measurement Worksheet. One survey, as it turned out, was not adequate for the job of qualifying different types of suppliers. The team, working from the "raw" criteria which they had brainstormed and gathered from people throughout the company, decided to develop four survey forms. They then established that a supplier had to score at least 70 out of 100 total points and at least 15 points for the first category, 7 points for the second category and 6 points for the third category to become qualified. It should be noted here that in a survey, it would be best if a supplier scored at least 70 percent in all ten categories. In this way, it becomes difficult for a supplier to qualify who is very strong in a few areas, but lacks strength throughout the business. You must keep in mind that you are rating the supplier's overall business.

Before the team set out on the task of surveying suppliers, the members decided to publish a memo in order to introduce the supplier survey process to all personnel. This was done so that the Supplier Certification program would become a "grassroots" movement in order to gain acceptance and commitment. The next step the team took was to publish this memo and the four surveys (note how the differences among them indicate areas of special importance to a particular company area):

SUPPLIER CERTIFICATION MEMO

To: All Employees
From: Supplier Certification Team
Subject: DYNACHEM SUPPLIER CERTIFICATION
                 PROGRAM

We have undertaken a process of Supplier Certification so that Dynachem will always receive quality product, purchased from suppliers dedicated to satisfying our needs.

SUPPLIER CERTIFICATION MEMO cont.

Supplier Criteria have been developed to use in the selection and measurement of suppliers. Criteria for Production, Non-Production, Transportation and Warehousing are posted below.

These Supplier Criteria were developed through a company survey that solicited opinions on what makes a "good" supplier. Our Criteria reflect those attributes we as a Company value in our internal and external suppliers.

The purchasing authority in each Dynachem location is using these standards when considering our external procurement requirements.

We encourage each of you to consider these criteria when evaluating your internal suppliers, and the service you give to your own internal customers.

Developing supplier selection criteria is the first step in our Supplier Certification Program; a process designed to ensure we have the high-quality, consistent supplier base required to compete in the 90's and beyond.

To learn more about the Certification Program, or to join the Team, please contact any of us:

Moss Point	Steve Gilmore, Phil Lofty, Henry Loper, Harrel Paul
Tustin	Mary Bennett, Sid Bloom, Lou Boffardi, Gene Collins, Kathy Parham, Cassandra Rice, Nick Segro, LeAnn Zunich
Woburn	Phil Hubis, Gerri Jackson, Tom McNamara

We would like to take this opportunity to thank the staff at Dynachem for sharing their supplier survey forms with us. It should save many companies a significant amount of time in preparing their own survey elements. The first survey below for Production Material Requirements represents suppliers who manufacture components considered direct material or inventory classification.

SUPPLIER SELECTION AND MEASUREMENT CRITERIA WORKSHEET
SURVEY ONE

Production Requirements

Supplier: _____ Rating: _____
Product(s): _____ Date: _____
Evaluator(s): _____

Evaluate the supplier, using the criteria below. A supplier may be awarded any point value within the range:

Criteria	Possible Points	Rating
1.0 **Product that meets Dynachem Specifications, providing Batch-to-Batch consistency**		
1.1 A documented system, including written specifications and/or requirements, for the control of out-going material quality	5	

Criteria	Possible Points	Rating
1.2 Non-conforming materials are identified clearly and segregated to prevent shipment to Dynachem	**1**	
1.3 A program for improvement and reducing variability of the quality of purchased and manufactured materials	**1**	
1.4 Analysis, including those requested by Dynachem	**5**	
1.5 Specification range for analysis is equal to or better than those requested by Dynachem	**5**	
1.6 Certification of analysis compliance	**3**	
1.7 Employees are familiar with Dynachem's requirements and expectations	**2**	
1.8 Test procedures are identified and made available for review	**2**	
1.9 Obsolete specifications, procedures, drawings and requirements are purged	**2**	
1.10 Proposed changes or raw material source changes affecting Dynachem products are communicated to Dynachem	**4**	
1.0 **TOTAL**	**30**	

Criteria	Possible Points	Rating
2.0 **Least Total Cost**		
2.1 Material meets specs	7	
2.2 On-time delivery	3	
2.3 Competitive price	2	
2.4 Favorable terms — N30 or better	1	
2.0 TOTAL	13	
3.0 **A Program of Statistical Process Control**		
3.1 Process of ongoing quality improvement in place	2	
3.2 Management, direct employees and indirect employees trained in SPC	3	
3.3 SPC is actively being used	2	
3.4 Processes maintain a process capability of at least 1.33 (Cp) for Dynachem products	3	
3.5 Cpk is within 20% of Cp	2	
3.0 TOTAL	12	

Criteria	Possible Points	Rating
4.0 **On-time, complete delivery**		
4.1 Material delivered within 1 day (24 hours) of due date	**4**	
4.2 Order 100% complete	**3**	
4.3 Supplier stocks one month's requirements	**2**	
4.4 Stocking warehouse within 150 miles	**1**	
4.0 **TOTAL**	**10**	
5.0 **Technical and Commercial Assistance with new and existing products**		
5.1 New Product development to meet future needs	**3**	
5.2 Technical recommendations for usage, improvement, and a willingness to do correlation studies	**3**	
5.3 Responsiveness to telephone calls	**2**	
5.4 Provide Technical seminars for Dynachem	**2**	
5.0 **TOTAL**	**10**	

Criteria	Possible Points	Rating
6.0 **A Commitment to Dynachem's Certification Program**		
6.1 Signed Letter of Commitment to Dynachem's Certification Program	3	
6.2 Program of Supplier Certification for raw materials	3	
6.3 Documented Program of Continuing Improvement	3	
6.0 TOTAL	9	
7.0 **Consistent, complete Quality documentation**		
7.1 Up-to-date procedures, specifications and drawings with a positive recall system for production and non-production, including tools which affect the final product	2	
7.2 Records of Inspection and Process Control	1	
7.3 Control and distribution of Documents — Process	.5	
7.4 Procedures for storage, segregation and timely disposition of discrepant materials	.5	
7.5 Up-to-Date Quality Manual	.5	
7.6 Cost of Quality Measurement System	.5	
7.0 TOTAL	5	

Supplier Certification II

Criteria	Possible Points	Rating
8.0 **Lot Continuity with a Minimum Number of Lots per Shipment**		
8.1 Minimum number of Lots	3	
8.2 Lots numbered consecutively	2	
8.0 TOTAL	5	
9.0 **Integrity**		
9.1 Published Code of Ethics	1	
9.2 Published Policy on Conflict of Interest	1	
9.3 Evidence of open lines of communication between management and other team members	1	
9.0 TOTAL	3	
10.0 **Regulatory and Environmental**		
10.1 Established mandatory training program for all personnel on: Handling of Dangerous Goods, Loading Compatibility, and Classification, Packaging, Marking and Labeling	1.5	

Criteria	Possible Points	Rating
10.2 Published emergency response procedures and guidelines, including: Chemtrec membership, updated MSDS availability, training and compliance with HM 126C	1.5	
10.0 **TOTAL**	3	

SUMMARY

Total Possible Points	**100**
Total Points Awarded	___
% Rating	___

OTHER: Number of Shipments: ____
      Number of Rejections: ____
      Reject % ____

This second survey for non-production items, usually called MRO items, has a wide range of use. In terms of time, it is also one of the longest process steps taken in certifying a supplier. Many of the items purchased in this area are bought one time or represent tooling, pens, paper, equipment, etc.

SUPPLIER SELECTION AND MEASUREMENT CRITERIA WORKSHEET SURVEY TWO

Non-Production Requirements

Supplier: _____   Rating: _____
Product(s): _____   Date: _____
Evaluator(s): _____

Evaluate the supplier, using the criteria below. A supplier may be awarded any point value within the range:

Criteria	Possible Points	Rating
1.0 **Product that meets Dynachem Specifications**		
1.1 A documented system for the control of out-going material	5	
1.2 Non-conforming materials are identified clearly and segregated to prevent shipment	5	
1.3 A program for improvement of the quality of purchased and manufactured materials	5	
1.4 Specification range is equal to or better than those requested by Dynachem	5	
1.5 Employees are familiar with Dynachem's requirements and expectations	3	
1.6 Obsolete specifications, procedures, drawings and re-quirements are purged	3	
1.7 Proposed changes or material changes affecting Dynachem products are communicated to Dynachem	4	
1.0	TOTAL	30

Criteria	Possible Points	Rating
2.0 **Least Total Cost**		
2.1 Material meets specs	7	
2.2 On-time delivery	3	
2.3 Competitive price	2	
2.4 Favorable terms — N30 or better	1	
2.0 TOTAL	13	
3.0 **On-time, complete delivery**		
3.1 Material delivered within 1 day (24 hours) of due date	4	
3.2 Order 100% complete	3	
3.3 Stocking warehouse within 150 miles	1	
3.0 TOTAL	8	
4.0 **Technical and Commercial Assistance with new and existing products**		

Criteria	Possible Points	Rating
4.1 New Product development to meet future needs	2	
4.2 Technical recommendations for usage, improvement	3	
4.3 Responsiveness to telephone calls	3	
4.4 Provide Technical seminars for Dynachem	2	
4.0 TOTAL	10	
5.0 A Commitment to Dynachem's Certification Program		
5.1 Signed Letter of Commitment to Dynachem's Certification Program	3	
5.2 Program of Supplier Certification	3	
5.3 Documented Program of Continuing Improvement	3	
5.0 TOTAL	9	
6.0 A Program of Statistical Process Control		
6.1 Process of ongoing quality improvement in place	2	

Criteria	Possible Points	Rating
6.2 Management, direct employees and indirect employees trained in SPC	3	
6.3 SPC is actively being used	2	
6.0 **TOTAL**	7	
7.0 **Consistent, complete Quality documentation**		
7.1 Up-to-date procedures, specifications and drawings with a positive recall system for production and non-production, including tools which affect the final product	2	
7.2 Records of Inspection and Process Control	1	
7.3 Control and distribution of Documents — Process	.5	
7.4 Procedures for storage, segregation and timely disposition of discrepant materials	.5	
7.5 Up-to-Date Quality Manual	.5	
7.6 Cost of Quality Measurement System	.5	
7.0 **TOTAL**	5	

Criteria	Possible Points	Rating
8.0 **Integrity**		
8.1 Published Code of Ethics	1	
8.2 Published Policy on Conflict of Interest	1	
8.3 Evidence of open lines of communication between management and other team members	1	
8.0 **TOTAL**	3	
9.0 **Regulatory and Environmental**		
9.1 Established mandatory training program for all personnel on: Loading, Packaging, Marking and Labeling	**1.5**	
9.2 Published emergency response procedures and guidelines	**1.5**	
9.0 **TOTAL**	3	

SUMMARY

Total Possible Points	**88**
Total Points Awarded	___
% Rating	___

OTHER: Number of Shipments: ___
       Number of Rejections: ___
       Reject % ___

The third survey is for providing the requirements used when evaluating transportation suppliers. It can also be used for all types of logistic suppliers — ocean, air and surface.

SUPPLIER SELECTION
AND MEASUREMENT
CRITERIA WORKSHEET
SURVEY THREE

Transportation Requirements

Supplier: _____ Rating: _____
Product(s): _____ Date: _____
Evaluator(s): _____

Evaluate the supplier, using the criteria below. A supplier may be awarded any point value within the range:

	Possible	
Criteria	**Points**	**Rating**
1.0 **On-Time Delivery**		
1.1 Agreed upon percentage for on-time delivery Percentage: _____	**15**	
1.2 Performance against published transit time Published time: _____	**10**	
1.0 [TOTAL]	**25**	

Criteria	Possible Points	Rating
2.0 **Pick-Up Service**		
2.1 Agreed upon percentage of on-time pick-ups, based on call-in cut-off times Percentage: _____	10	
2.0 TOTAL	10	
3.0 **Claims Handling**		
3.1 Timely investigation, within 15 days of delivery	1	
3.2 Claims acknowledgment in 30 days	2	
3.3 Disposition within 120 days	2	
3.4 Agreed upon percentage of claims to shipments handled Percentage: _____	5	
3.0 TOTAL	10	
4.0 **Billing Accuracy**		
4.1 Agreed upon percentage of correctly rated freight bills Percentage: _____	10	
4.0 TOTAL	10	

Criteria	Possible Points	Rating
5.0 **Tracing Response**		
5.1 Agreed upon response time to phone and written inquiries Time: _____	3	
5.2 Up-time of automated tracing systems	2	
5.0 ☐ **TOTAL**	5	
6.0 **Equipment Availability**		
6.1 Performance against agreed upon call-in cut-off times Time: _____	5	
6.0 ☐ **TOTAL**	5	
7.0 **Equipment Condition**		
7.1 Trailer cleanliness	1	
7.2 Condition of trailer: holes or nails in floor, roof leaks, etc.	2	
7.3 Compliance to established vehicle safety inspections	2	
7.0 ☐ **TOTAL**	5	

Criteria	Possible Points	Rating
8.0 **Personal Contact**		
8.1 Courteous employees: drivers, dispatchers, customer service, rate clerks, etc.	1	
8.2 Professional drivers	1	
8.3 Timely response to inquiries	2	
8.4 Sales representatives follow-up	1	
8.0 ☐ **TOTAL**	5	
9.0 **Management Reports**		
9.1 Compliance with agreed upon reporting requirements	1	
9.2 Timely, complete and accurate reporting	3	
9.3 EDI capabilities	1	
9.0 ☐ **TOTAL**	5	
10.0 **Cost Containment**		
10.1 Carrier performance against profitability goals Goals: _____	4	

Criteria	Possible Points	Rating
10.2 Competitive rates	10	
10.3 Impact of general rate increase	2	
10.4 Performance against contract terms	4	
10.0 TOTAL	20	

SUMMARY

Total Possible Points	**100**
Total Points Awarded	___
% Rating	___

OTHER: Number of Shipments: ___
Number of Rejections: ___
Reject % ___

As is true for other suppliers, a survey of warehousing or distribution facilities is also required. The fourth survey provides a starting point for developing criteria for this type of supplier.

**SUPPLIER SELECTION
AND MEASUREMENT
CRITERIA WORKSHEET
SURVEY FOUR**

SURVEY FOUR

Warehousing Requirements

Supplier: _____   Rating: _____

Product(s): _____   Date: _____

Evaluator(s): _____

Evaluate the supplier, using the criteria below. A supplier may be awarded any point value within the range:

Criteria	Possible Points	Rating
1.0 **On-Time/Accurate Order Completion**		
1.1 Same day pull of orders	5	
1.2 Shipment of open orders within one working day	5	
1.3 Orders accurate +2 percent per month	5	
1.4 Documentation accurate to one keystroke per page	5	
1.5 Facility has EDI capability	5	
1.0 **TOTAL**	25	
2.0 **Claims Handling**		
2.1 Objective investigation within 30 days	3	

Criteria	Possible Points	Rating
2.2 Disposition within 120 days	2	
2.0 **TOTAL**	5	
3.0 **Billing Accuracy**		
3.1 Bills 100% accurate	10	
3.0 **TOTAL**	10	
4.0 **Tracing Response**		
4.1 2 hour response to telephone inquiries	2.5	
4.2 7 day response to written inquiries	2.5	
4.3 In-house product tracking/tracing system	5	
4.0 **TOTAL**	10	
5.0 **Storage Facility Condition**		
5.1 Warehouse is clean	5	

Criteria	Possible Points	Rating
5.2 Warehouse and Equipment in good working order, including roof, racking, forklifts, etc.	5	
5.3 Warehouse has regular safety inspections	1.5	
5.4 Warehouse follows established safety rules	1.5	
5.5 Warehouse operates at least 10 hours a day, 5 days a week	2	
5.0 TOTAL	15	
6.0 Personal Contact		
6.1 Courteous employees: dispatchers, customer service, etc.	10	
6.2 Response to inquiries within 24 hours	5	
6.0 TOTAL	15	
7.0 Cost Containment		
7.1 Performance against profitability goals	5	

Criteria	Possible Points	Rating
7.2 Competitive rates	15	
7.0 ☐TOTAL	20	

SUMMARY

Total Possible Points	**100**
Total Points Awarded	___
% Rating	___

OTHER: Number of Shipments: ___
   Number of Rejections: ___
   Reject % ___

What may also be required by some companies is a survey form or addendum for suppliers of services. More time needs to be spent on these areas of Supplier Certification. Early developments in the field tended to focus on the inventory and direct material area.

IMPLEMENTATION OF A SURVEY

In Chapter Four, we shared a Presurvey Questionnaire and some samples of letters which would be sent to suppliers who qualified and those who did not. Let's now put this early step and last step into the total picture. The flow chart on Pages 175-176 will help you follow the sequence of actions described here.

First, the Supplier Liaison Team identifies suppliers that will be asked to participate in the company's Supplier Certification Program. These suppliers are then invited to a Supplier Symposium at which qualification criteria is outlined via a Supplier Certification Package and sample surveys. After the orientation, appropriate liaison teams schedule on-site surveys at the facilities of participating suppliers. These results are then evaluated and the supplier is advised whether they are "not recommended", "conditionally recommended" or "qualified". Those suppliers that are conditionally recommended are asked to meet with the team in order to establish a corrective action plan. After a suitable period of time, these suppliers are then reevaluated.

Suppliers which are qualified are added to the Purchasing Department's Qualified Supplier List (QSL) when the supplier has reached an agreement with the department on the terms in the Supplier Partnership Agreement. This agreement spells out the responsibilities of both parties in the certification process and is not a purchase order. It works in conjunction with other purchasing agreements, blanket orders or system contracts. The agreement is a mutually developed document which simply states that the supplier will deliver parts that conform to the company's requirements 100 percent of the time.

Recently, the legal department at one of our clients said that they had a problem with the use of the word "partnership." They felt that the word had a legal meaning all to itself. Our advice is to talk with your legal departments early in the program in order to clear up any problems like this.

The team may decide that the process of Supplier Certification should be the responsibility of a Buyer/Planner or team member. The process may begin with a memo like the one shown on Page 177 which is sent by the initiator who is recommending the candidate to the Supplier Certification Steering Committee.

SUPPLIER QUALIFICATION FLOW CHART

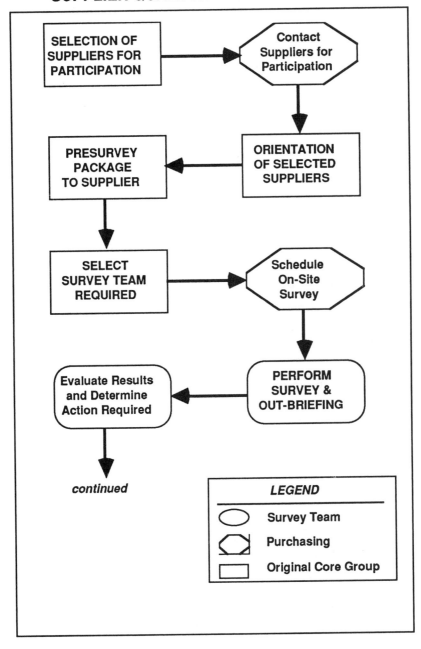

SELECTION OF SUPPLIERS FOR PARTICIPATION → Contact Suppliers for Participation

ORIENTATION OF SELECTED SUPPLIERS → PRESURVEY PACKAGE TO SUPPLIER

SELECT SURVEY TEAM REQUIRED → Schedule On-Site Survey

PERFORM SURVEY & OUT-BRIEFING → Evaluate Results and Determine Action Required

continued

LEGEND

◯ Survey Team

⬡ Purchasing

▭ Original Core Group

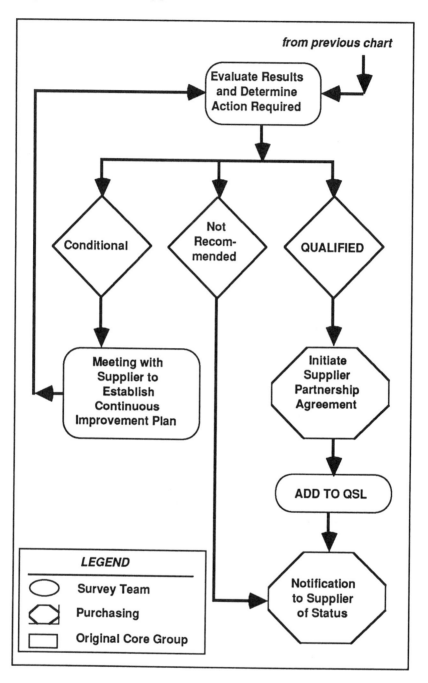

SUPPLIER QUALIFICATION CANDIDATE

DATE:
    TO: Supplier Certification Steering Committee
  FROM: Initiator (see below)
SUBJECT: Supplier Participation in Qualification Process

Please consider the supplier named below for participation in
the Supplier Certification Qualification Process:

Supplier Name	Supplier Code
Street Address	Phone Number
City, State, Zip	Contact/Title

- This supplier has ___ open Purchase Order, ___ part numbers.

- Yearly volume $ _____

- They presently have a ___% Delivery Rating and a ___% Quality Rating.

- The primary commodities this supplier provides are
  _____
  _____

- They have been awarded long-term contract on ___ part numbers.

- Schedule site survey.

Initiator's Name	Initiator's Title

This request, as you can see, only addresses a minimum of criteria. Also, before submitting such a request, be sure that there are no plans to remove the supplier from the Approved Supplier List. It is essential in today's business world to select suppliers that meet a minimum level of acceptance.

We have provided an actual survey used by a manufacturer of auto parts.

SUPPLIER QUALIFICATION
PROCESS EVALUATION

Category	Category Name	Possible Points	Actual Points	Scoring %
I	Management Commitment	30		
II	Finances/Total Cost Control	60		
III	Production Control	45		
IV	Capability and Capacity	30		
V	Facilities & Equipment	20		
VI	Statistical Process Control	35		
VII	Tool & Gage Maintenance	15		
VIII	Sub-tier Suppliers	15		
IX	Internal Measurements of Suppliers	30		
X	Configuration	25		

```
┌─────────────────────────────────────────────────────────┐
│              REQUIREMENTS for QUALIFICATION               │
│                                                           │
│  •   Minimum score of 60% in each category for initial    │
│      qualification                                        │
│                                                           │
│  •   Continuous improvement each year as agreed           │
│      upon at annual evaluation                            │
│                                                           │
│  •   Current Quality Rating of 99% minimum                │
│                                                           │
│  •   Delivery Rating of 95% minimum                       │
│                                                           │
└─────────────────────────────────────────────────────────┘
```

I. MANAGEMENT COMMITMENT

EXPECTATION: Management is the vital link in a supplier's organization, the key link that will ensure a successful Supplier Certification effort. A management philosophy which is totally committed to the goal of 100% QUALITY and DELIVERY with the involvement of all employees is necessary for a supplier to achieve qualification. It is the management's responsibility to establish these aggressive goals and targets which will drive a company to the level of a true world class supplier. The following criteria are designed to evaluate the supplier's commitment to the Certification program and to document the implementation of Total Quality Management in their facilities.

		Possible Score	Actual Score
1	Is the production performance communicated to management as well as employees on a regular basis? Describe method and frequency.	5	

_____

_____

_____

		Possible Score	Actual Score
2	Is management receptive to new ideas and change for continual quality improvements with employee involvement? Record examples below.	5	

_____

_____

_____

| 3 | Are employees involved in a training program? Record description, duration, frequency and percentage of involvement. | 5 | |

_____

_____

_____

| 4 | Has management identified a business plan describing commitments of capital and resources? Does the document plan for succession? | 5 | |

- Organization structure
- Capital
- Resources
- Current and future markets
- Future expansions

_____

_____

_____

| 5 | Does company have ethics policy committing the supplier to 100% quality and delivery? | 5 | |

_____

_____

_____

6   Does company support a Concurrent Engineering (CE) program at this facility with other customers?

Possible Actual
Score Score

If not, would supplier be willing to participate in
CE program?   5

_____

_____

_____

TOTALS
ACTUAL ÷ POSSIBLE X 100 = ___ %

II. FINANCES / TOTAL COST CONTROL

EXPECTATION: Financial stability is important when planning
for a long-term partnership with a supplier. It is also important to
know whether the supplier supports the company's commitment
to continuous improvement.

	Max Points	Earned Points
Section A — Sound Financial Condition	80	_____
Section B — Reinvestment Practices	<u>20</u>	_____
	100	

(TOTAL X .25) = ACTUAL SCORE

SECTION A: SOUND FINANCIAL CONDITION

Historical Ratio Analysis		
		Points
Current Ratio	Current Assets ÷ Current Liabilities =	_____
Quick Ratio	(Current Assets - Inventory) ÷ Current Liabilities =	_____
Acid Test	(Cash + Marketable Securities) ÷ Current Liabilities =	_____
Debt to Equity	Total Liabilities ÷ Net Worth =	_____
Return on Investment	Net Profit ÷ Total Assets =	_____

SCORING MATRIX					
POINTS	**CR**	**QR**	**AT**	**DE**	**ROI**
4	2.0	1.0	.4	.7	.14
3	1.7	.7	.3	1.0	.10
2	1.3	.5	.2	2.0	.07
1	1.0	.2	.1	4.0	.03
0	For any score less than level above				
TOTALS					

EVALUATION TOTAL VALUE	HISTORICAL RATIO ANALYSIS POINTS
12 and above	80
11	75
10	70
9	60
8	50
7 and below	0

SECTION B: REINVESTMENT PRACTICES

Trend Analysis

Historical	Prior Completed Fiscal Year	Most Recent Completed Fiscal Year	Less Than 5% Decrease Yes No		Points
(1) CASH FLOW			5	0	
(1) NET INCOME			5	0	
(1) RETURN ON SALES			5	0	
(2) CAPITAL EXPENDITURES RATIO			< 5% Increase		
			5	0	
			TOTAL		

Historical Scoring

(1)   If most recent completed fiscal year is greater than prior completed fiscal year times .95, then score 5 points, otherwise score 0 points.

(2)   If most recent completed fiscal year is less than prior completed fiscal year times 1.05, then score 5 points, otherwise score 0 points.

Terms Defined

Cash Flow   Net cash provided by (used in) operating activities.

Net Income   Income from continuing operations.

Return on Sales   Net Income + Sales

Capital Expenditures Ratio   Accumulated Depreciation + First cost of property, plant and equipment.

II. FINANCES / TOTAL COST CONTROL cont.

EXPECTATION: Financial stability is important when planning for a long-term partnership with a supplier. It is also important to know whether the supplier supports the company's commitment to continuous improvement.

		Possible Score	Actual Score
1	To what extent does the supplier have a cost accounting system?	5	
2	To what extent is the supplier willing to share cost data with the company, allowing examination of historical, actual and projected cost data?	5	
3	To what extent does the supplier develop and track operating budgets and forecasts estimating future costs in labor, overhead, capital expenditures, etc.?	5	
4	To what extent is the supplier willing to enter into long-term contracts with the company and our suppliers in order to extend cost reductions to us?	5	
5	To what extent does the supplier have a viable cost estimating and tracking system where they com-		

	Possible Score	Actual Score
pare actual performance to what was estimated?	5	

6   To what extent is the supplier willing to commit to product life cycle costing?   **5**

7   To what extent is the supplier willing to participate in performance incentives based on delivery, quality or holding costs in check?   **5**

TOTALS
ACTUAL ÷ POSSIBLE X 100 = ____ %

III. PRODUCTION CONTROL

EXPECTATION: Establishing what steps to take in order to adhere to the purchase order schedule is essential. Once a plan to meet the delivery date is implemented, all phases must be monitored and, if necessary, expedited, in order to assure the integrity of the purchase order agreement.

	Possible Score	Actual Score
1 How well does the supplier's production control system identify the steps needed to be taken to execute the committed purchase order date?	5	

	Possible Score	Actual Score

2 How well does the supplier monitor work-in-process in order to maintain schedule adherence?   5

_____

_____

_____

3 How well does the supplier manage capacity availability?   5

_____

_____

_____

4 How well does the supplier monitor and, if necessary, expedite subcontract orders?   5

_____

_____

_____

5 How well does the supplier track and monitor delivery performance to its customers?   5

_____

_____

_____

6 If schedule slippage occurs, how well does the supplier take corrective action in order to bring the project back on schedule?   5

_____

_____

_____

7 If schedule slippage is unavoidable from the supplier's perspective, is there a system to notify the customer and to solicit their input in order to correct slippage?   5

_____

_____

_____

		Possible Score	Actual Score
8	Is the Master Production Schedule centrally managed?	5	

_____

_____

_____

		Possible Score	Actual Score
9	How well is the Master Production Schedule executed?	5	

_____

_____

_____

TOTALS

ACTUAL ÷ POSSIBLE X 100 = ____%

IV. CAPABILITY & CAPACITY

EXPECTATION: In order to achieve 100% quality and 100% delivery, a supplier must have the appropriate manufacturing capability and adequate available capacity.

		Possible Score	Actual Score
1	To what extent does the supplier have documented process plans?	5	

_____

_____

_____

		Possible Score	Actual Score
2	To what extent does the supplier have the appropriate diversification of equipment to produce our planned products?	5	

_____

_____

_____

		Possible Score	Actual Score
3	To what extent are the employees qualified to perform their job functions? (Training/Experience)	5	

_____

_____

_____

		Possible Score	Actual Score
4	To what extent does the supplier have a set-up/ queue reduction plan or program in place?	5	

_____

_____

_____

| 5 | To what extent does the supplier have a capacity planning/tracking system in place? | 5 | |

_____

_____

_____

| 6 | How well does the supplier use its capacity planning/tracking system to determine availability of capacity to accept and meet purchase order delivery dates? | 5 | |

_____

_____

_____

TOTALS

ACTUAL ÷ POSSIBLE X 100 = ____ %

V. FACILITIES and EQUIPMENT

EXPECTATION: The condition of the supplier's facilities and equipment is reflected in the caliber of the products produced. It is important to determine the supplier's commitment to maintaining these fixed assets to assure the continued production of a high caliber product.

		Possible Score	Actual Score
1	How well are the supplier's facilities maintained?	5	

_____

_____

_____

		Possible Score	Actual Score
2	How well does the supplier maintain its equipment?	5	

_____

_____

_____

		Possible Score	Actual Score
3	Does the supplier have a preventive maintenance program in place for both the facilities and the equipment?	5	

_____

_____

_____

		Possible Score	Actual Score
4	To what extent does the supplier meet the state and federal environmental and regulatory requirements?	5	

_____

_____

_____

TOTALS
ACTUAL ÷ POSSIBLE X 100 = ____%

VI. STATISTICAL PROCESS CONTROL

EXPECTATION: Statistical Process Control (SPC) uses mathematical techniques to distinguish between natural and special causes of process variation. Once a process is operating with only natural variation, its capability of meeting specifications can be accurately determined. SPC is a system that helps prevent problems by logically analyzing/controlling processes and by identifying difficulties/solutions. Its goals are to eliminate waste, optimize processes and enhance predictability.

		Possible Score	Actual Score
1	To what extent have Pareto charts been used to determine areas/processes in need of statistical control?	5	
2	To what extent have process control limits been calculated?	5	
3	To what extent are control charts being used?	5	
4	To what extent has a control limit corrective action plan been implemented?	5	
5	To what extent have process capability studies been performed?	5	

		Possible Score	Actual Score

6 How adequately does process capability information affect manufacturing decisions?   **5**

_____

_____

_____

7 To what extent does final inspection rely on control chart/capability data?   **5**

_____

_____

_____

TOTALS
ACTUAL ÷ POSSIBLE X 100 = _____ %

VII. TOOL and GAGE MAINTENANCE

EXPECTATION: Good tool and gage control is instrumental in assuring that production requirements are met. It is important to assess the supplier's commitment to establishing a high level of tool and gage storage, control and maintenance.

		Possible Score	Actual Score

1 How well does the supplier's storage area accommodate the tooling and gaging issued to the facility?   **5**

_____

_____

_____

2 What type of tracking system does the supplier maintain in order to control the movement and

	Possible Score	Actual Score

calibration status of tooling/gaging within the facility?   5

_____

_____

_____

3   Does the supplier administer a routine maintenance
program to insure the proper functioning of tooling
and gaging?   5

_____

_____

_____

TOTALS

ACTUAL + POSSIBLE X 100 = ___ %

VIII. SUB-TIER SUPPLIERS

EXPECTATION: Control of sub-tier suppliers is important to the
successful manufacturing of products which meet customer requirements.

	Possible Score	Actual Score

1   To what extent are the methods used for selection
of suppliers based on the results of the following: 5
   a. Supplier System Evaluation
   b. Delivery Ratings
   c. Quality Ratings

_____

_____

_____

2   To what extent do Purchase Orders contain all
necessary information for compliance to the fol-

	Possible Score	Actual Score

lowing customer requirements:
  a. Customer contract flowdown requirements
  b. Complete definition of work scope   5

_____

_____

_____

3 To what extent are the results of Receiving Inspection documented and fed back to the appropriate
areas: 5
  a. Nonconformance data to the Supplier
  b. Acceptance data to the Supplier

_____

_____

_____

                                        TOTALS
            ACTUAL ÷ POSSIBLE X 100 = ____%

IX. INTERNAL MEASUREMENTS OF SUPPLIERS

EXPECTATION: A measurement system which provides information on trends which impact the supplier's business is essential
to a long-term partnership.

	Possible Score	Actual Score

1 To what extent does the supplier use customer
ratings of their business?   5

_____

_____

_____

		Possible Score	Actual Score
2	To what extent does the supplier maintain an internal delivery rating sytsem which is based on Purchase Order delivery date?	5	

_____

_____

_____

| 3 | To what extent does the supplier use milestones for continuous improvement on customer components? | 5 | |

_____

_____

_____

| 4 | To what extent does the supplier track scrap percentages and dollars?
  a. Internal?
  b. Sub-tier? | 5 | |

_____

_____

_____

| 5 | To what extent does the supplier track rework pieces and hours?
  a. Hours?
  b. Pieces? | 5 | |

_____

_____

_____

| 6 | To what extent does the supplier track nonconformances, both internal and external?
  a. Internal?
  b. External?
  c. Customer? | 5 | |

_____

_____

_____

TOTALS

ACTUAL ÷ POSSIBLE X 100 = ____ %

X. CONFIGURATION

EXPECTATION: Configuration Management is important in a long-term partnership in order to assure that product deliveries reflect customer needs. The system provides for controls over design, manufacture and hardware identification, all of which are key to customer satisfaction.

		Possible Score	Actual Score
1	How adequately does the system flowdown and control component revision ordered by customer?	5	
2	To what extent are the supplier's internal documents used for manufacturing components controlled for latest issue?	5	
3	To what extent can procured item purchases and special process information be traced to end item shipments?	5	
4	To what extent are there specific work instructions that assure the proper identification of hardware?	5	
5	How adequate is the configuration control system for supplier designed components and assemblies?	5	

TOTALS

ACTUAL ÷ POSSIBLE X 100 = ____ %

INTERNATIONAL
TOTALIZATOR SYSTEMS, INC.

Thanks to Fred Braun, executive vice president at ITS, here is a supplier survey which has been filled out while actually conducting a survey of one of ITS's suppliers. This example is particularly instructive because the supplier did not score very highly. As you will see, the company was especially weak in Quality Management, Procurement and Manufacturing Control. Pay careful attention to the individual scores and the comments at the end of each section and you will gain a very clear picture of why this supplier did not fare well in the survey. A fact sheet on the supplier is also included at the end of this survey to give you a better idea of what type of facilities and equipment the supplier has.

SUPPLIER SURVEY FORM

Supplier Name: Metal-Fab Co.   **Survey:** Yes   **Re-Survey:**
Address: Withheld   **Req. By:** Supplier Certification
                                           Team

Attendees: **Req. Date:**
                                 Survey Date:
Phone:
Contact: **Title:** President

QUALITY SYSTEM — PARAMETERS EVALUATED

	Available Points	Supplier Rating
1. Quality Management	13.5	3.7
2. Design Information	12.5	6.1

	Available Points	Supplier Rating
3. Procurement	11.0	3.0
4. Material Control	17.0	11.5
5. Manufacturing Control	25.0	8.5
6. Final Acceptance	6.0	1.5
7. Housekeeping	4.0	3.6
8. Quality Information	11.0	4.3
Total	100.0	42.2

ORGANIZATION

Name: Title: President
Name: Title: Senior Quality Official

Private or Public: Private, Corp. **Annual Report/10-K?** No
Total No. of Employees: Factory 12 Office 4 Quality 2

Primary Product Line: Job Shop

Total Company Sales Volume:
This Year (proj.): 1.5M **Last Year:** 1.5M **Previous Year:** 1.5M

Years in Business: 22 **Sq. Footage:** Manufacturing 8,000
                                     Office 440
Other Locations? No

Major Customers: Hi-tech firms

General Equipment Listing: **Attached?** Yes (see end of survey)

Do you have a Supplier Certification Program? No
Do you have a total organization chart? No

QUALITY MANAGEMENT

Key Contact: **Title:**

	Avail. Pts./ RATING	

1.1 Does supplier have a QA manual? Yes __ No X   **1.5   0**
Supplied _____ Latest Revision _____

1.2 Is supplier's QA manual reasonable for the product   **1.5   0**
complexity and quality requirements?

1.3 Are records kept of all inspection operations?
Yes __ No X

    1.3.1   Is Statistical Process Control used in the   **1.5   0**
        manufacturing operations?

1.4 Does quality monitor manufacturing, inspection, test-   **3.0   2.0**
ing and shipping?

1.5 How well are records maintained and stored?   **.5   .2**
Number of years? _____

1.6 How well are customer discrepant material reports   **1.0   0**
documented for the approval and rejection of all manufactured and processed goods?

1.7 How often are inspection stamps or other means used to   **1.0   0**
identify inspection status?

1.8 If used, how well does the Quality Dept. keep records of   **.5   0**
stamp assignments?

1.9 How often are inspection instructions, procedures and   **2.0   1.0**
other necessary tools, gages and equipment available
and being used?

    1.9.1   How often is precision measuring equipment cali-   **1.0   .5**
        brated and how well are records maintained?

                                            TOTAL   13.5   3.7

COMMENTS (Quality Management):

1.3 Only record of rejections kept, no point in keeping records for acceptable lots — too expensive

1.3.1   SPC — 6 months to 1 year to implementation

1.4 Operators responsible for monitoring

1.6 No formal paperwork on rejects

DESIGN INFORMATION

Key Contact: **Title:**

	Avail. Pts./ RATING	
2.1 How effective is the supplier's system for managing and storing customer supplied documentation (drawings and specifications)?	3.0	1.5
2.2 How reliable is the supplier's change control process for customer initiated revisions?	3.0	1.5
2.3 How well is the customer documentation distributed internally to all departments that require it?	1.0	.7
2.4 Rate the status of prints in active customer files (i.e. illegible, obsolete, marked-up).	1.0	.5
2.5 Rate the status of the supplier's copies of all pertinent customer specifications on file.	.5	.4
2.6 How effective is the supplier's mechanism for notifying ITS of documentation problems, resolving them and documenting the solution?	2.0	1.5
2.7 How adequate is the supplier's disaster recovery capability to minimize down time, i.e. process documentation, etc.	2.0	0
TOTAL	12.5	6.1

COMMENTS (Design Information):

2.1 One copy of the print is circulated to each area/dept.
2.2 If a revision is received, the new print is stapled to the front of the old print.
2.6 Documents changes and notes directly on the print. Notifies buyers of all conversations with various ITS personnel.
2.7 No off-site storage, fire-proof safe or back-up information kept.

PROCUREMENT

Key Contact: **Title:**

	Avail. Pts./ RATING	
3.1 How well are procurement sources evaluated and monitored (i.e. on-time deliveries, quality and pricing)?	3.0	1.5
3.2 How adequate are records maintained regarding approved sources?	2.0	1.0
3.3 Are records of rejections/defects tracked and logged?	2.0	0
3.4 How accessible are the records regarding discrepant material?	1.0	0
Subcontractors		
3.5 Does supplier have a list of qualified subcontractors?	1.0	0
3.6 Does supplier have a procedure implemented to inspect subcontracted work performed (i.e. tooling, plating, painting, machining, assembly work)?	1.0	.5
3.7 Does supplier have adequate traceability with regards to subcontractor's past history?	1.0	0
TOTAL	**11.0**	**3.0**

COMMENTS (Procurement):

3.1 President keeps mental records — no hard copies.
3.4 Not applicable.
3.5 Mental listing. Keeps standard suppliers.
NOTE: President approves all the buying.

MATERIAL CONTROL

Key Contact: **Title:**

	Avail. Pts./	RATING
4.1 How well are stores controlled and supervised?	3.0	2.0
4.2 How well is material segregated and identified by part number/customer/other?	2.0	1.5
4.3 How well is material with limited shelf life identified and controlled?	1.0	0
4.4 How adequate are procedures to detect transit damage, correct counts and correct parts?	1.0	0
4.5 How adequate are procedures to assure proper storage conditions and to guard against damage from handling?	2.0	1.5
4.6 How adequate are procedures to identify and trace raw materials?	1.0	.5
4.7 How well are raw materials protected from the environment?	1.0	1.0
4.8 How well are incoming materials quarantined while under test?	1.0	1.0
4.9 How well are in-process materials identified and controlled?	3.0	2.0
4.10 How well are materials in inspection identified and controlled?	2.0	2.0
TOTAL	**17.0**	**11.5**

COMMENTS:

4.1 No real stores area. Some material stored outside.
4.3 Not applicable.
4.8 Not applicable.
4.9 Not applicable.
4.10 Not applicable.

MANUFACTURING CONTROL

Key Contact: **Title:**

	Avail. Pts./ RATING	
5.1 Is there a formal E.S.D. procedure?	2.0	2.0
5.1.1 Is it followed?	1.0	1.0
5.1.2 Is there a plan for E.S.D.?	.5	.5
5.2 Are there written procedures for manufacturing?	2.0	0
5.2.1 Are process sheets used?	1.0	0
5.2.2 Are batch sheets used?	1.0	0
5.3 Are manufacturing lots traceable throughout the process?	2.0	.5
5.4 Is there a formal in-process inspection procedure?	2.0	0
5.4.1 Is in-process inspection conducted by the operator?	1.0	.5
5.4.2 Does in-process inspection promote the appropriate corrective action?	1.0	0
5.5 Is Statistical Process Control used?	2.0	0
5.5.1 How well is it followed?	1.0	0
5.5.2 Is there a formal Statistical Process Control training program?	1.0	0
5.5.3 Is there a plan for Statistical Process Control?	.5	.5
5.6 Is there a system for preventive maintenance on manufacturing equipment?	2.0	1.0
5.6.1 Is preventive maintenance work documented and are records maintained?	1.0	0
5.6.2 Is there a written procedure for performing preventive maintenance?	1.0	0
5.7 Does the supplier control tool life per the manufacturer's specifications?	1.0	1.0
5.8 Is there evidence of a set-up reduction program to allow quick changes?	1.0	1.0

	Avail. Pts./ RATING	
5.9 How well are the drawing and specification changes controlled?	1.0	.5

TOTAL	**25.0**	**8.5**

COMMENTS (Manufacturing Control):

5.1 - 5.1.2   Not applicable.

5.2 No written procedures or travelers used.

5.6 Waits for in-process of final inspection to discover discrepancies in product to flag maintenance needs.

5.7 Not applicable.

NOTE: Converting to computer system which determines time allotments necessary for each machine and the machine's capability. Trying to implement this new system to improve scheduling requirements.

FINAL ACCEPTANCE

Key Contact: **Title:**

	Avail. Pts./ RATING	
6.1 Is final inspection performed to confirm compliance to all purchase order requirements	2.0	1.0
6.2 Are final acceptance procedures used and are they adequate?	1.5	0
6.3 Do inspection and test records contain the necessary observations, defects, dispositions and corrective actions?	1.0	0
6.4 How well are the records maintained?	.5	0

	Avail. Pts./ RATING
6.5 How is packing for shipping controlled to ensure adequate protection from damage?	1.0 .5

TOTAL	6.0	1.5

COMMENTS (Final Acceptance):

6.3 Only documentation is scribbled notes on prints.
6.4 Judgment call, but mostly paper. Subcontracted products are kept in their original packaging received in.

NOTE: Prefers to use metal stamping rather than rubber.

HOUSEKEEPING

Key Contact: **Title:**

	Avail. Pts./ RATING
7.1 Are all areas of the plant kept clean and free of non-essential items?	1.0 .8
7.2 How safe are manufacturing areas in which to work (i.e. proper ventilation if chemicals are used, safety glasses)?	1.0 .8
7.3 How adequate is the work environment?	1.0 1.0
7.4 How well is conformance to regulatory agencies (i.e. EPA, OSHA, etc.) monitored and controlled?	1.0 1.0

TOTAL	4.0	3.6

COMMENTS (Housekeeping):

No safety glasses required.
OSHA approval hanging on wall.

QUALITY INFORMATION

Key Contact: **Title:**

	Avail. Pts./	RATING
8.1 Does supplier have a Material Review Board for the control of non-conforming material?	3.0	2.5
8.1.1 What departments are represented in MRB? President _____ _____ _____ _____ _____ _____		
8.2 How well are records maintained and used to detect recurring discrepancies?	2.0	1.0
8.3 Does procedure exist for segregation, disposition and identification of rejected material?	2.0	0
8.4 How active is the corrective action feedback system to suppliers?	1.0	.5
8.5 Is the corrective action report returned in a timely manner?	1.0	.3
8.6 Is there a corrective action procedure/system and is it followed?	1.0	0
8.7 How well is the holding area secured and identified for non-conforming goods?	1.0	0
TOTAL	**11.0**	**4.3**

COMMENTS (Quality Information):

President is entire MRB.
No actual corrective action report.
Does not inspect incoming material prior to actual start of production.

The following is a listing of the equipment and facilities:

METAL-FAB CO. MACHINERY LIST

1   Shear 8' 3/16 CRS Capacity

1   Shear 4' 166 GA Capacity

2   Pierce all hydraulic duplicating punches 40 ton 1" dia.
    hole 1/4" cold rolled steel

1   US Amada CNC duplicating punch "Pega" with
    computer back-up system

1   Time Saver sander

1   Straight line sander

1   Mill Cincinnati

1   PEM nut inserter automatic feed (PEM)

1   PEM nut inserter automatic feed (HAGER)

1   Chicago press brake 40 ton

1   Wisconsin press brake 120 ton

1   Cut off saw

1   Spot welder (Steel)

2   Corner notchers and coping

2   Welding booths/metallic arc TIG MIG A/C Hi
       frequency up to 300 amps

1   6' press brake

MISCELLANEOUS

Compressors (2) with cooling and drying capability
High production or prototype
Business in same area since 1969

In the next chapter, we will look in even more detail at quality
management and Statistical Process Control in your suppliers'
plants. This is an essential part of the Supplier Certification
process.

SUPPLIER QUALITY MANAGEMENT

6

Supplier Certification rests on the bedrock of quality. This is something that the Japanese first learned in the 1950s when Deming was invited to present his quality philosophy. Up to that time, Japanese companies had a reputation for producing low quality items. Then they realized that, in order to compete, they would need to start paying attention to quality. Deming showed the Japanese how to improve quality. Most importantly, the Japanese listened while their American counterparts seemed content to rest on their laurels. Not so ironically, the threat of competition is now driving North American and European companies to embrace Total Quality Management for their survival.

As manufacturers, we need to commit ourselves to working with suppliers to ensure customer satisfaction through total conformance to quality requirements. At the same time, we should be developing suppliers who are dedicated to the continuous improvement of quality. In essence, a Supplier Certification program requires:

KEY QUALITY REQUIREMENTS

1. **Reliability over a period of time, meaning consistent deliveries, product and conformance to customer requirements.**

2. **Burden of quality is on the supplier's control of its process, not on inspection techniques.**

BASIC PRINCIPLES OF QUALITY

These rules are the operating philosophy for improving supplier quality through a certification program. This philosophy requires basic principles which will govern both short-term and long-term activities. These principles are as follows:

• *A control process by which to check, measure and report.*

Statistical Process Control (SPC)
Statistical Manufacturing Control (SMC)
Acceptable Quality Level (A Quick Look) (AQL)
Six Sigma Adherence

The determination of what is to be measured is equally as important as the method or technique used. SPC and

SMC are quality tools used by various industries and mathematical techniques which determine where a process is in relation to upper and lower control limits.

Although you may use AQL, we don't view it as the primary measuring tool for the long run. AQL is an evolutionary step we will go through before we move on to SPC. We recommend using AQL as a problem-solving technique to determine the differences between causes and effects, rather than as a way to segregate bad from good parts as we do today.

• *A program that is visible to all levels of operation.*

The results of a quality program should be visible to all levels of personnel. This information must be displayed, clearly defining the goals we are trying to achieve and the measurements we use. As quality levels improve, the movement upward on a chart is an effective impetus to further improvement. Some companies are hesitant to display graphs or charts on the walls of their factories because customers often tour their plants. One company told the receptionist to alert the factory floor whenever an inspector or customer would make a visit. Factory personnel then had fifteen minutes to take the charts down.

We believe this is wrong for two reasons. First, it sends the wrong message to the workers on the floor that the company has something to hide. Second, whether it is an inspector or a customer, most people are understanding and supportive of a company which is trying to improve its quality. Honesty, therefore, is not only the morally right thing to do, but it is also the economically right thing to do. Don't display charts one week and fail to post progress on them. This only provides a mixed message to employees who will begin to question your company's commitment to excellence.

• *Compliance of material requirements and specifications.*

This principle can be easily understood. A company should have the materials, fixtures, tools and equipment in place which is required to perform the job within specifications.

• *The support of management.*

Management support is the oil which keeps the machinery of quality improvement functioning smoothly. Its presence is critical to the morale and engagement of all levels of the organization. If the different levels of the company don't feel that management is involved and committed, then their support and contributions will be limited.

• *A new mind-set and culture.*

This principle fosters a culture which accepts new projects and changes. It assumes that there are no sacred cows in a company and that all operations and procedures are open to scrutiny and improvement. Furthermore, a zero-defect mentality must permeate all levels of a company. There must be established and clear lines of authority. Only when operators are given the authority and responsibility for quality will it have an effect on improvements. If that requires stopping the production line to fix the true causes of a problem, then *production lines must be stopped.*

POINTS OF THE AGREEMENT

ZERO-DEFECT PROGRAMS

The principles of a zero-defect program support the philosophy of Total Quality Management:

- **Conformity** — meeting all customer requirements.
- **Process** — delivering only what you need.
- **Tracking** — knowing the results and how they compare to the goal.
- **Measurement** — being able to measure the results of the program.
- **Corrective action** — fixing the problem.

CONFORMANCE TO REQUIREMENTS

Much is said about conformance to requirements, but most of it assumes that conformance is exclusively a management problem. We view conformance more broadly. What other questions are implicit in the accepted definition that conformance is a product meeting the requirements set forth by the specifications?

- **Does it meet the customer's requirements?**
- **Does it meet the Engineering specifications?**
- **Does it meet the manufacturing process requirements?**
- **Does the product meet the test requirements?**

We believe that products meet their customer requirements. The problem with many manufacturers is that they are not inclined to determine what is needed or wanted by their customers. A good example is custom corrugated cartons. We know of a situation in which a company using custom cartons could fit their product into standard cartons simply by adjusting one dimension. They had difficulty changing the dimension because it wasn't in the specifications and had to be sent to Engineering Change Control. They then have to see whether the change makes any difference to their customers. In many cases, the change made no difference and they were able to lower the total cost.

It pays to make it right the first time, but this requires close communication and documentation of the actions between Engineering and Manufacturing. Supplier Certification addresses this by demanding:

- A flexible system in which every company level, not just management, is responsible for quality.

- Accurate and timely maintenance of route sheets, processes and Bills of Material.

- Accurate and timely maintenance of effectivity dates.

- A system of no variances to specifications.

QUALITY AT THE SOURCE

Employees should be held accountable for performing their job correctly. For example, a client manufacturing a product noticed that cartons coming down the production line were being filled with various components. At the end of the line, an inspector would open the box to make sure everything was inside and packed carefully. This is inspection after the fact. The company established a system so that each worker would be held accountable for making sure the components from the previous person were there to begin with. This is quality at the source.

The source of quality must originate at both the supplier's and company's production level and then work its way to the customers. Ground-level participation also boosts morale. People feel as though they are contributing to the production of quality materials. Thus, we should eventually eliminate sampling techniques such as AQL (MIL STD 105D). Implementing quality at the source with the involvement of workers is the objective. A 2% AQL is not good enough in today's competitive environment. One only needs to look at the chart below to see the consequences of operating at this level:

WHAT TO EXPECT FROM A 2% AQL

- **At least 20,000 wrong drug prescriptions each year.**

- **More than 15,000 newborn babies accidentally dropped by doctors or nurses each year.**

- **Two short or long landings at O'Hare airport each day (also New York, Los Angeles, Atlanta, etc.)**

- **Nearly 500 incorrect surgical operations per week.**

When customers demand 100% quality and provide the testing, education and training, we can compete. By accepting 2 out of 100 parts as bad, we have established a policy of self-destruction. In fact, the first pass yield is only 17% for a product comprised of 100 parts which are subject to a 2% AQL. To go beyond a 2% AQL and reach 100% accuracy 100% of the time means paying attention to three major areas:

Operator — Internal and external suppliers must be trained in quality techniques like Statistical Process Control (SPC). A quality manual must be used and not sit on a manager's shelf. Operators should know exactly what quality means and its effect on the operation.

Machine — Operators must be capable of demonstrating how SPC is conducted on a machine. There must be documented evidence that the machine is capable of performing within the established control limits 100% of the time.

Process — There must be documented evidence that the entire process is under control. SPC provides a tool for measuring process variables.

These three areas lay the groundwork for one of the cornerstones of Supplier Certification — Statistical Process Control (SPC).

STATISTICAL PROCESS CONTROL

> **"15% of the faults belong to the workers. 85% of the faults belong to the system. Management owns the system, therefore they own 85% of the faults."**
>
> **W. Edwards Deming**

We can no longer conduct business in an environment which accepts previous high levels of scrap, rework, waste and delays. Establishing process control is the new level of excellence. Before we start defining this new level, let's take some time to see at what level your knowledge of SPC stands. The quiz on Page 218 asks for definitions of terms commonly used in work involving SPC. (Answers are on Page 542.)

Statistical Process Control is an effective method of evaluating a process to identify both desirable and undesirable changes. Armand V. Feigenbaum's **Total Quality Control** contains an excellent discussion of statistical methods. The result of statistical process control is to produce a product which conforms to requirements while the product is in process.

STATISTICAL

Statistical means using numbers and data which are recorded from observations. Some types of data collection or measuring are:

- Run charts.   • Check sheets.
- Graphs.   • Histograms.
- Pareto charts.

PROCESS

SPC can also measure the effectiveness of a *process* by using statistical data to determine what is the capability of the machine or its operational activities (machines, people and material):

- Sampling.   • Data collection.
- Stratification.   • Standard deviation.
- Normal frequency distribution.
- Control charts.

Define the Following Terms:

Assignable Cause _____

_____

Average _____

_____

C-Chart _____

_____

Capability _____

_____

Common Cause _____

_____

Cp _____

_____

Cpk _____

_____

Loss Function _____

_____

Mean _____

_____

Pareto Chart _____

_____

Population _____

_____

$\overline{X}$ and R Chart _____

_____

CONTROL

Control makes the process behave the way we want it to.

Employees trained in SPC use process control charts while charting a process in order to keep it under control. Operators need to learn only four rules in order to chart processes. First, they must know what is a correct part and why. Second, they must have ways of determining if a part is right. Third, they must have the means to monitor a change over time in order to prevent defects. Fourth, they must have instructions on how to adjust or change the process before defects occur.

Now you are ready to let operators benefit from the training by keeping statistical records of their machine's operation. These will take the form of a control chart. But, before operators at a supplier start using control charts, they must establish that the process is capable. We need to set some precontrol rules for a simple and effective method of allowing them to control the process. Given sample sizes of five parts for set-ups and five consecutive parts at regular intervals or continuous during run time, the precontrol rules say:

SET-UP:
> OK to run when six readings are inside the target area. The target is defined as the area within an upper and lower control limit. This requirement is for the set-up portion only.

RUNNING:
> 1. If results are inside target area, continue to run.
> 2. As results tend toward control limits, operator may continue to run until one falls outside of control limits.
> 3. No parts are allowed to go beyond the specification limits and remain with good parts.

Results are tabulated on a control chart like the one depicted here for a machined steel shaft whose limits are plus or minus .003 inches. Tests are conducted to determine where the upper and lower control limits are placed in order to insure with greater than 99.73% accuracy that only acceptable parts are produced.

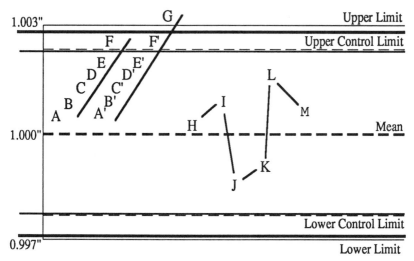

PROCESS CONTROL CHART

The operator of this particular machine which makes the shafts would then begin to make parts as soon as six consecutive parts fall within the area between UCL and LCL. This would complete the set-up. Now the operator would begin the run.

The first part (A) measures slightly more than 1 inch. B through E gradually deviate further from the mean, but in a predictable pattern. In this case, it would probably indicate that the cutting tool was wearing. Repeated use allows the part to grow as the tool wears down. Predictably, the sixth part (F) falls beyond the upper control limit. It is still, however, within specification limits.

Therefore, the part is not rejected, but the process is adjusted. What happens when the operator measures a part that falls at G? The operator then physically separates the part from other produced pieces and **STOPS** the process. She calls over her supervisor or consults a troubleshooting guide to see why the process went wrong. She should not make another part until the problem is corrected. She does not treat the symptom and hope for the best.

Finally, what does it mean when an operator charts measurements which appear like H through L? They are all in the control limits, all perfectly acceptable. But, they do not depict a predictable pattern. Such a chart indicates that the process may be out of control. Here, too, the operator stops her run and finds out why the machine is performing erratically.

As we have said before, JIT and TQM require that we provide the operator with responsibility and authority. These charts clearly show how this works in real-world situations. Each operator is responsible for charting his or her own machine's process and has the authority to stop the machine when parts fall out of predictable patterns or beyond acceptable limits.

If your supplier has SPC in place, you can be assured of two things — higher quality parts and, most importantly, a process which will continue to produce zero-defect parts. That is why SPC at the supplier's plant is such an important part of Supplier Certification.

However, it doesn't stop here. There must be on-going education and a program to promote quality. Quality must be a way of life or, as Ford says, "Quality is Job 1." A poorly designed product fights an uphill battle, maybe even a losing battle, against quality. If you are going to make it right the first time, you must design it right the first time.

THE SPC SYSTEM

Now that we have talked about how an operator must use SPC to chart a process and keep it under control, let's review the process of implementing SPC as a means of continuous improvement. First, take a look at the flow chart on the opposite page to get an idea of how the different parts relate to each other as well as the sequence of events.

There are several statistical concepts which must be understood in order to fully comprehend what follows. The two terms commonly used in statistics are populations and samples. Populations are groups containing items which share common characteristics. For example, parts which share the same characteristics, dimensions, sizes, etc. A population, in terms of the manufacturing process, is all the products made during a repetitive process, since a repetitive process, by definition, is supposed to produce identical parts.

A sample is a group of randomly selected items from a population. Its purpose is to provide information about the whole population without having to sample every member of that group. Samples, when taken off a machine, should form a bell curve when enough of them are plotted. As you can see from the illustration on Page 224, the vast majority of the samples will fall inside the curve with only a few deviations at either of the extreme ends.

In fact, 99.7 percent of the curve lies within the furthermost limits shown below. These limits would correspond to your upper and lower limits. In a bell curve, the characteristics of the desired condition are that the samples are at the target point or with a spread less than the allowable tolerance. This insures that there are no nonconformances.

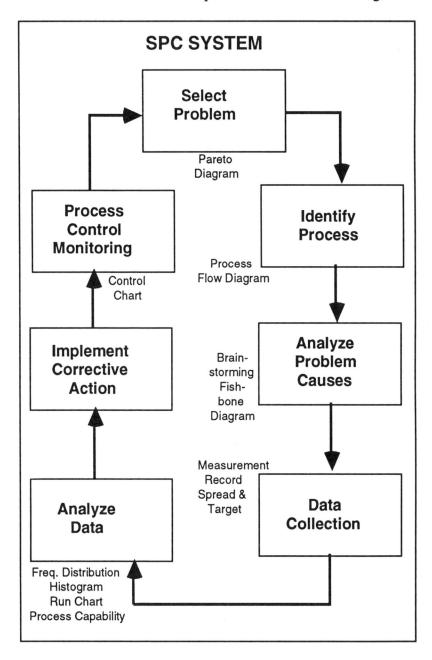

SPC SYSTEM

Select Problem

Pareto Diagram

Process Control Monitoring

Control Chart

Identify Process

Process Flow Diagram

Implement Corrective Action

Analyze Problem Causes

Brain-storming Fish-bone Diagram

Analyze Data

Measurement Record Spread & Target

Data Collection

Freq. Distribution
Histogram
Run Chart
Process Capability

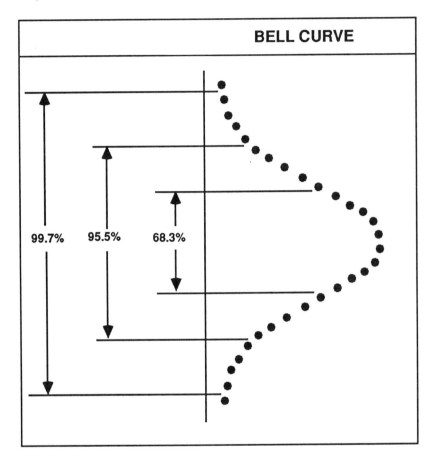

Back now to the SPC System flowchart. The first step is to **select a problem.** A fundamental mistake of many problem-solving teams is that they begin problem solving without having defined the problem. Definition is essential so that we do not end up selecting a symptom rather than the true problem. We can help identify the specific problem by looking for assignable causes and that is further helped by breaking a problem down into "bite-size" chunks.

Selection of a problem is greatly aided by preparing a **Pareto chart** which allows you to set priorities for problems and their causes. It provides a basis upon which you can make a decision about which contributing factor to tackle first. All Pareto charts, including the one below, indicate the relative importance of causes to each other and to the total problem. Somewhere between 5 and 20 percent of the contributing factors (the vital few) account for approximately 60 to 85 percent of the total effect.

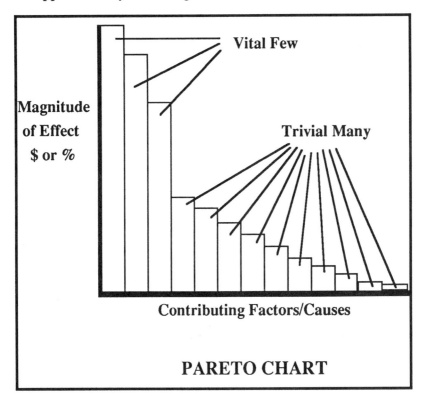

PARETO CHART

IDENTIFY THE PROCESS

The next step in the SPC system is to **identify the process**. The best technique for undertaking this step is to prepare a **process**

flow diagram which is a schematic diagram that shows the important operation and steps in a process. More importantly, it is used as a tool to suggest points in the process where problems may exist. It serves as a picture of how and when work gets done.

In our work with clients, we have always found that reviewing each step of a process helps determine what is necessary and what are areas of potential opportunity. The advantage of using a process flow chart as shown on the opposite page is that develops a **common understanding** of the process as it exists today and can, in fact, provide assurances that this is the method that everyone will follow step by step.

ANALYZE PROBABLE CAUSES

The third step in the SPC process is to **analyze problem causes**. Our preferred method of analysis is to brainstorm and then construct a fishbone diagram. We will be detailing fishbone diagraming in a few pages.

Let's turn our attention here to naming the objectives and setting some rules for how to do creative **brainstorming**. (More on using brainstorming in a team situation is discussed in our book, **People Empowerment:** *Achieving Success from Involvement*, PT Publications, Palm Beach Gardens, FL, by Michael W. Gozzo and Wayne L. Douchkoff.)

The principal objective of brainstorming is to get everyone to participate equally. Every person in a group (team) must give an idea as their turn arises in the first rotation. Only during subsequent rotations can somebody pass if they have nothing to add. This process continues until the group cannot add to the list.

	Analysis Why?	
QUESTION *EACH* *DETAIL*	Where When What How	

SUMMARY	Present # Time	Proposed # Time	Diff # Time	
◯ Operation				Job
⇨ Transport				
☐ Inspection				Person Or Material
D Delay				Chart begins
▽ Storage				Chart ends Charted by
	Ft.	Ft.	Ft.	Date

Details of Present or Proposed Method	Operation	Transport	Inspection	Delay	Storage	Distance	Quantity	Time	Eliminate	Combine	Sequence	Place	Person	Improve	Notes
	◯	⇨	☐	D	▽										
	◯	⇨	☐	D	▽										
	◯	⇨	☐	D	▽										
	◯	⇨	☐	D	▽										
	◯	⇨	☐	D	▽										
	◯	⇨	☐	D	▽										
	◯	⇨	☐	D	▽										
	◯	⇨	☐	D	▽										

Here are some basic rules for brainstorming:

NO CRITICISM
A member of the group cannot criticize either ideas or another member.

FREEWHEELING
The objective is to get as many varied ideas out on the table as possible. The number of ideas is important.

PARTICIPATION IN SEQUENCE
Each member has a turn so that everyone has an opportunity to participate. The shy person has the same opportunity as the outgoing person.

IDEAS ENCOURAGED
What may appear to be a dumb idea may be the solution to the problem. The more ideas we have, the better.

IDEAS RECORDED
Always record the ideas to insure that we capture each and every person's input.

ALLOW IDEAS TO INCUBATE
There may be something we have overlooked. Thinking about the ideas can help add items to the list later.

DATA COLLECTION

Now we are at the **data collection** step of the SPC system. The first question to answer is just what is the purpose of data in the manufacturing or administration areas. Data allows us to review the manufacturing process by collecting information about operations. Data will tell us the degree and range in which a process is now operating. This gives us information to define the problem before we start plotting control charts.

SPC data also serves the process of providing us with a rating system by which we can objectively evaluate supplier performance and effectively select and manage the supplier base. Data collection will also indicate the present control settings within which the process is operating. When the process is at this level of operation, then we have reached the point of lowest total costs. Data collection will show us when a process is starting to drift away from optimum levels before it goes out of acceptable ranges.

Some more considerations to keep in mind when collecting data is to know the types of errors often made. Lack of precision occurs in a number of different ways, but most often when an operator does not take an accurate reading. Operator accuracy and neatness must be stressed at all times. Another error is a bias or system error. These errors need to be addressed with more problem-solving techniques, but like all continuous improvement endeavors, there should be an adequate amount of planning so that system errors do not occur. Yet one more error occurs when there is a failure to maintain constant conditions. This is absolutely necessary to any data collecting.

A powerful tool not widely used during the SPC process is the **Spread and Target Worksheet** (see Page 235). A Spread and Target worksheet is used to create distribution patterns by calculating the target and spread of a process and then to determine whether a shift or spread problem exists. The worksheet is a tool which can provide us with a precise and quick overall picture of what a process is producing as well as indicate analytical paths to pursue when problems do exist. The key information provided by a completed form includes:

- Spread.
- Target point.
- % of tolerance.
- % over SPEC.
- % under bell curve.
- Bell curve.

There are six steps to take in filling out this very valuable tool.

SPREAD & TARGET WORKSHEET
SPC Measurement Record — Step 1

The first step is to complete the SPC Measurement Record Sheet shown on the opposite page. You begin by obtaining a minimum of 25 sample readings from the manufacturing or administrative process which you have identified for evaluation.

Establish the Cell Width — Step 2

If you determine that the number of cells in which readings occur falls between 6 and 16, then the cell width on the Spread & Target Worksheet will be equal to one gradation of the gage used when measuring the sample population. For example:

Number of cells = 7
Gage graduated in .001 increments
Cell width = .001

If the number of cells is greater than 16 or less than 6, then the cell width must be adjusted accordingly. From the SPC Measurement

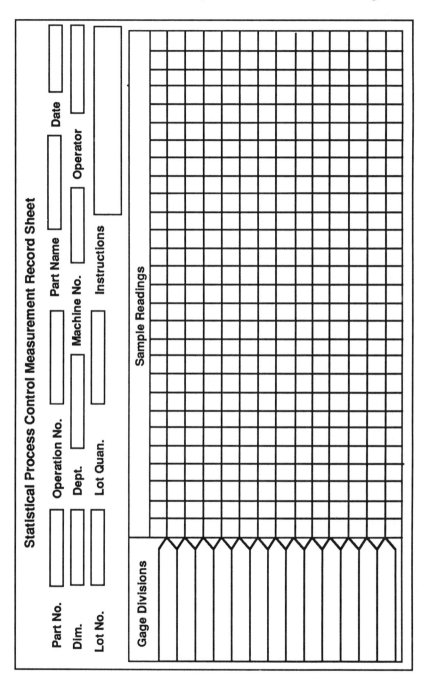

Record, you should next determine the center of the distribution pattern and establish the appropriate boundaries around the darkened cell. Then, establish the remaining cell boundaries in both the plus and minus directions in order to encompass the full range of readings as well as the tolerance limits. Under the column headed "Gage Divisions," enter the mean of the samples taken in the middle of the first column and, proceed in order to enter the other measurements until you reach the highest and lowest sample sizes, keeping basic centered. Now, take your sample readings and place a check in the appropriate box in the array to the right of the "Gage" column for each reading in that range. If a dimension falls on a boundary line, always record it in the row closer to the basic. If a dimension falls right on basic, balance your checks by placing one in the row immediately above basic and one in the row immediately below. This will create a more normal bell-shaped curve on the Spread and Target Worksheet.

Once the SPC Measurement Record is complete, we must transfer data to the appropriate column on the Spread and Target Worksheet. Working from left to right, record the measurements in the cell column. Then, enter hash marks in the tally section and fill in the cell to the mid-point of the column (one-half the difference between any two consecutive cells). Lastly, fill in the frequency column and total it. The total should equal the number of samples which were taken. (See completed chart on Page 235.)

Calculate the Accumulated Frequencies — Step 3

After you have entered the frequencies for each cell, take the Spread and Target Worksheet and place a zero above the first number in the column labeled "Frequency" as well as a zero under the last number in that column. At the same time and level with the first nonzero figure in the "Frequency" column, put a zero in the column labeled "Accumulated Frequency." Now determine the accumulated frequency for each cell by adding the accumulated frequency of the prior cell to the frequency of the current cell. Continue on down the column until the final entry in the "Accumulated Frequency" column is made. This final entry will equal two times the sum of the "Frequency" column.

To determine the "% Over," use the following formula to determine the percentage over for each figure in the accumulated frequency column:

$$\frac{\textbf{Accumulated Frequency}}{\textbf{2 x Sum}} \quad \textbf{x} \quad \textbf{100} = \textbf{\% Over}$$

Record the figure for the percentage over in the appropriate column next to the figure for the accumulated frequency from which it was determined.

Plot the Graph — Step 4

The right half of the Spread & Target Worksheet has figures which represent the percent over. We use these figures to plot the "% Over" figures just calculated. We use a small circle to mark the point when the "% Over" figure is less than 10 and greater than 90. We use an "X" to mark a point when the "% Over" figure is between 10 and 90. When this is completed for all of the "% Over" figures, we now draw a straight line that best fits the "X" points only. This best-fit line should be continued through the lines marked "Left Cell" and "Right Cell" on either side of the graph. (See completed chart on Page 235.)

Record the Information — Step 5

The bottom section of the Spread & Target Worksheet is for entering the number where the "best-fit" line crosses the extreme left and right lines of the "% Over" graph just plotted. Enter the Left Cell number in the appropriate box and the Right Cell number in its box and then determine the difference as indicated. Multiply the figure in the "Difference" block by the cell width and record that number in the "Spread" block. Next, we divide the figure in the "Spread" block by the total tolerance on the blueprint or engineering drawing and multiply this figure by 100. This number is the total percent of tolerance the process is consuming.

Let's go back again to the "% Over" graph and extend a horizontal line from the intersection of the "best-fit" line and the "50% over" line to the "A" line on the left side of the graph. This figure is then entered in the "50% Over Point" block.

Now extend a line from the maximum blueprint (engineering drawing) tolerance cell until it intersects the "best-fit" line. From this point of intersection, extend another line upward to the "% Over" line at the top of the graph. Enter that figure in the "% Over Spec." block in the bottom right-hand corner.

Last of all, extend a straight line from the minimum blueprint (engineering drawing) tolerance cell until it intersects the "best-fit" line. From this point of intersection, extend another line downward to the "% Under" line at the bottom of the graph. Enter that figure in the "% Under Spec." block in the bottom right-hand corner.

Plot the Curve — Step 6

The next step is to plot the curve by determining where the "best-

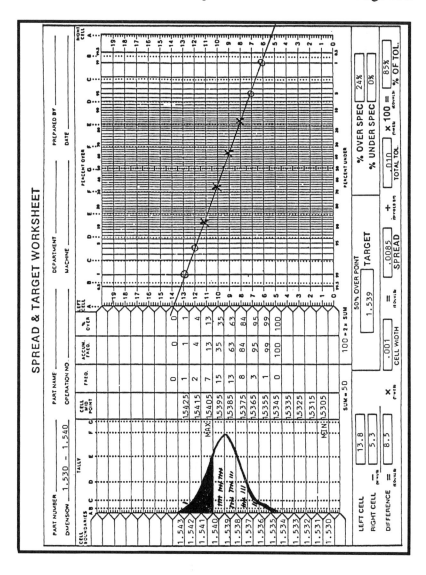

fit" line intersects with each of the dotted vertical lines that begin under the letters at the top of the "% Over" graph. Match these points with corresponding points in the "Tally" area on the left-hand side of the Spread & Target Worksheet. Connect the points to plot the curve.

ANALYZE THE DATA

The fifth step on the SPC system process is to **analyze the data**. Analysis actually begins as you collect and plot data. Two of the charts you will prepare from the data are the $\overline{X}$ and R charts. The $\overline{X}$ chart detects shifts in the process average and makes them visual. The R chart detects changes in the process spread. A process is in control when all the points representing samples are within the upper and lower control limits and there are no assignable causes. In other words, there are approximately the same number of points on each side of the centerline with the majority of those points near the center. Look at the examples on the opposite page.

Out of statistical control is signified on the $\overline{X}$ chart when:

- One or more points are beyond the upper or lower control limit.
- Six to eight points in a row are either above or below the process average ($\overline{X}$).

Out of statistical control is signified on the R chart when:

- One or more points are beyond the upper or lower control limit.
- Six to eight points in a row are either above or below the average range (R).

IN STATISTICAL CONTROL

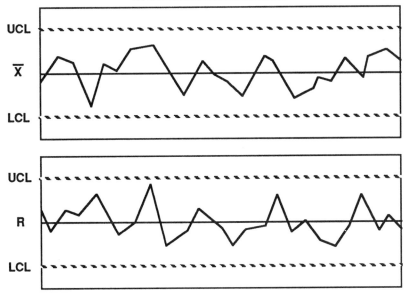

Out of statistical control examples are shown below:

OUT OF STATISTICAL CONTROL

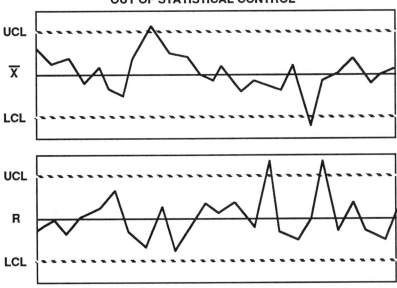

The R chart will show a decrease in process spread (which is an improvement) when:

- One or more points are below the lower control limit (as long as the sample size is 7 or more.
- Six to eight points in a row are below the average range (R).

The example shown here illustrates a decrease in process spread:

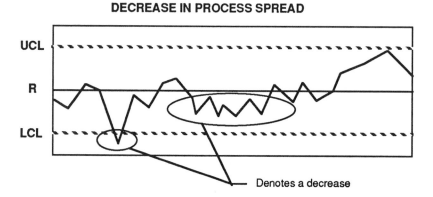

DECREASE IN PROCESS SPREAD

The last two stages in the SPC system, **implement corrective action** and **process control monitoring** take place in the problem-solving area which we shall discuss next.

QUALITY PROBLEM-SOLVING — CAUSE AND EFFECT DIAGRAMS

The major problem that manufacturers encounter when using statistical methods is an inability to define the process and the characteristics to be studied. We don't know how to use statistical reporting to find the real causes of problems. This is because the responsibility for problem-solving is poorly defined by management. Most control systems are inadequate or misunderstood and the approaches to problem-solving are unstructured.

You may also be guilty of attacking the whole problem instead of sizing up the problem and then attacking its parts. We also tend to treat symptoms instead of curing causes. Management often focuses on short-term solutions which miss treating the real cause of a problem.

One effective problem-identification technique is the cause and effect (fishbone) diagram as shown below. The intent is to identify a problem and its possible causes and then to note which causes are being worked on and which are done.

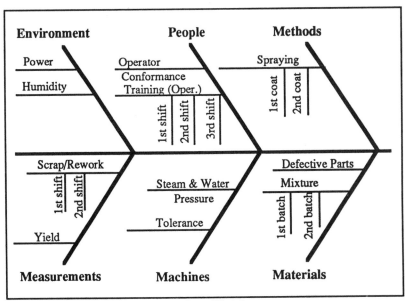

Cause Enumeration Fishbone

In our example, you can undoubtedly see that one problem may have causes in a number of areas. For example, is "inaccurate measurement" a machine problem, a measurement problem or a manpower problem? It is not so important where you place the problem on the fishbone as it is to identify the problem and causes. If you spend too much time deciding what goes where, you could contract the dreaded disease of "paralysis through analysis." We warn you not to study a plan to death. Problem-solving is more than identification; it is action.

PROJECT PLANNING WORKSHEET

Here is an action plan for problem-solving used by many companies. It begins with a concise statement of the problem and how the solution to that problem will contribute to the Continuous Improvement Process. There is a space to put the start date and a space, as we have said so many times before, for the finish date. A list of the team members follows and a summary of all the meetings which tells what problem-solving step was taken. Below that is a space to designate when each problem-solving step was taken and another area for comments on how each step was done. Near the bottom of the worksheet there is one very important question: Can this be replicated at another location? The answer to that question, if affirmative, serves to move the Continuous Improvement Process forward.

TEAM PROJECT PLANNING WORKSHEET

Problem Statement:

How does solution contribute to CIP goals?

Type of team
  __ Functional   __ Task   __ Cross-functional
Team work location: Dept: Team name:
Start (Mo/Yr):   Finish (Mo/Yr):   Total Months:

TEAM MEMBERS

Name (Leader first)

MEETINGS

			Problem	
No.	Date	Hours	Solving Step	# of Attendees

PROBLEM-SOLVING STEPS

Project Schedule (Mo/Yr)   **Comments (how each step was done)**

1. Problem identification
2. Root cause analysis
3. Identify solution/corrective action
4. Plan/trial implementation
5. Standardization
6. Future plan

Cost of quality impact: $
Can this be replicated at another location? __ Yes   __ No
If so, where and how:

Members in Attendance: Number absent:

Signatures: Team Leader   Manager

Presentation Dates: (1)   (2)   (3)

PROBLEM-SOLVING FLOWSHEET

And when all else fails, here is the world-famous problem-solving flowsheet. Take a look at the flow chart on the opposite page. Obviously, we are pulling your leg. But the humor points out something that is very true. A lot of companies use some variation of this system instead of the ones we advocate. So you can choose to stay with what is below or you can try one of our other suggestions for solving problems which *really* work.

WARNING: The flowsheet on the opposite page is a joke. Do not attempt this stunt on your own.

CORRECTION STEPS FOR DEVIATION

Once the problem is identified, then we are ready to work with the supplier to correct the deviation using the following steps:

CORRECTION STEPS FOR DEVIATIONS

* **Develop specific goals and have the right tools.**
* **Identify exactly what is out of control.**
  Accumulate data (reports)
  Summarize data on one sheet of paper
  Chart data so it is understandable to the layperson
  and the operator
* **Discuss a solution.**
  Break diagnosis into manageable units
  Analyze data
  Define problem and brainstorm

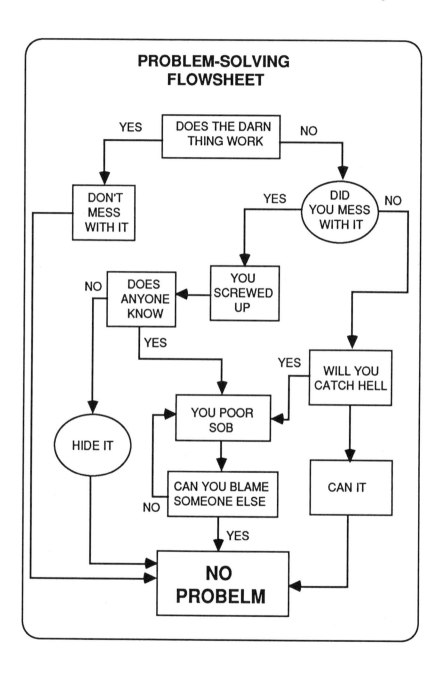

**CORRECTION STEPS
FOR DEVIATION (cont.)**

• **Initiate action.**
Develop a plan for new standards
Utilize feedback
Monitor
Establish control so action remains consistent with
overall process and timely completion (target date)

THE COST OF QUALITY

Continuous improvement of quality not only moves you toward zero-defect products, but increases savings as well. The cost of quality divides into three classifications — Failure Costs, Appraisal Costs and Prevention Costs which appear on Pages 245-247. A baseline formula is a dollar value assigned to an area to insure that a point in time is documented. It acts as a benchmark in order to note progress.

The first two classifications, failure and appraisal, are typical of costs incurred by manufacturers using traditional quality methods. They are the costs associated with products which do not conform to requirements. Prevention costs, on the other hand, are more in keeping with TQM. Not surprisingly, spending more on prevention and less on failure and appraisal costs will increase savings as the toaster chart on Page 248 (published in an article we wrote for *Production and Inventory Management Review*) shows.

Failure Costs	Base Line Formula	Month Actual Dollars	YTD Actual Dollars
Scrap			
Rework			
Warranty			
Product liability			
Corrective action			
Service			
Purch. change orders			
Eng. change orders			
Redesign			
Customer relations			

The prevention cost chart can be used for budgeting purposes. It will clearly show the dollars required in this area and certainly put pressure on management to commit themselves to spending those dollars.

The cost of quality is usually greatly underestimated by most companies. The chart on the next page shows that when a company has a low level of quality understanding, actual costs increase dramatically. As the company grows more mature, the more realistic reported costs will become.

Appraisal Costs	Base Line Formula	Month Actual Dollars	YTD Actual Dollars
Prototype inspection			
Acceptance testing			
Supplier qualification			
Product inspection			
Marketing service survey			
Incoming inspection			
Pkg. inspection			
Inventory audit			
Matl. review board			
Process control tests			
Production spec.			

QUALITY COST
(% of sales or operations)

Level	Reported	Actual	% Accurate
First (Hidden Inspector)	Unknown	Unknown	0
Second (Firefighter)	3	10	33
Third (Involved Managers)	8	12	50
Fourth (Effective Officers)	6.5	8	81
Fifth (TQM: Method of Operation)	2.5	2.5	100

Prevention Costs	Base Line Formula	Month Actual Dollars	YTD Actual Dollars
Design reviews			
Qualification testing			
Parts qualification			
Supplier qualification			
Supplier quality seminars			
Specification reviews			
Process control studies			
Tool control			
Eng. quality training			
Operational training			
Quality orientation			
Acceptance planning			
Zero-defect pgms.			
Statistical training			
Quality audits			
Drawings reviews			
Preventive maint.			
Automation			

Prevention and Supplier Certification become a way of life when the reported cost of quality equals the actual cost. At this level, we have control over the process. This is also the level at which we want suppliers to be. The quality agreement spells out the goals

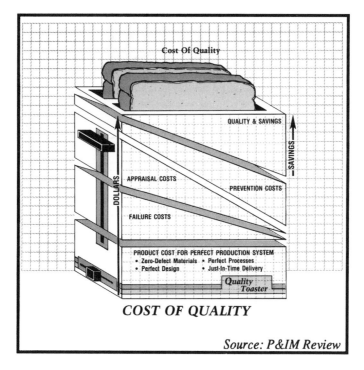

COST OF QUALITY

Source: P&IM Review

and the intervening steps which suppliers agree to take in order to become certified. Certification can be accomplished easily and quickly with the proper support.

DUTIES OF THE SUPPLIER QUALITY ENGINEER (SQE)

The position of Supplier Quality Engineer has several critical duties. The most important is establishing a line of communication between the supplier and customer. The SQE acts as an interface between the customer and the supplier's departments.

At the start of a quality program, both sides must sit down and clearly define what is expected in the demonstrated process areas.

The first area is establishing performance goals. Here, we should make clear exactly what we want from the supplier in terms of conformance to requirements and in the establishment of correct specifications. The next area is establishing the existence of procedures and process documents. The goal is to receive components at our plants which require no inspection. The third area is the implementation of control procedures. This includes defining procedures and how to use them in the supplier's organization. The fourth area is defining what goals we want the supplier to achieve. The most important goal is to continuously work toward improving the product and total cost. The last area is procedure improvements. Here, we want to establish the procedures which are needed to improve the overall process.

Prior to a supplier certification program, most of these activities were covered by inspection. This meant inspection of the end result of a process and little communication between the supplier and the manufacturer. This is also true of First Article inspection. All too often this means the inspection of the best samples culled from a production run. This is not a true indication of the quality of a part. The SQE must be an integrated part of the process who assists in improving the product. Let's review some of the SQE's duties:

Duties of the Supplier Quality Engineer

- Audit supplier product and process.
- Perform dimensional/functional tests.
- Maintain qualification status.
- Communicate with customers/suppliers.
- Verify completeness of specifications.
- Provide engineering interface.
- Specification adherence.
- Guarantee accountability.

In the next chapter, we will discuss the contents of a supplier partnership and how it is essential to your eventual success with Supplier Certification.

SUPPLIER PARTNERSHIP AGREEMENTS

7

The Supplier Partnership Agreement spells out the responsibilities of both the manufacturer and the supplier in the certification process. It is not a purchase order. It works in conjunction with purchasing agreements, blanket orders or system contracts. Instead, it is a mutually developed document which simply provides that the supplier manufactures and delivers components, raw material and assemblies which conform to requirements 100% of the time. Its purpose is to state responsibilities before the product is made and to create an understanding of the working relationship.

THE CONTENTS OF A SUPPLIER PARTNERSHIP AGREEMENT

The agreement's purpose is to map out how the customer and the supplier will integrate all of the issues discussed in this chapter. As explained earlier, it will contain a statement of purpose and scope and set objectives:

Terms and Conditions

- Sets quantity levels for raw material, work-in-process, assemblies or services which reflect flexible production schedules.
- Defines quality level as zero-defects.
- Controls price fluctuations and conditions for cost/price changes.
- Establishes delivery schedules and windows as well as shipping terms and packaging specifications.
- Defines terms of payment.
- Establishes responsibilities for corrective action in the event of non-conformance.

In order to have a true partnership, each side must be committed to meeting certain responsibilities. This is the core of any successful agreement. Neither side should feel as though they are being taken advantage of. It is important to stress that a partnership must achieve:

- 100% Quality
- 100% Delivery
- 100% Quantity
- 100% of the Time

The following chart illustrates some of the responsibilities of a partner:

RESPONSIBILITIES OF A SUPPLIER PARTNERSHIP

Manufacturer	Supplier
1. Process-achievable specifications	Evaluate process capability to meet customer specifications
2. Clear standards — Quality, Quantity, and Delivery	Evaluate standards/methods
3. Clear line of communication	Clear line of communication
4. Notification of organizational changes	Notification of organizational changes
5. Discussion of potential changes in requirements	Discussion of potential changes in requirements
6. Assist supplier in solving quality, production problems	Notify customer of quality, production problems and capacity
7. Provide timely feedback and corrective action	Provide timely feedback and corrective action
8. Provide audit schedule	Notify customer of sourcing or process changes
9. Share audit results	Close feedback loop

RESPONSIBILITIES (cont.)

Manufacturer   Supplier

10. Resolve supplier questions   Inform customer of new
                                  processes and /or materials

11. Commit to continuous   Commit to continuous
    improvement program   improvement program

All is now set for the supplier certification process. We can't emphasize enough the necessity of building a solid foundation before you begin to qualify a supplier's process and components. An Olympic diver, for example, may make his sport look so graceful as to appear effortless. But he spends many long hours practicing the dive, exercising to get into peak shape and consulting with his coach on the finer points of technique. Great divers and great dives don't just happen. They are earned by long hours of commitment and dedication. It is just this type of mind-set that these beginning chapters have attempted to establish. They may have been lessons which demanded much practice before they became part of a total quality mentality, but the rewards will be great. We, too, can make the plunge into the Phases of Certification appear as graceful as the most complicated dive.

SAMPLE SUPPLIER AGREEMENTS

In this section, we have included four sample supplier agreements. Some are long and some are short, but all support the Continuous Improvement Process and Supplier Certification. We have helped the clients develop these agreements with an eye to incorporating all of the basic principles of Supplier Certification while modifying the agreement to the needs of each individual company.

ARCHIVE CORPORATION
Costa Mesa, California

The Archive Supplier Agreement beginning on the next page was prepared by Don Zannotti, Director of Quality Assurance. We wish to thank him for allowing us to use this agreement.

COMMITMENT AGREEMENT

Representatives from Archive have the requirements of certification. We understand that the purpose of this agreement is to provide a basis of understanding whereby we, as suppliers of materials to Archive, commit to developing a plan for process control and improvement, which will be applied to parts and/or components produced for Archive in addition to complying with the basic defined elements of certification:

- We understand and agree to the supplier responsibility as defined in the Archive Certification Process document.

- If we have not achieved certification status, or we find defects in manufacturing or through incoming audits, we agree to 100% inspect/test nonconforming parameters until process controls are (re)established and verified.

- We will not alter manufacturing processes, quality control procedures, or components that affect appearance or mechanical/electrical interface with Archive products without prior notification and approval in writing from Archive.

- We will permit Archive personnel access to our facilities for the purpose of reviewing quality and manufacturing procedures, processes, and records, except those areas which are: 1. Proprietary, 2. Company confidential, or 3. Government classified.

- We will maintain product acceptance records for all materials shipped to Archive. The product acceptance records should include, but not be limited to, the following items: part number, P.O. number, revision level, lot size, process capability studies, control charts, quantities inspected, defects description, lot disposition, etc.

- We understand that Archive's functional reject rate for materials used in product assembly shall be reported in parts per million.

- We understand that Process Capability Indexes on mutually agreed upon processes and/or criteria will meet or exceed a Cpk of 1.33.

- We understand that certified material will be shipped to stock, and/or using facilities, and should any defective material be identified, we assume liability for screening, rework or replacement.

- Archive acceptance level for delivery performance shall be 100% on time.

- We agree to complete Statistical Process Control (SPC) training, and to implement SPC in our facility, as defined in the Archive Certification Process document.

Company   **Approved By**
Date   **Title**

INTERNATIONAL TOTALIZATOR SYSTEMS, INC
Carlsbad, California

SUPPLIER QUALIFICATION PROGRAM AGREEMENT

Representatives from International Totalizator Systems, Inc. (ITS) have explained the requirements of qualification. We understand that the purpose of this agreement is to provide a basis of understanding whereby we, as suppliers of materials to ITS, commit to developing a plan for process control and improvement, which will be applied to parts and/or components produced for ITS in addition to complying with the basic defined elements of certification:

- We understand and agree to the supplier responsibility as defined in the ITS Supplier Qualification Program booklet.

- If we have not achieved certification status, or we find defects in manufacturing or through incoming audits, we agree to 100% inspect/test nonconforming parameters until process controls are (re)established and verified.

- We will not alter manufacturing processes, quality control procedures, or components that affect appearance or mechanical/electrical interface with ITS products without prior notification and approval in writing from ITS.

- We will permit ITS personnel access to our facilities for the purpose of reviewing quality and manufacturing procedures, processes, and records, except those areas which are: 1. Proprietary, 2. Company confidential, or 3. Government classified.

- We will maintain product acceptance records for all materials shipped to ITS. The product acceptance records should include, but are not limited to, the following items: part number, P.O. number, revision level, lot size, process capability studies, control charts, quantities inspected, defects description, lot disposition, etc.

- We understand that qualified material will be shipped to stock, and/or using facilities, and should any defective material be identified, we assume liability for screening, rework or replacement.

- We understand that the ITS acceptance level for delivery performance is 98% on time.

- We agree to pursue the principles of Statistical Process Control (SPC) and to ultimately provide training and implementation in our facility, as defined in the ITS Supplier Qualification Program booklet.

Company: **Date:**
Representative's Signature:
Title:

As can be seen from both the ITS and Archive agreements, both companies have taken a similar approach. The difference is that the Archive agreement is significantly stronger.

GENERIC MANUFACTURER

Generic Manufacturer and (Supplier's Name) are entering into a partnership as defined within this Supplier Agreement. Both of us, as parties, will endorse, communicate and execute the provisions stated in this agreement throughout their respective organizations and to each other.

Our organizations recognize the need to continually improve product and service quality to their successive customers in order to compete in today's marketplace. Both of us agree that total quality is a journey, rather than a one-step process, and will pursue continuous improvement in all areas of their operations in order for mutual support to exist in a supplier-customer relationship.

The following criteria are the requirements which both parties agree to uphold.

Generic Manufacturer Shall ...

1. Execute an on-time payment for received products and services in accordance with agreed upon terms.

2. Contract process-achievable specifications on all products and services.

3. Not accept products and/or services with deviations from the original statement of work, contract and/or engineering requirements. Errors of communication will be corrected in the most expedient manner in order for the supplier to produce quality material.

4. Offer, whenever possible, long term agreements on products and services with a forecast of future requirements.

5. Establish a clear line of communication, and a focal point of contact with a formal notification of any changes, to the supplier.

6. Assist supplier in solving quality and production problems as necessary.

7. Share all evaluation results at the close of the survey.

8. Commit to continuous improvement in all areas of operations and in the supplier interactions.

9.   Agree to uphold the criteria for certified part numbers.

Supplier Shall ...

1.   Deliver all contracted products and/or services 100% on-time in accordance with the purchase order delivery date. Deliver all products with a 100% level of conformance.

2.   Maintain a fair cost basis on all contracted products and services. Maintain a cost control program throughout the facility.

3.   Not accept products and/or services with deviations from the original statement of work, contract and/or engineering requirements. Errors of communication will be corrected in the most expedient manner in order for the supplier to produce quality hardware.

3.   Establish a clear line of communication, and a focal point of contact with a formal notification of any changes, to the company.

4.   Notify the company of potential quality, production and capacity problems.

5.   Provide timely feedback on all improvement actions regarding qualification and certification.

6.   Inform the company of new and additional processes in the facility.

7.   Commit to a continuous improvement program.

8.   Agree to uphold the criteria for certified part numbers.

At this point in a Supplier Agreement, many companies put in survey requirements while other companies include survey results to show what type of improvement is required.

DATA CONFIDENTIALITY AGREEMENTS

This document is an agreement drawn up by a company and is designed to be used with a supplier when it is necessary to "disclose, furnish or exchange data in which the disclosing party identifies a proprietary interest or a desire for confidentiality... The agreement establishes the rights and obligations regarding such proprietary interests and confidentiality and procedures for handling and protecting the data." The document covers a number of areas, such as:

* **Termination date of agreement.**

* **Continuing effectivity of the provisions of the agreement regarding confidentiality to any data remaining in receiving party's possession after the agreement terminates (when appropriate).**

* **Destruction of data by receiving party and written certification of destruction to disclosing party, or return of all data to disclosing party.**

* **Restriction on disclosure to third parties.**

* **Restrictions on use by receiving party.**

* **Procedure in the event of legal action.**

In the agreement, the company makes it clear that any confidentiality agreement binds the whole company and all its elements. That is why it is necessary to carefully draw up the document so that the restrictions "do not interfere with the normal operations of other parts of the corporation."

The following is a confidential agreement that we were asked to sign by a client. We thought it was a good example to include in this book.

AGREEMENT OF CONFIDENTIALITY

This agreement made and entered into as of the _____ day of _____ by and between The Company, a corporation with offices in _____ and (Name of supplier).

WITNESS THAT:

WHEREAS, both parties for their mutual benefit, anticipate the possible need to disclose to and receive from the other party, from time to time, information which the furnishing party considers to be proprietary and which relate to the Supplier Certification Program (hereinafter called "Program").

NOW THEREFORE, _____ and _____ do hereby mutually agree as follows:

1. MARKING OF INFORMATION
    Any information exchanged by the parties and entitled to protection hereunder shall be identified as such by an appropriate stamp or marking on each document exchanged designating that the information is "Proprietary," and if oral disclosure of such protectable data is made, such data shall be so identified at time of disclosure. Within thirty (30) days thereafter

a written notice with complete summaries of all
oral disclosures desired to be protected,
appropriately stamped or marked, shall be
delivered to the receiving party addressed as
noted hereafter in this Agreement. Transmittal
of documents exchanged shall be evidenced by
written notice from the disclosing to the
receiving party.

2. PROTECTION AND USE
The receiving party shall hold each item of
proprietary information so received in confidence until ___ years after the expiration of
this Agreement. During such period the receiving
party shall use such information only in
connection with the purpose of the this Agreement
and shall make such information available only
to its employees having a "need to know" with
respect to said purpose. In connection therewith
the parties shall advise each such employee of
obligations under this Agreement. Except when
authorized in writing by the disclosing party,
the receiving party shall not otherwise use or
disclose such information during the aforesaid
period, except that it may without the other
party's consent be disclosed by the receiving
party to the cognizant U.S Government agency in
connection with proposals related to the Program; provided, however, that any such disclosure bears the restrictive legend as applicable
of FAR 15.509, Use and Disclosure of Data, or FAR
52.215-12, Restrictions on Disclosure and Use of
Data in effect on the effective date of this
Agreement, or a successor provision substan-
tially the same. No data provided under this
agreement shall be delivered under a contract or
otherwise made subject to a contract "rights of
data" clause.

Neither party hereto shall, without the prior
written consent of the other, use in whole or in

part proprietary information disclosed by the other to manufacture or enable manufacture by third parties of the disclosing party's products, products similar thereto, or products derived therefrom. The disclosed information and all copies thereof shall, upon the expiration or termination of this Agreement, be returned to the respective party, or be destroyed and a written certificate of destruction shall be provided to the disclosing party.

3. EXCLUSIONS FROM PROTECTION
Information shall not be afforded the protection of this Agreement if, on the effective date hereof, such data was or subsequent hereto that such data is:
(a) developed by the receiving party independently of the disclosing party; or

(b) rightfully obtained without restriction by the receiving party from a third party; or

(c) publicly available other than through the fault or negligence of the receiving party; or

(d) released without restriction by the disclosing party to anyone including the United States Government; or

(e) known to the receiving party at the time of its disclosure.

4. LEGAL ACTIONS AND GOVERNMENT REGULATIONS
Should the receiving party be faced with legal action or a requirement under U.S. Government regulations to disclose information received hereunder, the receiving party shall forthwith notify the disclosing party, and upon the request of the latter, the receiving party shall cooperate in contesting such disclosure. Except

in connection with a failure to discharge the responsibilities set forth in the preceding sentence, neither party shall be liable in any way for any disclosures made pursuant to judicial action or U.S. Government regulations, or for inadvertent disclosure where the customary degree or care has been exercised by the receiving party as it normally uses to protect its own proprietary or confidential information; provided that upon discovery of such inadvertent disclosure or use it shall have notified the disclosing party and shall have endeavored to prevent any further inadvertent disclosure or use.

5. NO RIGHTS GRANTED
   Nothing in this agreement shall be construed as granting or conferring any rights on the part of either party by license or otherwise, expressly or implied, to any invention or discovery or to any patent covering such invention or discovery.

6. INDEPENDENT CONTRACTOR
   Each party in undertaking its responsibilities hereunder shall be deemed an independent contractor and nothing in this Agreement shall constitute, create, or in any way be interpreted as a joint venture, partnership, or formal business organization of any kind.

7. TRANSMISSION AND CONTROL POINTS
   The exclusive points of contract with respect to the transmission and control of information furnished by either party to the other hereunder shall be as follows:

           (Name and address of other party)
           (Name and address of the Company)

   Either party may change the above points of contract at any time providing written notification to the other party.

8. EXPIRATION/TERMINATION

This Agreement shall expire ____ year(s) after
the day and year first above written except that
it may be terminated earlier by 30 days prior
written notification of either party to the other
or extended by mutual agreement. The provisions
of paragraph 2 above shall survive such expiration or termination.

IN WITNESS WHEREOF, the parties hereto have caused
this agreement to be duly executed and in effect on
the day and year first above written.

Your Company	Name of other party
By: _____	By: _____
Title: _____	Title: _____

ACCEPTANCE

Supplier Signature:
Title:
Company Supplier Code:
          Purchasing Manager:
          Procurement Quality Assurance Manager:
          Manufacturing Engineering Manager:
          Controller:

SHAREBASE CORPORATION
Los Gatos, California

The following agreement is the master for all procurement quality
agreements used by ShareBase in their Supplier Certification
program. This particular agreement owes much of its work to two
individuals at the company: Peter Garcia, Materials Manager and
Nick Farana, Purchasing Manager. Along with the Supplier
Certification team, they have developed an excellent example of
what such an agreement should contain. Like all legal documents
in this book, however, we do not advise you to use any until you
have contacted your own legal department or counsel.

SHAREBASE/SUBCONTRACTOR
MASTER AGREEMENT

PREAMBLE

This agreement is made on the _____ day of _____, 19__,
by and between ShareBase Corporation wholly owned
subsidiary of Teradata Corporation and _____
hereby referred to as the "Subcontractor," under which
the work, the subject of this agreement, shall be
conducted.

1. **SCOPE**

    Both ShareBase and the Subcontractor will work
    toward the ultimate that the Subcontractor will
    supply ShareBase with those Printed Wiring Board
    Assemblies designated in APPENDIX 1 (PWBAs) and
    which fully conform to specifications appli-
    cable to each type of PWBA.

    Subcontractor will provide a turnkey service
    utilizing their manufacturing, process and
    procurement expertise to produce and supply
    PWBAs to ShareBase's unique design requirements
    and specifications. The mutually agreed respon-
    sibilities are defined in the body of this
    Agreement.

2. **TERM OF AGREEMENT**

    This Agreement will be valid for a period of one
    year from and by the consent of both parties may
    be extended annually for one year periods.

3. **RESPONSIBILITIES**

    a) ShareBase will be responsible for providing
       the Subcontractor with the following:

       i) Engineering Documentation and related
           specifications which includes ShareBase
           authorized deviations.

ii)   Approved Supplier List (A.S.L.)
      It is the intention of ShareBase to
      advise the Subcontractor of new
      designs at least six months before
      manufacturing is scheduled to com-
      mence.

b)   The Subcontractor will be responsible for
     the following:

     i)   Manufacturing, testing (all printed
           circuit boards must be electrically
           tested for open and short Fabs) and
           supplying to ShareBase the PWBAs all
           of which must conform to specifica-
           tion including ShareBase authorized
           deviation(Subcontractor) applicable
           to each type of PWBA. Refer to
           appendix for listing or appropriate
           specifications.

     ii)   Maintaining and regularly calibrat-
           ing all equipment involved in the
           PWBA processing.

     iii) Utilizing only those components as
           specified in the ShareBase provided
           A.S.L. or sources listing for assem-
           bly of completed PWBA. (ShareBase
           Corporation reserves the right to
           approve the replacement of any sup-
           plier (or addition of second source)
           on its A.S.L. by another source at the
           request of the Subcontractor. Sub-
           stitute of an alternative or replace-
           ment is prohibited without approval
           in writing by ShareBase Corpora-
           tion).

     Note: It is understood that the responsi-

bilities defined in this section are
of general nature and are more fully
covered in various other sections.

4. **ENGINEERING CHANGE ORDERS (ECOs)**
   a)   All ECOs supplied by ShareBase will be
         implemented in a time scale and at a cost
         to ShareBase agreed by both parties.

   b)   The Subcontractor will procure and stock
         components to minimize any potential
         obsolescence arising as a result of the
         implementation of ECOs. This practice will
         be based on Subcontractor's standard
         processing cycle, minimal quantities due
         to packaging suitable for automatic equip-
         ments and best commercial practices (i.e.
         supplier's flexibility rules).

   c)   The Subcontractor undertakes to redirect
         to other uses where possible any surplus
         materials arising from implementation of
         ECOs.

5. **QUALITY**
   The Subcontractor accepts zero-defects as a
   quality standard and does not subscribe to the
   philosophy of acceptable levels of defective
   materials (A.Q.L.).

   a)   PWBAs which do not conform to specifica-
         tion including any ShareBase authorized
         deviation will upon documented verifica-
         tion be returned to the Subcontractor at
         its expense for repair/replacement and
         failure analysis.

   b)   The Subcontractor will provide ShareBase
         with Process and Failure information
         monthly.

c) The Subcontractor undertakes to develop and implement a process of continuous quality improvement to achieve and maintain a zero defect quality rating.

d) The Subcontractor will permit ShareBase free access to its PWBA manufacturing facility to carry out inspection of work being performed on PWBAs, such access to be on a non-interference basis and at dates and times to be mutually agreed.

6. INSPECTION

The Subcontractor will be responsible for inspection of material required per the bill of material associated with each contracted PWBA. The inspection of material will fall under two categories of parts:

a) Standard component — off the shelf devices (i.e. Subcontractor ics, resistors, capacitors, connectors) with ShareBase supporting documentation provided called the Standard Component Specification.

b) Custom fabricated — material built to ShareBase specification (i.e. printed circuits, stiffeners, etc.) in which supporting fabrication drawings are supplied by ShareBase Corporation.

Inspection criteria is provided in the above referenced documentation for each part category. The Subcontractor will enforce adherence to all specifications and inspect accordingly. The Subcontractor will be responsible for maintaining a complete set of documentation at all times as well as supplying the appropriate documentation to its vendors.

7. **DELIVERY**

The subcontractor shall be responsible for meeting its delivery commitments as specified on individual purchase orders* for PWBAs incorporated under this master manufacturing agreement. In addition to its commitment for on time delivery the Subcontractor is responsible for delivering each PWBA complete for all components (standard and custom) designated by the PWBA bill of material. It will be incumbent upon the Subcontractor to notify ShareBase of any component whose lead time exceeds the Subcontractor's prescribed lead time and which could potentially impact the Subcontractor's ability to deliver on schedule or complete. This Notification should occur with the Subcontractor's authorization via ShareBase purchase order to begin work and periodic updates to ShareBase are expected.

*ShareBase purchasing will issue purchase orders for individual PWBAs as designated by the master manufacturing agreement. ShareBase in house delivery dates will be exhibited on the purchase order as well as contract pricing. The terms and conditions of the master manufacturing agreement will take precedent. Non-conflicting terms and conditions will be accepted per the purchase order.

8. **WARRANTY**

a)   The Subcontractor warrants that the PWBAs supplied to ShareBase shall conform to the relevant specifications and any ShareBase authorized deviations.

b)   The Subcontractor warrants that PWBAs supplied to ShareBase be free of component failure and workmanship defects for a period of 12 months from date of shipment from the Subcontractor's facility.

c)   In the event of failures occurring within the warranty period, ShareBase may elect to return defective PWBAs to the Subcontractor (as set out in Para. 5a) or alternatively to repair in house or at customer sites. Such components as are necessary to effect repairs, will be supplied by the Subcontractor free of charge. ShareBase undertakes to return faulty components (where possible) to the Subcontractor for failure analysis.

d)   This warranty shall not apply to breakdown, malfunction, or other failure of PWBA if it is:

     i)   Used, operated or maintained in a manner, or subjected to any condition, not consistent with the intended purpose of the PWBA.

     ii)   Improperly repaired by ShareBase.

     iii)   Damaged or affected by the negligence of ShareBase or the end user, or by causes external to the equipment, such as but not limited to, air conditioning failure, or negligent acts or conduct of third persons.

9. PRICING/PAYMENT CONDITIONS

a)   All PWBA pricing is defined in Appendix 2.

b)   PWBA pricing is valid for the calendar year on the basis that the total volume of PWBAs purchased by ShareBase is between __ and __ units over a twelve month period. Refer to appendix.

c)   In the event that the purchase orders

placed by ShareBase over a twelve month period exceed or fall short of the stated volume, both parties will meet to review the situation and agree to price revision if appropriate.

d)   Since the sources specified by ShareBase for fabrication of printed circuits and assembly of the finished PWBA are already in place all nonrecurring test and fixturing costs have been previously absorbed by ShareBase. New designs will be addressed separately. ShareBase Corporation does not anticipate the need for the following N.R.E. costs and terms for their payment (as outlined) unless functional testing at the instruction of ShareBase Corporation is to be installed and performed by the Subcontractor. Should functional testing be required the following would apply:

i)   30% of cost upon receipt of Purchase Order.

ii)   30% of cost upon shipment of First Article PWBAs.

iii) 40% of cost upon First Article Approval by ShareBase.

e)   All invoices by the Subcontractor to ShareBase will be paid by ShareBase forty-five days after shipment from the Subcontractor facility.

10. COMPETITIVENESS

ShareBase and the Subcontractor will cooperate to reduce the costs of ShareBase PWBAs.

Cost improvement plans will include the following:

a) The Subcontractor will manufacture the PWBAs using the most competitive component prices consistent with quality and commercial conditions obtainable.

b) The Subcontractor will apply best industrial processes at its disposal or as committed to by the Subcontractor via its demonstrated capabilities and proposed methodologies to reduce the manufacturing costs consistent with meeting ShareBase's specifications.

c) The Subcontractor will provide cost details of major components on a confidential basis so that cost trends may be monitored.

d) ShareBase undertakes to give full consideration to the Subcontractor requests to add alternative suppliers to the ShareBase A.S.L. ShareBase reserves the right to approve the replacement of any supplier on its A.S.L. by another (or additional or second source) at the request of the Subcontractor. Substituting of an approved supplier by one not approved is prohibited without written approval from ShareBase.

e) Benefits of any cost improvements implemented will be reflected by negotiation in PWBAs pricing.

11. FORECASTING AND ORDER PROCESS

1. On the third week of each calendar month, ShareBase will provide the Subcontractor with firm orders covering the following 90 days requirements, together with a non-commitment forecast of requirements through a further 180 days.

a)   Quantities of PWBAs ordered for delivery within 0-30 days are noncancellable and no reschedule is allowed.

b)   Quantities of PWBAs ordered for delivery within 31-60 days are noncancellable; however, orders may be increased or decreased by up to 25%. Reschedules as a result of decreases may not extend initial delivery dates by more than 90 days.

c)   Quantities of PWBAs ordered for delivery within 61-90 days are noncancellable; however, orders may be increased or decreased by up to 50%. Reschedules as a result of decreases may not extend initial delivery dates by more than 90 days.

d)   Activities carried out under paragraphs (a) to (c) are without charge to ShareBase.

e)   In the event of cancellation (or hold placed on this order by ShareBase) ShareBase's liability shall be limited to the applicable cost of those items scheduled for delivery on this order during the ninety days following the date of cancellation (or hold date) or the actual cost of material completed or in work. ShareBase liability should be limited to the final costs that would be subject to ShareBase audit.

12. FIRST ARTICLE QUALIFICATION

a)   Each PWBA type will undergo a First Article Qualification Program as detailed in Appendix 3.

b) Upon successful completion of the Qualification program for each PWBA type, ShareBase will authorize the Subcontractor in writing to commence production.

c) The time scale prior to Production Authorization will be referred to as Pre-Production Phase.

13. LEAD TIME

Lead time for supply of First Article PWBAs will be __ weeks from receipt of order together with relevant documentation. First production deliveries will commence a maximum 3 weeks after First Article Approval. Thereafter, the order process outlined in Section 11 will apply.

14. END OF LIFE

a) It is the intention of ShareBase to provide the Subcontractor with a minimum of __ days notice of the end of life to the PWBAs which are covered by this Agreement and any extension thereof.

b) ShareBase will supply the Subcontractor with a purchase order __ days prior to the end of life of specified PWBAs.

Such order shall be noncancellable; however, quantities may be decreased/increased or rescheduled as set out in Article 11 of this Agreement. Such purchase order(Subcontractor) are governed by prices pertaining at that time.

c) Excepting for the provision in Sub Para. (b) above, should ShareBase require PWBAs after the determined end of life, the Subcontractor will accept purchase orders to provide products at prices and lead times to be arranged.

15. REVIEW MEETINGS

a)   Monthly meetings will take place between
     the two parties at agreed to locations to
     review performance and delivery or other
     issues (see article 7 delivery).

b)   ShareBase or the Subcontractor, with the
     other party's agreement, may at its option
     alter the frequency of these meetings if
     conditions so warrant.

16. COMMUNICATION

a)   All communications during First Article
     Pre-Production Phase will be coordinated
     through Managers appointed by both par-
     ties.

b)   Production issues will be communicated by
     the Subcontractor through material con-
     trol to purchasing.

17. CONFIDENTIALITY

This Agreement and all supplements and data
(verbal and written) of both a technical or
commercial nature, all pricing and associated
information and any such information relating
to the work subject to this Agreement, either
generated by or provided by ShareBase to the
Subcontractor and the Subcontractor to ShareBase,
shall at all times and for a period of five years
following the expiration of this Agreement, be
treated in fully confidential manner and shall
not be divulged to third parties whatsoever
without written permission of the other party,
including but not limited, to any parent company;
associated , affiliated or subsidiary companies
division and departments of all such companies
and the like of the Subcontractor. The dissemi-

nation of all said documents, data and the like, shall be limited to the Subcontractor employees and then only on a need to know basis.

18. EXCLUSIVELY

The Subcontractor will supply the PWBAs covered by this Agreement only to ShareBase and to other designated companies specified by ShareBase in writing.

19. FORCE MAJEURE

Neither party shall be liable in any way whatsoever to the other party in the event that the performance of this Agreement, or any part thereof, is delayed through causes beyond the reasonable control of the delaying party, such as but not limited to, acts of God, acts of civil or military authorities, fires, industrial disputes, floods, wars, riots. In the event of such delay, the performance of this Agreement or any part affected by such cause (Subcontractor) shall be suspended for so long and to the extent that such cause (Subcontractor) prevents or delays its performance. The delaying party shall immediately and fully inform the other party of such delay. In the event the delay exceeds 30 days (or is anticipated to exceed 30 days), the parties shall meet to mutually decide what action should be taken in respect of the work and this Agreement. Both parties undertake to make "best efforts" to recover from such situations as timely as possible with minimal impact on the other party.

20. LIMITATION OF LIABILITY

a)   Excepting as provided for in Sub Para (b) below, neither party shall be liable in any way whatsoever to the other party for any collateral, consequential, indirect or

incidental damages of any nature arising
out of or related to the transactions the
subject hereof.

b)   The Subcontractor shall be liable to
ShareBase or any other party for any
collateral, consequential, indirect or
incidental damages of any nature arising
out of or related to any activity deemed
to be the Subcontractor responsibility,
including but not limited to, processes,
non-conformance to specification, the
Subcontractor substituted components, even
though such activities may have been
approved by ShareBase.

21. MOST FAVORED CUSTOMERS

The Subcontractor undertakes to give ShareBase
highest priority if and when demands are made on
the Subcontractor from whatever source which
could result in shortages of materials (including components) and/or labor likely to adversely
affect the timely performance of this Agreement
and/or deliveries of PWBAs to ShareBase.

22. GOVERNING LAW

This Agreement shall be construed and interpreted in accordance with the law of the State
of California.

23. APPROVALS

In witness whereof the parties hereto have caused
this Agreement to be duly and properly executed
by the duly authorized representatives as of the
day and year written below.

On Behalf of ShareBase

On Behalf of Subcontractor

APPENDIX III

FIRST ARTICLE QUALIFICATION AND PRODUCTION QUALITY ASSURANCE

1.0 INSTRUCTION

ShareBase requires from each initial lot one each first article sample PWBA indicative of that production run and all subsequent production.

The same inspection procedures will apply for First Article and production PWBAs. Upon successful completion of the following steps, ShareBase will approve the Subcontractor for the first release of each board type under qualification.

a)   All PWBAs will be inspected against the requirements specified in common PCB assembly instructions and ShareBase workmanship standards manuals. Specifications unique to a particular PWBA will be cited on the assembly drawing for that PWBA.

b)   First Article PWBAs will be functionally tested on ShareBase premises utilizing a Zehntel 860 in circuit test (IC) device. This ICT will detect for open and short, component incompatibility, component functionality and improper installation of components.

c)   All PWBAs will be visually inspected for any deterioration in solder bonding or component attachment.

d)   Components on each PWBA type will be checked against the ShareBase A.S.L. or sources listing. Only agreed deviations from the ShareBase A.S.L. are acceptable.

e)   In the event of any failures found during inspection or test, a failure analysis and corrective action will be required. The Subcontractor will receive written notification of failures. Subsequent releases of production may be withheld pending their resolution.

In the next chapter, we take a look at the phases of Supplier Certification which have now become the standard followed by most companies when implementing a Supplier Certification program.

PHASES
OF
CERTIFICATION

$$\overline{\overline{}}\ 8$$

Quality at the source and shipping parts that conform to requirements and require no inspection are the primary objectives of
supplier certification. We can achieve this by entering into a
partnership with a supplier which is based on trust and cooperation. Establishing that partnership is a five-phase program. It
entails gathering facts about a supplier, designing quality improvement processes, putting them into practice, and then auditing and maintaining the process based on results which are
continuously gathered and jointly interpreted.

In this program, we can think of ourselves as medical researchers
who take a patient and not only find a cure, but find the means for
the patient's continued well-being. The five phases of supplier
certification are similar to the compilation of a medical history,
the implementation of a nourishing diet and a schedule of exercise, and the institution of regular check-ups. Our goal is to
develop a relationship in which a healthy supplier will act according to the regimen of TQM and World Class objectives.

PHASE ONE: History, Status, Documentation

In the first phase, we must determine if each supplier who was qualified earlier is in shape to work in a symbiotic relationship. To determine this, we assess the present health of quality, processes and controls. There are a number of areas to probe for each supplier and part number to be certified:

First Article Inspection Status

The first question we want answered is whether or not a first article inspection was performed on the part. A first article inspection requires that a production component be checked for each attribute and then determine if all standards and specifications have been met. We want to be sure that a sample or culled-out component is *not* sent for review. In many instances, an outside, independent service can be used to conduct the inspection.

If a first article inspection was performed, we want to be sure that its results measure up to requirements. In other words, does a part taken from the production line today match the original first article? Often, first articles do not accurately reflect production parts. For this reason, we may elect to perform a first article on a later point in the process depending on the criticality of the part number or production lot.

Incoming Quality Control History (IQC) and Line Fallout

Companies usually have compiled considerable information in this area. The problem is that the data is rarely organized. Our first step is to gather all available information so we can determine the major areas in which rejects occur. Equally important is determining whether parts are rejected for the same reason every time despite notices of previous corrective action notification to correct the problem. The supplier's responsibility is to inform us about line rejects they experience on each component. What you will most likely find is that much of the available data is marked **DW** ("Don't Work") without real cause being established. The major objective is to gain an understanding of all the available quality data and present this data in an orderly fashion to the supplier. The supplier's role is to provide us with the data needed for correlation. Quality problems must help us determine cause and effect on the production line. By reviewing the percentage of reject types, we can begin to isolate where the disease is located and what courses of action are required.

Part Documentation Review and Update

In this step, we insure that all specifications, blueprints or drawings we send to the supplier are accurate and understood. There are few things more annoying and eventually detrimental than incorrect specifications from which the supplier must then build.

While Peter Grieco was working at Digital Equipment Corporation (DEC), he ran across a good example of how to solve a problem in part documentation. A supplier was having difficulties building a part to specifications. For a while, the problem was assumed to be the supplier's, until Pete asked the supplier to visit the plant with his copies of DEC's blueprints for the part. The supplier came in and spread several sets of blueprints on the table. "Which set do you want me to follow?" the supplier asked. "The one without the red marks," Peter replied. "They all have red marks depending on which engineer visited my plant," was the supplier's reply. It soon became apparent that the problem was not solely the supplier's.

Over 50% of the time, you will find that when comparing your prints or specifications with a supplier's that the problem is yours.

Numerous purchasing functions do not even include a current print with each purchase order. It is no wonder, then, that a supplier doesn't know which specification is correct.

Packaging Specification/Method of Shipment

With each supplier, we must identify the type of packaging required for each line item as well as the standard number of parts per unit. Standard packaging speeds delivery and greatly increases data accuracy. The classic example is a carton of eggs. We don't count the eggs to see if there is a dozen; we simply look for empty spaces. In addition to packaging, we must determine the best inbound routing and shipment method for each part.

Status of Production Tooling

Every tool has a production life expectancy. Each tool is also designed for a specific job. Most companies, however, have no idea of how many parts were produced off of a certain tool. Nor do they hesitate to use a prototype tool for a production job. But this data is required to insure control over the process. Worn tools do not make quality parts. It is far better to replace an old tool before it reaches its production life, than it is to push the tool beyond its capability. Since this data is often hard to find, or nonexistent, we can estimate the status of production tooling by asking the supplier for tool purchase orders. From this data, we can determine how many tools were bought and when and then we can estimate how many parts can be produced off of a tool. We must remember that hard and accurate data is not always available, but that intelligent estimates will initially suffice.

Status of Inspection Tooling and Gauges

This area is similar to the above in that we need to know how often and when inspection tools are calibrated? We also need to determine whether the present inspection tools are tied into the process. In other words, do they test the part in process or do they inspect after the fact?

Remember: a tool must never be totally out of calibration before it is adjusted back into specification. A control chart may be applicable here. Lastly, we must survey the existing inspection tools to see whether they are adequate for the job and whether the supplier may need duplicate tooling or more advanced fixtures.

Delivery Performance

Here, we look for the delivery performance of a part over a period of time to find out if the supplier delivers on time. If a delivery window has been established with a +/- tolerance, then a review of adherence to the exact date is required to see what the actual performance is. On-time delivery can only be measured against a committed delivery date with the supplier. If you ordered without lead-time consideration, a supplier cannot be punished. Again, the idea is to establish a beginning point from which we can measure progress toward narrowing the delivery window.

Teamwork and Timing

Phase 1 is the longest phase because it lays the foundation for what follows. It is most often slowed down because of poor specifications, incomplete data and lack of support. There are ways to quicken the process even though supplier certification is not a short-term commitment. One way is to perform a risk analysis. Obviously, we can't take 13,000 months to conduct Phase 1 for 13,000 different part numbers. This will mean concentrating first on the major parts or commodity and taking a risk with suppliers who have demonstrated quality in the past. At a computer manu-

facturing plant, for example, they were able to certify 67% of their suppliers' part numbers in the first year. In the third year of the program, they were up to 80%.

The second way to hasten Phase 1 is to form a team of people from Purchasing, Engineering, Manufacturing and Quality Assurance. They are the minimum required to support this phase.

The other important member of the team is, of course, the supplier. The leader of the supplier's team should be the person with the most enthusiasm and interest for the program. Often, we have found, it is also the busiest person, the one who gets things done. If your goal is quality at the lowest level of the organization, then the leader should *not* be the Quality Manager. He or she can be a consultant to the project or a catalyst on the team, but we believe that the leader should be someone who has the final responsibility for the product.

Teamwork also means numerous visits to the supplier's plant to review the supplier's manufacturing and quality process. Evaluation by a multi-disciplined team means that details will not be overlooked.

Selection of Part Numbers for Certification Process

The list generated by the form on Page 290 can be sorted by part number, descending dollar value or category code. Purchasing will review the list of part numbers with the supplier and determine which parts are eligible for potential certification. The Supplier Certification Steering Committee must approve all selections before the "Kick-Off" meeting.

Part Number Certification Initiation Checklist

The checklist on Page 291 can be used to track the activity throughout this phase as well as designate what the responsibilities are for each department. The Certification Team is responsible for collecting the data from each department, reviewing it and then determining whether the part number should proceed into the Certification Process. The Team also determines how much time is necessary to gain the pertinent information in this phase.

PHASE TWO: Supplier Program Review and Process Evaluation

Submit Phase 1 Findings to Supplier

The preliminary research done, it is now time to take your data and review it with the supplier. Concurrently, the supplier submits its

SUPPLIER PART NUMBER SELECTION

Qualified Supplier		Supplier Code		Part Family Matrix (Y or N?)	
Part Number		SIC Code			

Dollar Value (per unit)		Quality History Percent	
Current Requirements (units)		Forecast Quantity (units)	
Contract Number			

CERTIFICATION TEAM MEMBERS

Buyer:	
Administrator:	
Manufacturing Engineer	
Quality Assurance:	

STEERING TEAM COMMITTEE APPROVALS

Manufacturing Engineering:	
Procurement Quality Assurance:	
Purchasing:	
Administration:	

KICK-OFF MEETING

Date:	
Time:	
Place:	

```
COMPONENT CERTIFICATION
INITIATION CHECKLIST
```

Part # _____   Supplier _____   V/C _____

Date Initiated _____   Supplier Code _____

Buyer requesting Certification Initiation

_____

                                                        Yes   No

Has supplier been qualified?   ☐   ☐
If yes, on what date _____   Date
                                                        Com-
Purchasing shall obtain the following: pleted
    Delivery History   ☐   ___
    Cycle time requirements   ☐   ___
    Supplier History   ☐   ___

Quality Assurance shall obtain the following:
    Quality History   ☐   ___
    Specification Adherence   ☐   ___
    Supplier Inspection Records   ☐   ___
    Process Capability   ☐   ___

Mfg. Engineering shall obtain the following:
    Supplier Process Planning and History   ☐   ___
    Packaging Requirement   ☐   ___

_____

Team agrees that component should   ☐   ☐
proceed to Phase 3.

Review Meeting Date: _____

data to you. This documentation consists of process and quality data either required or existing on a part number. The next step is to sit down at a table and review all the documentation and analyze all the data so as to establish an understanding of the performance of the part in the past.

Supplier Process Review

The first review step determines whether the supplier's process is under control and what areas need to brought under control. If you find that the process is not under control, you must then determine the steps required to achieve process control. At this point, you may determine that SPC be employed.

Quality Survey and Continuous Improvement Plan

In this step, we go back to the supplier selection criteria we developed earlier and determine whether the supplier meets the minimum requirements we established. If he doesn't, then we look for ways to work with that supplier to improve their position or look for a new source. At this point, you should review the supplier's response to your original survey.

Evaluation Memo

Once these surveys are completed, we will undoubtedly find problems and weak areas which need strengthening. Our next step is to document all differences of opinion in an Evaluation Memo. Both sides sign this agreement which summarizes all corrective actions and constructs a time frame for their completion. The memo also assigns the responsibility and authority for addressing each issue to one specific person. That person commits to a finish date and a start date as well. This insures that the person does not wait to the last minute to complete the task.

Review of Supplier Responses

This step is a review of all the documentation until it is mutually agreed that the specifications can be met. By that, we mean that both parties agree that it is accurate and free of ambiguities.

Phase 2 takes time to complete. By the end of this time, the question arises of whether or not the supplier is committed and capable of making the part to specification each time. If the answer is "no," then we either keep negotiating over the documentation, change the specifications so that the supplier can meet them or find another supplier. On Pages 294 to 297, we have provided a checklist for process validation. Before you can proceed to Phase 3, an agreement must be reached on the specifications.

PHASE THREE: Finalization

In this phase, we have reached an agreement that the supplier can make parts that conform to our requirements. We must ensure that all the courses of corrective action delineated in the Evaluation Memo have been completed. We must then agree on how to handle testing and methods of inspection for the supplier's product in order to reach full certification.

Finalization is the most difficult phase of supplier certification. The team must determine the number of acceptable lots that will prove a supplier can consistently deliver zero-defect parts. Our task is to set a level of lots which must come in to our factory with no defects before the supplier can be certified. One technique for implementing this phase is to use a number of approaches which gradually move us away from Incoming Inspection. For example, establish 20 lots of zero-defect parts as the criteria. For the first 10 lots, perform a standard sampling plan to determine if the supplier is making the part to print. The next 10 lots could then be skip lots, that is, every other lot gets reviewed.

The number of lots must be established with the supplier as well as the type of inspection. Full certification and the absence of incoming inspection depends upon the criticality of the part. The number of lots and the type of inspection will be determined by

Date:		**PROCESS VALIDATION**

Company Name:	
Supplier Code:	
Supplier Contact:	
Part Number:	
Description:	

SECTION ONE: Review of the Supplier's Commitment	YES	NO
1. Is the supplier's sequence of operations adequate to assure compliance to the design's requirements?		
2. Is the supplier utilizing the latest blueprints, specifications and other processing information as applicable?		
3. Does the supplier utilize separate work instructions for each part number?		
4. Is the part manufacturable as depicted on the Engineering specification?		
5. Would the manufacturability of the part be improved with a change to the Engineering Design?		
6. Has a Change Request been submitted or discussed with the Concurrent Engineering Coordinator, for the appropriate product line, to enhance the manufacturability? CHANGE REQUEST #: _____ DATE SUBMITTED: _____ COORDINATOR CONTACTED: _____		
7. Does the supplier maintain adequate testing points for detection of nonconformances?		
8. Are the machines and process depicted capable of producing conforming material?		

SECTION TWO: Identification of key operations, services, processes and characteristics	YES	NO
1. Has the supplier identified the key operations, within the manufacturing process, that present the greatest potential for opportunity?		
2. List the supplier identified operations that present the greatest potential for opportunity. (Attach a separate sheet if necessary.) _____ _____		
SECTION THREE: Process changes requiring notification	YES	NO
1. Has the supplier been advised that changes to the critical processes/operations identified in Section 2 require prior notification to the company?		
2. Has the supplier been advised that changes to the above stated processes without prior notification will result in decertification of this part number?		
SECTION FOUR: Statistical Process Control	YES	NO
1. Has the supplier identified the key characteristics for all critical operations for monitoring via control charts?		
2. Have the process control limits been calculated for all key characteristics?		
3. Has the supplier performed process capability studies?		
4. Does the supplier rely on control charting and capability data for acceptance?		

SECTION FOUR: Statistical Process Control	YES	NO
5. Is the Detailed Testing Plan to the latest Blueprint revision on file?		
6. Is there a First Article Inspection Report on file?		
7. Are the supplier's sampling levels and testing techniques adequate?		
8. Is there a better or more economical way to test the characteristics? If YES, state below and communicate them to supplier: _____ _____		
9. Does the supplier have clear specifications and instructions available and do they include clear accept/reject criteria?		
SECTION FIVE: Requirements to Second Tier Suppliers	YES	NO
1. Does the supplier provide to their second tier suppliers detailed work instructions to insure compliance to the specifications?		
2. Are the blueprints, specifications and other processing information flowed to the second tier supplier, at the correct revision level defined on the Purchase Order?		
SECTION SIX: Tooling and Gaging	YES	NO
1. Does the supplier have adequate tooling and gaging?		
2. Will additional tooling and/or gaging be required ? If YES, make a list with costs.		
3. Is the tooling in good condition and capable of producing conforming components?		
4. Is the gaging in good condition and within calibration limits?		

SECTION SEVEN: Packaging and Shipping Requirements	YES	NO
1. Does the supplier utilize adequate Material Handling devices before and during manufacturing to prevent damage to the material and components?		
2. Does the supplier package and ship in the prescribed methods as stated in the Purchase Order?		

SECTION EIGHT: Supplier/Company Agreed Upon Corrective Actions	YES	NO
1. Has the supplier been briefed on the actions necessary to complete Process Validation on this part? AGREED UPON DATE FOR REVIEW:		
2. Has the supplier agreed upon a date to verify that the corrective actions have been completed and implemented? VERIFICATION DATE:		

SECTION NINE: Verification of Completed Action	YES	NO
1. Is the supplier in compliance with the agreed upon specification and process? COMPLIANCE DATE:		

ADDITIONAL COMMENTS/OBSERVATIONS:

	Signature	Date
Supplier's Acknowledgment		
Team Verification		

what it takes to satisfy our requirements. The first two phases are there to gain control over the supplier's process for making the part. If they have been done correctly, we can trust the supplier to make zero-defect parts that meet the requirements of the customer. Therefore, we can make the inspection criteria as tough or easy as we want, based on what we are buying and how critical that is to our own production processes. Supplier certification does not get rid of all incoming inspection. We will always have reliability labs and failure testing. But, supplier certification can and will greatly decrease our reliance on incoming inspection. We must simply change our frame of mind from inspecting parts to verifying processes.

There are some companies that set a time period for inspection, rather than the number of lots. For example, they might say that if there are no rejects in six months, then the supplier will be certified. We have problems with this method. It is conceivable that a six-month supply of parts can all be from one lot. The supplier has produced and warehoused the entire amount. This tells us very little about how much control he has over the process since there is only documentation for one lot. We want to see that a supplier can consistently make zero-defect parts and deliver them to us in smaller lots at more frequent delivery dates. Remember that Just-In-Time is based on flexibility which smaller lots and reduced set-up times provide to the manufacturer.

Phase 3 completion, as outlined above, depends on the frequency of deliveries. The more frequent they are, then the more lots that can be inspected in a shorter period of time. Depending on the level of trust, we can move some suppliers through the process more quickly. For example, if a supplier has a history of few rejects, then it may be possible to jump ahead and do five skip lots in order to reach certification. Again, this is something that only you can determine.

FINALIZATION AND CERTIFICATION

Part # _____   Supplier _____

Date Initiated _____   Supplier Code _____

Certification

	Yes	No
Has Process Validation been completed?	☐	☐
Have all agreed upon actions for validation been completed? Date: _____	☐	☐
Have required # of lots been accepted? Date Complete _____	☐	☐
Has ongoing periodic audit plan been defined? Date Complete _____	☐	☐
Add part number to certified list? Date Added _____	☐	☐
Has the acceptance plan been revised? If yes, send copy to buyer/planner.	☐	☐

Manufacturing Engineer: _____

Quality Engineer: _____

Purchasing: _____

PHASE FOUR: Certification

This phase is the easiest to achieve. The first three phases dealt with the efforts required to clarify specifications and establish the testing procedures to receive parts that conform to established requirements. Once this has been performed successfully, we are now ready to certify the supplier for each *specific part number*.

Before the actual presentation of a certification award, we need to review the following for the last time:

• **RESULTS OF INSPECTION**

• **RESULTS OF IN-PLANT MANUFACTURING**
     • **Material Review Board activity**

     • **Part application audit within the plant**

     • **Field return activity**

     • **Repairs conducted**

• **CORRECTIVE ACTION**

          • **Follow up results of fallout**

          • **Documentation follow-up**

          • **Bills of material, blueprints, specifications**

• **RESULTS OF PHASE 1, 2, 3**

• **AGREEMENT OF TEAM MEMBERS**

Now that our review has been completed and the entire team is satisfied that all areas have been met, we are ready to certify the supplier for that specific part number which has achieved excellence. Once certified, we should acknowledge the achievement with a certificate or some type of ceremony. This can be a letter or plaque. If it is a plaque, we suggest that it be hung on the walls of your lobby, not the supplier's. First, this will be the place where the supplier's competition will view the plaque and hopefully initiate a request to become certified themselves. Second, we want to avoid plaques in a supplier's lobby that announce they were certified 10 years ago. This is what L'Oreal decided to do as the photograph below shows. This plaque which is in their lobby reads "L'Oreal Certified Suppliers."

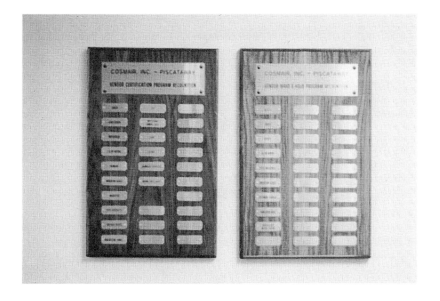

A letter like the one shown on the next page should then be sent to every supplier that has achieved certification as well.

Ms. Mary Aaron
President
Travel Access
2727 Okeechobee Blvd.
West Palm Beach, FL 33409

Dear Ms. Aaron:

I am pleased to announce that Travel Access has met all the requirements of Pro-Tech's Supplier Certification Program and is now a Certified Supplier.

As a Certified Supplier, Travel Access is Pro-Tech's supplier of choice. We expect our working relationship to foster the development of new technologies relating to travel that will benefit both of our companies.

In becoming a Certified Supplier, Travel Access has demonstrated its superiority in quality, delivery, service, and pricing in providing Pro-Tech with the lowest cost for travel.

Being a Certified Supplier changes the way Pro-Tech will do business with Travel Access. Effective with this letter, we will no longer inspect 100% of Travel Access's tickets and itinerary.

We look forward to working with all of our Certified Suppliers. The consolidation of our supplier base allows us to reduce the occasion for special cause variation in our product. We believe that with Travel Access and our other Certified Suppliers we can concentrate on adding value — not adding cost with inspections.

Congratulations. We are pleased Travel Access has become a Certified Supplier. Travel Access is important to Pro-Tech and we value our relationship with you.

Sincerely,

Leslie Boyce
Assistant to President

Certification is not earned and then forgotten. A supplier must continuously improve to maintain that certification. Companies have different ideas about certification. Some of them are short-cuts which will not provide us with a long-term position to be competitive. The results we demand are a quality product at the lowest total cost delivered on-time. The methods used in the past for building supplier relationships have not been effective. If you are not ready for change, don't try to tackle this issue.

PHASE FIVE: On-going Audit and Maintenance

In Phase 5, we audit and maintain the supplier certification program by conducting random audits of material and the supplier's process. It helps greatly to designate one person to be responsible for documentation and monitoring the certification process for each supplier. While auditing, this person should take samples from lots and inspect 1) to see that the product meets the print, 2) to see if capability ratios have changed or not, and 3) to see that the supplier's process is under control. You may want to set up a specific frequency for audits.

Disqualification

A supplier loses its certified status if it ships a lot with any discrepancies. In this eventuality, you must alert the supplier with a Memo of Disqualification which outlines the problem and suggestions for how it can be solved. Problems will, of course, occur from time to time, but how the supplier handles them makes all the difference. For instance, let's say that a certified supplier informs us that a tool slipped on one of the machines while making parts. He has culled the rejects, fixed the tool and documented precisely what happened. Now, let's say another certified supplier has had a similar problem, but he ships the lot without telling you what happened. Which supplier do you disqualify? The second supplier should be disqualified. He has not demonstrated that his process is under control or that he is interested in being a partner who shares information.

Requalification

After spending many months to achieve a certified status, we believe a supplier deserves some consideration in this area. Our belief is that, once disqualified, a supplier should be given *one* more opportunity to succeed. If disqualified again, then we should start to look for a new source. A certification program must have some teeth in it. Previous supplier programs *did not* show suppliers that we meant business. We sorted, repaired, borrowed and used "as-is." Certification means quality from the top of a company to the bottom. Quality is important. Shipping products which do not conform is what we need to avoid.

The two checklists on Page 305 show how decertification and recertification can be handled.

Introducing Supplier Certification

The booklet (beginning on Page 306) was developed and printed by International Totalizator Systems, Inc. of Carlsbad, California to introduce its suppliers to Supplier Certification. From supplier symposium and on-site surveys to quality system requirements to product qualification, ITS has set out in sufficient detail the steps which need to be taken in their program. At the same time it explains Supplier Certification, it lets the supplier know what is expected of his or her company. Such completeness is highly recommended. Although Supplier Certification is simple in concept, its steps do need explanation so that you do not lose a

PART NUMBER DECERTIFICATION

Part # _____ Supplier _____

Date Initiated _____ Supplier Code _____

DELIVERY 100% ☐
(For Certified Parts Only)

PROCESS ☐

QUALITY ☐

When all information is completed, forward to Procurement Quality Assurance.

PART NUMBER RECERTIFICATION

Part # _____ Supplier _____

Date Initiated _____ Supplier Code _____

PROCESS REVALIDATION ☐

CLEARING INTERVAL ☐
(Mfg. lot acceptance)

DELIVERY ☐
(3 consecutive months above 98%)

Quality Assurance: _____
Manufacturing Engineering: _____
Purchasing: _____

When all information is completed, forward to Procurement Quality Assurance.

potentially excellent supplier from confusion. What follows is the text of the ITS booklet:

INTERNATIONAL TOTALIZATOR SYSTEMS, INC.
PARTNERS IN QUALITY
Supplier Certification Program

1.   PURPOSE

The purpose of this booklet is to introduce suppliers to the International Totalizator Systems, Inc. Supplier Certification Program. It defines the basic quality system and procedures required for suppliers to become CERTIFIED suppliers to International Totalizator Systems, Inc. (ITS).

1.1   THE SUPPLIER CERTIFICATION PROCESS

1.1.1   SUPPLIER SYMPOSIUM

Suppliers with the potential to become certified will be invited to attend one of several ITS Supplier Symposiums which will introduce them to the ITS Supplier Certification Program and certification requirements.

1.1.2   INITIAL ON-SITE SURVEY

Following the symposium, ITS suppliers who wish to participate in the certification process will be scheduled for an on-site survey by the ITS Supplier Certification Team.

1.1.3 CERTIFICATION PROCESS

Following the initial on-site survey and evaluation by the Supplier Certification Team, suppliers approved by the Team will become a "qualified" supplier with **certification subject to the requirements as defined herein.**

1.2 FOLLOW-UP SURVEY OF EXISTING SUPPLIERS

A follow-up or repeat survey of an ITS certified supplier or qualified supplier shall be considered appropriate when any of the following conditions exist:

1.2.1 When the supplier has documented evidence of improvement on recommended or required certification parameters.

1.2.2 When supplier conformance to drawing an/or specification requirements is not consistent though all other certification requirements have been met.

1.2.3 When the supplier's organization/management has been changed.

1.2.4 When the supplier has changed location.

1.2.5 When the supplier has significantly changed processes and, as a result, process capabilities.

1.3 ON-SITE AUDIT

ITS reserves the right to perform periodic appraisals of the supplier's quality systems, audit quality records, and source audit any parts ready for shipment.

2. GENERAL POLICIES

Since purchased parts constitute a significant percentage of the components included in every ITS product, it is necessary to define and describe the performance requirements for ITS Certified Suppliers. The following is a brief description of such requirements:

2.1 Suppliers are responsible for comprehension of the drawings and specifications. Any questionable area must be immediately clarified by contacting ITS Engineering through the ITS Purchasing representative.

2.1.1 ITS documentation adheres to the specifications of ANSI Y14.5 1982 and Geometric Dimensioning and Tolerancing is used throughout. Suppliers are expected to fully comprehend the symbology and interpretation of this standard.

2.2 Compliance with the requirements defined herein is required of certified suppliers to ITS and exemptions or exceptions shall be permitted only when noted on the purchase order or otherwise granted by ITS — in writing.

2.2.1 In situations where the requirements of ITS engineering drawings or specifications conflict with this document, the drawing/specification shall supersede the corresponding requirements of this specification.

2.3 Suppliers are responsible for setting up and maintaining a quality system which will ensure that every part complies with the requirements of the drawing and any specifications which are defined on the purchase order.

2.4 The supplier's facility, process, and quality systems are subject to review and evaluation by the ITS Supplier Certification Team. This document will serve as the basis for such a review.

Suppliers who meet certification requirements as defined in this document and provide quality parts, in a timely fashion that are competitively priced, will continued to be used as source for current and new ITS orders.

2.5 Suppliers are to furnish parts and materials that comply with current engineering drawings and specification. Suppliers must emphasize process control, utilizing techniques such as SPC to maintain control and quality and not rely on ITS receiving inspection or our Supplier Certification Team to determine the quality level of the parts. Suppliers are to use any sampling plan which utilizes "ZERO DEFECT" principles.

2.6   Suppliers are to direct their long-term quality approach to the prevention of defects through process controls rather than defect detection through inspection techniques. Process control systems not only increase productivity, they also promote continuing quality improvement, which benefits both ITS and the supplier.

2.7   Suppliers are fully responsible for the initial and follow-up qualification layout activity of the tooling plus the end product shipped to ITS.

2.8   Certain purchased parts may include dimensions and/or specifications which significantly affect the form, fit, and functional characteristics of the final ITS product. These dimensions and/or specifications when identified by the symbol ◊ on the ITS engineering drawings shall be subject to additional requirements as outlined in this booklet.

2.9   Improved methods of quality assurance, including SPC, are recommended to all suppliers seeking certification.

3.   QUALITY SYSTEM REQUIREMENTS FOR ALL PURCHASED PARTS

3.1   SUPPLIER RESPONSIBILITIES

The supplier has the responsibility to develop and maintain an effective system for control of quality, utilizing defect prevention methods such as SPC.

3.2 ORGANIZATION

The supplier is to establish and maintain an effective quality assurance organization commensurate with the size and complexity of the facility and the type of product being manufactured.

3.3 DOCUMENTED QUALITY PROGRAM

The supplier's quality program shall be documented and shall include a definition of each established control system with procedures for delegating responsibilities and directing performance for each quality assurance operation plus a description of and instruction for completing any forms used in the program.

3.4 DRAWING OR SPECIFICATION CHANGE, AND DEVIATION CONTROL

3.4.1 DRAWING AND SPECIFICATION CHANGE CONTROL

The supplier is required to have a documented system for assuring that the latest applicable ITS engineering drawings and specifications are available to manufacturing, inspection, and test. The supplier must maintain a record of change effective dates and change authority. All changes affecting ITS parts must have ITS written approval/authorization prior to being incorporated.

3.4.2　DEVIATION CONTROL

When a drawing or specification deviation is authorized by ITS Engineering or Quality Control it is to be coordinated through the ITS Purchasing Department and the supplier must maintain the necessary records to insure and validate compliance with the original document and superseding deviation.

3.5　MEASURING AND TESTING EQUIPMENT CONTROL AND CALIBRATION

The supplier shall provide and maintain adequate gaging and test equipment as necessary to provide for sufficient process control.

The supplier shall develop and implement a written plan to verify the accuracy of such devices at sufficient, frequent intervals (normally at least once per year) to ensure continued accuracy.

This documented plan shall cover all measuring and test equipment, including production tools, fixtures, and personal gages used as a medium of inspection. Calibration control documents shall be traceable to National Institute of Standards and Technology, formerly know as National Bureau of Standards, or equivalent international standard. Control documents are to be maintained, listing location, date, last inspection results, and date of next scheduled inspection.

3.6   MANUFACTURING STATUS CONTROL

The supplier's quality assurance system shall assure compliance with drawings, manufacturing process specifications and quality standards during fabrication and testing of the manufactured article.

Quality requirements shall be specified on all work orders or process cards. Any characteristics controlled or affected by the operation shall have written inspection instruction and frequencies established for operators and/or inspectors. The established frequencies are to be based upon the process capability studies and/or the supplier's experience in controlling the process. *Results of the inspection shall be recorded.*

3.7   PRODUCT STATUS CONTROL

The supplier shall identify the status of the product (accept, reject, sort, rework, scrap, hold, etc.) through all stages of the process by means of stamps, tags, routing cards, color codes or other effective control devices.

3.8   FINAL INSPECTION AND TEST PLAN

The supplier is fully responsible for outgoing products and documentation of their conformance such as: chemical, mechanical, raw material, and heat treat process certifications done to comply with ITS drawings/specifications. The supplier's control plan shall include a final inspection plan sufficient to provide an accurate measure of the quality of the completed article. Control of outgoing product quality can be demonstrated by any one or combination of the following:

3.8.1   WHERE SPC IS NOT ESTABLISHED

Final inspection/test utilizing either 100% inspection/test or an appropriate statistically valid acceptance sampling plan based on a zero defect acceptance number.

Acceptance of product by any sampling plan does not relieve the supplier of the responsibility that all parts must meet specifications. Also, documentation/records such as: acceptance of outgoing product quality, physical and chemical property test records on all components/materials used and furnished to ITS, heat treat certification, etc. must be available for review by the Quality Control or Purchasing representatives of ITS. When requested by ITS, documentation and records are to be included in shipments to the receiving ITS location.

3.8.2   WHERE SPC IS ESTABLISHED AND MAINTAINED

In-process statistical control records, indicating parts were manufactured with processes operating under statistical control and capable of meeting plus or minus three standard deviation (± 3.0). Periodic audits are required to confirm that in-process controls are adequate.

3.9　NONCONFORMING MATERIAL CONTROL

Material that does not conform to drawing/specification requirements shall be identified as nonconforming, segregated, removed from operation, and stored in a separate area designated for that purpose only.

The supplier shall determine immediately the extent of the problem and take prompt action to correct the condition and prevent shipment of all nonconforming material.

The supplier shall immediately notify the ITS Purchasing representative or Quality Control department of any suspected quality problems in shipments already released and of the corrective actions being taken to eliminate the condition.

If the problem cannot be corrected immediately, shipments must be held, pending specific instructions or deviation authorization from ITS.

3.10　CORRECTIVE ACTION

The supplier's quality program shall provide a plan for timely corrective action on all conditions detrimental to product quality including product deficiencies encountered during processing, fabrication, assembly, or test.

The prime objective of corrective action is to preclude the recurrence of nonconformance by identifying and correcting the causes and contributing factors. This plan shall be prevention oriented and shall include follow-up measures to assure that the action was lasting and timely.

3.11 SUB-SUPPLIER CONTROL

The supplier shall assume full responsibility of all purchased materials and services. The responsibility includes:

3.11.1   Evaluation of the sub-supplier's quality system.

3.11.2   Selection of qualified sub-supply sources.

3.11.3   Communication of all design and quality requirements to the sub-suppliers.

Each supplier shall establish procedures to carry out this responsibility using methods listed below:

3.11.4   By receipt of satisfactory factual data and/ or certification.

3.11.5   By performing (or contracting) the required inspection and testing with adequate frequencies to assure conformance to ITS drawings and specifications.

The supplier shall initiate corrective action with sub-suppliers on all nonconforming parts.

The supplier shall have all the necessary documents on file, subject to review and acceptance by ITS for a period of five (5) years from the date of purchase.

3.12 RETURNED PRODUCT ANALYSIS

The supplier is to analyze defective products returned from ITS (dimensional, metallurgical, physical, chemical or material nonconformance), determine the cause of the problem and implement appropriate corrective action. This action is to be communicated to ITS and the records are to be maintained on file for review.

3.13 QUALITY SYSTEM SELF AUDIT

The supplier is responsible for auditing the total quality system in the supplier's facility. As a minimum, the supplier shall audit all quality systems and control plans annually. Internal audit results and documented corrective measures shall be retained on file for review upon ITS request.

3.14 MATERIAL CERTIFICATION REQUIREMENTS

This requirement applies to all designated purchased material/parts obtained through ITS purchase orders.

The applicability of each specification type can be determined by reviewing the specification noted on the drawings or the ITS purchase order.

3.15 PRESERVATION, PACKAGING AND SHIPMENT

The supplier is to provide controls that will assure satisfactory protection against damage, contamination, and corrosion during manufacturing, subsequent storage, and shipment. When not included on the ITS drawing or specification, packaging, preservation, and identification requirements and instructions can be obtained from ITS Engineering or Quality Control through the ITS Purchasing representative.

4.   ADVANCED QUALITY PLANNING REQUIREMENTS

4.1   PROCESS CONTROL PLANNING

Process control planning provides an effective way for the supplier and ITS to achieve a consensus on the quality planning for new products and review any system changes made thereafter.

Suppliers are to develop and submit process control plans which describe the quality planning for a specific part or family of parts. These plans should cover all effected designated characteristics specified by ITS.

Plans should include, but not be limited to, the manufacturing processes within the supplier's facility and all sub-contracted material and services. Each plan is to be approved by ITS upon the initial submittal and for any follow-up changes.

Proprietary process details included on the plan should be identified as such. On such occasion, the supplier may reserve the right to maintain these plans at their facility subject to review by ITS representatives.

4.2 PROCESS FLOW DIAGRAM

A process flow diagram is a planning tool used to depict the sequential flow of material through the receiving, manufacturing, assembly, and final process.

4.3 PROCESS-POTENTIAL STUDIES

Process-potential studies assess the short-term influence on part dimensions emanating from the machine/operation/process alone when the study is performed.

4.4 STATISTICAL PROCESS CONTROL (SPC)

ITS expects its designated suppliers to use SPC techniques in order to achieve defect prevention and pursue continuous improvement through the application of statistical techniques. It is only through such a systematic approach that consistency of performance in a capable process can be achieved.

4.5 CRITICAL PRODUCT FEATURES

Critical Product Features established by ITS Engineering will be identified on the drawing or specification using the ◊ symbol. Any features so identified are critical to the integrity of the ITS product.

5. PRODUCTION PRODUCT QUALIFICATION (INITIAL SAMPLE)

ITS requires a qualification of new production parts in advance of first production shipment. Required ITS report forms will be provided to the supplier by the ITS Quality Control group.

5.1 CONDITIONS REQUIRING INITIAL SAMPLE

5.1.1   Upon initial production of a part.

5.1.2   Whenever an engineering, process, or tooling change occurs that may affect dimensional, metallurgical, chemical, functional, or appearance parameters.

5.1.3   Change in supplier's manufacturing location or facility. In this instance, the supplier shall notify ITS Purchasing Department for instructions.

If temporary or preproduction tooling is required to meet the initial production schedule, the supplier shall notify the ITS purchasing representative; however, a secondary sample qualification is to follow upon completion of production tooling.

5.2 INITIAL SAMPLE INSPECTION AND TEST

The supplier shall perform any inspection and/or tests necessary to assure that the samples conform to specification. Dimensional and laboratory tests such as chemical, mechanical, and others required by the document and/or specifications are to be performed and certification of the testing is to be supplied to ITS.

Initial samples evaluated because of engineering, process, or tooling changes, or parts resubmitted due to nonconformance, need only the evaluation of the affected characteristics.

5.3 INITIAL SAMPLE QUALITY AND TYPE

5.3.1 DIMENSIONAL SAMPLES

Unless instructed by ITS, the supplier is responsible for a complete dimensional evaluation of a designated sample quantity. In the event that parts are being produced on multiple cavity dies or cavities, at least one "layout sample" will be required from each cavity and shall be so identified.

5.3.2 LABORATORY SAMPLES

The supplier is to initiate and perform the necessary laboratory testing in accordance with ITS drawings and specifications. All tests and required specifications are to be listed and the results for each test are to be identified. When necessary, a legible attachment which clearly states the nature and results of testing may be affixed to the report form.

ITS reserves the right to witness the qualification activities through a Supplier Certification, Quality Control, or Engineering
representative or by the layout audit function at the receiving facilities.

The supplier will be advised of the preliminary results upon the completion of the
witnessed layout activity or by an ITS
Purchasing representative. In the event
that corrections must be made, ITS will
provide the supplier with new forms and/
or instructions.

ITS Engineering, Quality Control, and
Purchasing representatives will be ready
to provide any assistance to the supplier to
resolve questions or misinterpretations regarding the product qualification.

5.4   SAMPLE IDENTIFICATION AND SHIPPING INSTRUCTIONS

When instructed, the evaluated/identified parts and
reports are to be shipped to the designated ITS
location and addressed "Receiving Audit Department." The package is to be clearly marked SAMPLE
PARTS and REPORTS. Shipping information will
be indicated on the ITS purchase order.

5.5   RELEASE OF FIRST PRODUCTION SHIPMENT

5.5.1   Production shipments with any nonconformance must be held by the supplier pending ITS disposition instructions.

5.5.2 Unless otherwise specified, first article production shipments need not be held by the supplier pending final approval by ITS, providing the evaluated or submitted sample conforms to specifications during the preliminary review.

5.5.3 ITS reserves the right to disposition an entire production lot based upon the results of initial sample appraisal.

5.5.4 ITS may entertain a supplier request for a temporary departure from ITS drawings and specifications by submitting a written request for material review action.

5.5.5 The request will be considered for a specified number of parts or a specific period of time as required to implement corrective action to the supplier's process or the ITS drawings/specifications.

6. SPECIAL PROCESSES

Special processes are those that cannot be adequately evaluated for conformance to requirements through audits or non-destructive tests alone. For example, welding, plating, heat treating, etc. The supplier is responsible for assuring compliance to ITS specifications. As applicable, the supplier shall provide detailed process procedures, destruct test of the samples, and training of the involved personnel.

AEROJET ORDNANCE COMPANY
Tustin, California

The following brief summary of Aerojet's certification process shows, in the words of President Charles R. Sebastian, that the key to their "long-term success is for Aerojet Ordnance to be the *leader* in our industry." Sebastian goes on to define a leader as a "preferred company," that is, a company "preferred by our employees as *the place* at which they want to work; by our subcontractors as *the company* they want to work with; and by our customers as *the company* they know they can count on to get quality products delivered on-time, every time, at a competitive price." If more company presidents felt this way, we would be moving steadily toward the future. It is this type of commitment and thinking which lies behind Aerojet's Supplier Certification process as described below in the literature they give to their suppliers:

THE PROCESS:

The certification process begins when Aerojet Ordnance selects a supplier to provide a particular product or service and includes a review of the supplier's quality history. An on-site survey is also conducted to determine if the supplier does, in fact, have the capability to produce consistently a quality product.

During this initial survey, the Aerojet Ordnance Certification Team will meet with the supplier to introduce the Certified Supplier Program, explaining the requirements and benefits, and ascertaining that the supplier has a clear understanding of all purchase order requirements. Subsequent to a contract award, the supplier then must submit a Quality Plan to Aerojet Ordnance for review and approval by the Certification Team. The team will return to the supplier during the early phase of production to conduct an audit to assure implementation of the Plan and to resolve any problems identified earlier.

A first article inspection on a sample of the initial lot produced is conducted by Aerojet Ordnance Source or Destination Inspection personnel to verify the ability of the supplier to produce material in conformance with purchase order requirements. Determination is based on 100 percent inspection of all characteristics of the sample parts. Lots delivered during the next six months are inspected by Aerojet Ordnance personnel. When the nonconformance rate during each of the six months is zero percent, the Certification Team recommends that the supplier be recognized as a Certified Supplier. When the nomination is approved by the Aerojet Ordnance Company Vice President for Quality Assurance and Test and the Director of Procurement, arrangements are made for presenting the Certification Award plaque to the supplier at his facility.

Once a supplier is officially certified, subsequent lots of material will be accepted on the basis of supplier inspection and test reports, and statistical documentation that the manufacturing processes are in control. An on-site audit of the manufacturing process and quality program will be conducted annually by Aerojet Ordnance personnel to monitor the supplier.

Aerojet Ordnance will respond to any degradation of the supplier's performance by providing on-site assistance to the supplier. If the noted degradation is not rectified within 30 days or any degradation is noted twice within a one-year period, Aerojet Ordnance will revoke the supplier's certification.

As you can see, Aerojet Ordnance's statement about their program is concise and thorough. Companies either use a "short form" like this or a "long form" such as the one shown for International Totalizator Systems, Inc. The next form falls somewhere in between the two.

ARCHIVE, Inc.
Costa Mesa, California

The following are the six steps taken by Archive in certifying suppliers. Like all such programs, the emphasis is on meeting quality objectives and in controlling the manufacturing process. In many ways, being asked by a customer to become a certified supplier is the best thing that could happen to your company. The results of any successful program are increased productivity, lower total cost and higher quality which invariably leads to higher profits and a larger market share. Think over, as you read Archive's steps, how each could help your company.

SIX STEPS TO QUALITY:
The Archive
Supplier Certification Process

STEP 1

Supplier Selection

Selecting the right supplier for the job is one of the most important steps in the certification process. The decision will require a visit by Archive representatives to the supplier's facility. To be effective, the visit must include a

---

meeting with top management and staff. The purpose is to review and assess capabilities, resources, and corporate commitment to quality assurance. Matters to be addressed during the visit would include:

- Attitude on Statistical Process Control (SPC) techniques.
- Certification process with:
  a. Materials and part suppliers.
  b. Other customers.
- Training programs.
- Measurement equipment and capabilities.

An official supplier survey will be completed at this time.

STEP 2

Requirement Review

A selected supplier must fully understand Archive's requirements. The objective of this step is to communicate all the requirements that must be fulfilled to become a certified Archive supplier. Any exceptions to the requirements identified by the supplier must be satisfactorily resolved prior to contract commitments. Specific subjects to be covered in detail:

- Review of prints and specifications.
- Exceptions to prints and specifications.
- Acknowledged acceptance of exceptions in writing.
- Mutual agreement of initial production quantities.

- 100% inspection of initial sample.
- Packaging to protect built-in quality.
- On-time deliveries.

STEP 3

Quality Plan

When all the requirements have been communicated, the supplier must devise a plan defining how process control and capability are achieved. The quality plan submitted to Archive for approval should be oriented to a specific part (or group of common parts) manufactured to Archive's requirements. Overall process flow and step-by-step descriptions of each operation are to be provided.

In addition, the process control plan for each operation is to be defined. SPC techniques should be utilized whenever applicable. Data which is to be taken at designated check points must be submitted with each lot in the form of $\overline{X}$-R charts or other SPC techniques until process control and capability are established. The plan must also include how the supplier will handle in-process rejects, corrective action, and Ongoing Reliability Testing (ORT).

STEP 4

Qualification

Samples representing the production process will be 100% tested and evaluated by Archive to qualify design, process, capability, and correlation. The purpose of this qualification step is to assure that the design and production process, including tooling and inspection equipment, are correct and capable. Inspection and test methodology will also be evaluated during this phase.

All critical components, mechanical and electrical, will require additional qualification procedures. By definition, the failure of a critical component renders the equipment incapable of performing its intended operational function. Initial production samples of critical components must be accompanied with inspection and test data that correlate with Archive's own data. After data correlation and process capability are completed, the qualification process will continue at Archive. Based on the type of part involved, the qualification process could include additional life testing and other reliability tests.

STEP 5

Process Control

After successful qualification, the supplier can proceed to ship production parts. However, ongoing process control based on SPC concepts must also be implemented and maintained. The objective is to assure that process control and capability exist for the production process on an ongoing basis. It is important that the patterns of variability be known and correct.

This phase is basically the implementation of the quality plan identified in Step 3. SPC information is to accompany each production lot or is to be submitted at regular intervals as mutually established between Archive and the supplier. The SPC information must continue to be provided until process control and capability are demonstrated. The supplier is expected to continue SPC methods even after the need to send data to Archive has ended. It is recommended that each supplier designate an SPC resource person to assure effective implementation of sound process control techniques and methods.

STEP 6

Certification

After SPC has been effectively implemented and five successive production lots have been accepted by Archive, certification will be granted the supplier. Parts will then be shipped directly from the supplier to the point of use at Archive (dock to stock). Certification means that the supplier's quality system is able to deliver parts that conform to Archive's requirements, the process is capable and under statistical control, evidence of quality (control charts, process capability data, and actual parametric measurements) is available for immediate review, and continuous reduction of variability is being pursued. In keeping with our Partners-In-Quality relationship, it is vitally important that proposed process changes or problems be communicated to Archive. Archive, in turn, will provide suppliers timely feedback of quality performance, and will expect prompt corrective action when problems arise.

Now, let's turn our attention to how you can rate your suppliers in the next chapter.

SUPPLIER RATINGS

9

Although many companies rate suppliers before initiating a supplier certification program, we view this process as a tool to be used in helping suppliers improve their performance. One of the principal goals of supplier certification is to reduce the supplier base, to eliminate those suppliers who are incapable of conforming to our specifications. We must provide all our suppliers the opportunity to become certified. This is a prudent strategy because many suppliers who are presently not performing above the minimum level become significantly better in this program. The incentive to gain a larger share of business and more profit motivates suppliers to improve. Supplier rating, as shown in our VideoEducation Series, *Supplier Certification, The Path to Excellence*, is a way for us to determine which suppliers are committed and capable.

Ratings should be performed monthly or at regularly scheduled times. They are designed to help both the customer and the supplier to anticipate and prevent problems with quality, delivery and process control. In this sense, they are very similar to audits which, by definition, are performed after a product is built or a process is completed. As with the criteria described in our supplier survey, rating criteria must also *only* be measurements which can be quantified. We want to avoid situations where suppliers are ranked by "warm and fuzzy" criteria.

For example, cooperation is a desirable result of a supplier certification program. How do we quantify this criteria? Do we simply award points because a supplier returns telephone calls? There are more quantitative questions to ask. For instance:

---

1) How many new products have we developed with the supplier?

2) Are corrective actions implemented and documented within 48 hours?

3) How long does it take the supplier to phase in an engineering change?

BENEFITS OF SUPPLIER RATING

One more of the principal benefits of supplier rating is that it establishes a baseline from which you and the supplier can track future improvements. In establishing this present base, areas that need improvement will be revealed as well as areas which are performing according to requirements. This baseline and the subsequent data which is gathered must be quantifiable and objective performance criteria. We explain to our clients that the baseline can help to foster in-company competition as workers and managers strive together to enhance the company's performance beyond what was measured when they began. In addition to that advice, we also have come up with a list of "do's and don'ts" for developing a suitable rating system:

THE "DO'S" OF SUPPLIER RATING

- Use the team approach in developing the program.
- Use quantifiable data.
- Use supplier rating in selective situations initially.
- Present the system to suppliers before beginning to rate them.
- "Coach" your suppliers so as to improve their performance.

THE "DON'TS" OF SUPPLIER RATING

- Develop a program without cross-functional consensus.
- Use subjective data.
- Use mass mailings to present the system to the supplier.
- Rate without warning suppliers.
- Use ratings as a club on your suppliers so as to improve their performance.

Above all, we recommend that you and your company remember that supplier rating is a tool to help the supplier succeed because when the supplier succeeds, you succeed. Suppliers are not the enemy, so we shouldn't be beating them with a stick to improve performance. Supplier rating works more like a carrot in that it extends the reward of more business if the supplier can improve and conform to requirements.

ELEMENTS REQUIRED
FOR A SUPPLIER RATING SYSTEM

Our experience has led us to develop a supplier rating system based on seven elements and two modifiers. As shown on the next page, the emphasis is on quality since supplier certification is a quality-oriented program.

We recommend that each company assign values according to their importance to the company. For example, if on-time delivery is the biggest problem at your plant and quality issues have been eliminated, then you should raise the point value for on-time delivery from 20 points to 30. Similarly, if quantities are a problem, we should raise quantity discrepancy from 5 points to 10 or 15. Neither do we need to use the same point values or criteria for all commodities or suppliers. We can devise rating systems by commodity or class of suppliers and we can phase in criteria which may be critical to one supplier and not another. The point is to develop a rating system which we can use as a tool to make the supplier better. Whatever measurements we use, however, should be aimed at improvement, not at maintaining the status quo.

DEFINITIONS OF THE ELEMENTS

Before we explain how to use the rating system and its results, let's

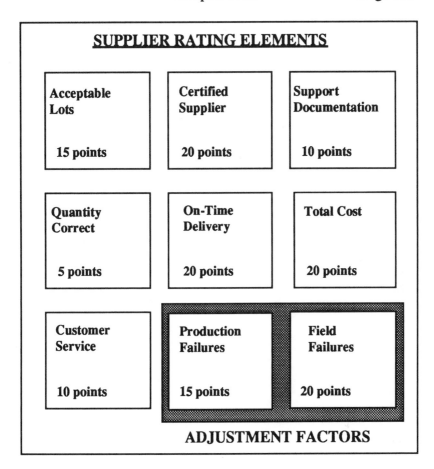

first look at the elements in more detail and how to assign points for different supplier actions.

ACCEPTABLE LOTS — Maximum Points = 15

This element measures the percentage of acceptable lots to total lots submitted by a supplier. As we described earlier, a supplier who notifies us of a discrepancy, documents the error and initiates corrective action may not be penalized. The same holds true for a supplier who requests a deviation ahead of shipment. However, a supplier who requests a deviation after production is begun, should receive far less points than the supplier in the first example. Our aim is to encourage communication between suppliers and customers before action is taken. If we return the product, the supplier receives no points.

CERTIFIED SUPPLIER — Maximum Points = 20

A rating of 20 points signifies that the supplier is certified for that component or process. If a supplier is in Phase 1 of the program, it would receive 5 points and so on as the chart below suggests:

PHASE	RATING
Not in program	0
Phase 1	5
Phase 2	10
Phase 3	15
Phase 4	20

SUPPORT DOCUMENTATION — Maximum Points = 10

This rating element measures the presence and quality of documentation, certification data, inspection/test results and instruction manuals for operations and maintenance. The more complete this material is, the greater the amount of points the supplier receives. Lack of proper documentation received on time should result in zero points. Also, this support documentation should never replace TQM. Examples of support documentation are a control chart or metallurgical, chemical and various other data.

QUANTITY CORRECT — Maximum Points = 5

Quite simply, this element measures how close the quantity shipped is to what was requested. We need to establish a scale which indicates the level of tolerance. Plus or minus 10% is no longer tolerable in a World Class company. Suppliers who ship orders with this margin of error should receive zero points. Suppliers who ship with 100% accuracy receive five points.

ON-TIME DELIVERY — Maximum Points = 20

This element measures on-time delivery and the tolerance level within which a supplier must ship product to the plant. The closer a supplier is to delivering products within a specified window, the more points are given. Those suppliers who can deliver on-time, 100% of the time, will be given 20 points.

TOTAL COST — Maximum Points = 20

This element should be measured by determining all the costs associated with a supplier's product, not price alone. Then, using the profit equation, we determine what level those costs should be in order to earn a fair profit. How close a supplier comes to paring down costs to the level we set determines the number of points received. Suppliers with costs that exceed this level will have the most points taken away from the total allowed.

CUSTOMER SERVICE — Maximum Points = 10

Here, we are looking for suppliers who cooperate and communi-

cate and who meet certain interface requirements. The less cooperative in the following areas, the fewer points are awarded:

- **Lack of Research and Development**
- **Lack of design support**
- **Non-sharing of testing methods**
- **Infrequent and incomplete progress reports**
- **Withholding of technical information**
- **Insufficient assistance in problem-solving**
- **Poor timing — assistance too late**
- **Applicability — assistance not pertinent to subject**

As a customer, you must determine which of the above areas
affects you the most. If you are in a growing or a high-tech
industry, you may assign more value to Research and Development.

ADJUSTMENT FACTORS

The following two adjustment factors provide a means to take
away points for both process and field failures. If you elect to use
a demerit program, you would add points to the supplier's total.
For a merit program, you would take away point value.

PRODUCTION FAILURES — Maximum Points = 15

This adjustment measures the inherent reliability of a supplier's
production or a moving average calculation of manufacturing
failures. In order to support shipments being delivered to work-in-
process, a system of production failure feedback must be in place.
The production area must report defects which should carry a
severe penalty.

FIELD FAILURES — Maximum Points = 20

This adjustment measures the operating reliability of a supplier's product in the field. It isolates and detects field failures and their related costs directly to the supplier. As with production failures, ratings should be severe and may be reason for a supplier to lose its certified status. Every effort must be made to eliminate field failures.

HOW TO CONSTRUCT
A SUPPLIER RATING CHART

A supplier rating chart simply lists the rating elements in one column, the maximum points for each element in another column and the number of points earned by the supplier in a third column. See the illustration in the next section for an example. The difficult part is gathering data and determining responsibilities.

First, let's look at data. If your supplier has a software package and a capable computer system which can generate performance reports, like an MRP or MRP II system, then both your jobs will be easier. Even so, you will need to make sure that all the different functions within the supplier's company are aware of their part in the data gathering. This is where the supplier must develop a program to convey to internal departments the requirements of supplier rating. This will entail prior notifications and meetings in order to build a strong level of commitment. At this point, the company doing the rating, the customer, must come in and explain and promote the use of the rating system. They must make it clear that this is an unbiased system. Lastly, your company will need to determine the frequency of supplier rating. Certainly, it should be employed whenever there is a process change at the supplier's facility. But the frequency otherwise will depend upon whether the company is a major or minor supplier, how many dollars are spent and whether they supply a critically functional part or material. Based on these criteria, you will make weekly, monthly, quarterly or yearly appraisals.

HOW TO USE THE SUPPLIER RATING CHART

If we use the preceding elements to rate a number of companies, we now have a way to objectively compare the performance of one supplier against another. We now have the basis for a report card which can be sent out to our suppliers. Such a report card for a particular product would look like this:

ELEMENT	MAX. PTS.	RATINGS		
		A	B	C
Acceptable lots	15	12	6	5
Certified supplier	20	15	9	2
Support documentation	10	8	6	6
Quantity correct	5	4	2	1
On-time delivery	20	14	12	9
Total cost	20	13	8	7
Customer Service	10	8	5	4
Totals	**100**	**74**	**48**	**34**
% of business		**60%**	**20%**	**20%**

We would send this report card to each of the suppliers. Supplier A's report would have the ratings of B and C, their competition, but they would not be identified by name. This chart makes it clear to each company where they stand in relation to other suppliers and where they stand in each category. We then make it clear to everybody that if they want a larger percentage of business, they must improve their supplier ratings with respect to their competition. In other words, supplier B and C must be better than A to get more business. For supplier A to keep this percentage, however, he cannot stand still. He, too, must improve.

As the report card reads now, supplier C is in danger of losing business or being removed from the supplier base. But, if six months from now the results read as A = 74, B = 48 and C = 74, then supplier A is in danger of losing his share of business. He still has a high total, but it has not changed in six months. In such a case, we must begin to doubt his ability to improve on a continuous basis which is the foundation of a supplier certification program. This measurement of supplier performance must press for continuous improvement.

A similar chart can be used to compare a supplier's performance from month to month:

ELEMENT	MAX PTS.	MONTHS											
Supplier: _____		1	2	3	4	5	6	7	8	9	10	11	12
Acceptable lots	15												
Certified supplier	20												
Support documentation	10												
Quantity correct	5												
On-time delivery	20												
Total cost	20												
Customer Service	10												
Totals													
% of business													

MANAGING THE SUPPLIER RATING SYSTEM

We consider supplier rating as a 50/50 proposition. Plans must be made and administered by both your company and the supplier which means that meetings between both sides must be held throughout the program. Meetings must be seen as a way to further the win/win philosophy of Supplier Certification. That makes full preparation and full participation equally important in order to agree upon a rating system that will help the supplier perform better and will help your company control variability. Meetings will help both of you establish goals with clear start and completion dates as well as a system for monitoring progress. In short, we are talking about the establishment of a corrective action loop for managing the supplier rating system. Consistent follow-up is the key to such a program of managing change.

Above all, the key to supplier rating and Supplier Certification as a whole is communication. It is imperative that you make your goals known to the supplier and that the supplier makes them known to its workers and managers. Success requires active supplier participation. Communication also requires the ability to listen. We emphasize this point over and over in every client meeting and seminar we give, whether here in America or in Europe, the Far East or the Mideast. Communication means having the ability to listen. As we always point out to people, the same letters that spell the word "listen" also spell the word "silent."

THE TEAM'S ROLE

Reporting data without analysis is self-defeating in our view. That is why we not only advocate giving authority but responsibility to Supplier Certification teams which work with suppliers. Such teams should be held accountable for the performance of the suppliers in their purview. At the same time, these teams should be preparing quarterly reports for top management which draw conclusions and suggest action plans for continuous improvement in the area of supplier rating. This will mean that the teams must keep an eye out for suppliers who are heading into a "danger zone." You will know this is happening when:

- **Supplier ratings stagnate or drop.**

- **Supplier's management never becomes involved or involvement begins to lag.**

- **Sales representatives begin to make less and less contact.**

- **Supplier equates increased prices with improved performance.**

When any of the above danger signs come up, it is time for the team to take action. This could mean identifying suppliers who may need to be eliminated from the Supplier Certification program or, better yet, by trying to work with the supplier in improving their performance. The final goal is to maximize the business relationship for both sides. That is the essence of the win/ win philosophy of doing business.

One of the more pleasant duties of the team is to take a success (a supplier who works to keep consistently high ratings) and publicize it within the company and within the supplier base in order to clone the performance. When this happens, look for areas of transferability, that is, procedures, actions or ideas which the successful supplier has used which can be used by other suppliers.

We suggest strongly that you arrange for this kind of cross-pollination among your suppliers (that is, of course, if they are not competitors). Have suppliers visit each other's plants and, as we keep emphasizing, communicate with each other.

SUPPLIER SELF-RATING
AND CUSTOMER RATING

Supplier self-rating can work if there is a very high level of trust. This does not mean that a supplier is necessarily going to misreport data, but that there is a tendency to overrate when there is no impartial observer. We would say that the best method is to begin by doing the rating together and, as the supplier learns what is necessary and a baseline is firmly established, to let the supplier take over more and more of the task. The other side of self-rating is having the supplier rate your company as a customer. Customer rating makes it clear that you believe that Supplier Certification is a partnership in which both sides are seeking to improve. Some of the areas for a supplier to judge are:

- **How difficult is it to do business with the customer?**

- **Is the payment pattern fair and consistent?**

- **Are lead-time requests accurate or are they always less than actual due date?**

- **Does the customer involve the supplier early in the development of new products?**

Again, you can see the presence of a win/win philosophy. Giving feedback to each other works hand-in-hand with this philosophy and is essential to the improvement of both sides of the customer/ supplier partnership. In the next chapter, we will look at how to implement this partnership in the form of a successful Supplier Certification program.

IMPLEMENTING THE PROGRAM

$$\equiv 10$$

The most successful way to implement a supplier certification program is to gain top management commitment. Total cost, not standard cost or purchase price, is the important criterion. There are three ways in which we can make management listen. One way is to forward articles, books, reports and pieces of information about the tangible benefits of TQM to the top levels of our companies. A second way is to arrange for on-site visits to plants which have embraced TQM so management can see a total business concept in action. Peter Grieco remembers that there were so many requests for visits to the Apple Macintosh plant when he worked there that a limit had to be imposed. Pro-Tech was also witness to the commitment companies were putting into

Supplier Certification programs during its involvement with Sterling Engineered Products and Loran. Both Sterling and Loran are Q1 certified suppliers in the Ford Motor Company's "Quality is Number One" program. The third way is to select a small part of our company and implement a pilot project before tackling the whole company.

In the case of the last suggestion, we recommend choosing an area with the most visible paybacks. It could be an area which is most in need of improvement and/or it could be one in which you are assured of success. One way to locate such an area is to use a Pareto approach. By listing all the parts used in manufacturing a product, we will generally find that a relatively small number of items and suppliers account for a large percentage of the product cost. At one client, we were able to free up 35% of the total warehouse space simply by certifying these "A" parts first and getting the suppliers to deliver them as the client needed them. Almost immediately, the champions of the certification program could point to some impressive results.

There is a fourth way to get management commitment. When we address this last method with clients or at seminars, we use the following story to make our point:

> Two business people, one Japanese and one American, are at an international manufacturing conference held in Africa. One afternoon, they decide to explore a nearby national game park. They drive up to the entrance where there are signs everywhere: DON'T FEED THE ANIMALS, DON'T LEAVE YOUR VEHICLE, DANGEROUS WILDLIFE, DON'T DRIVE OFF THE ROAD.

They drive into the park and they see a herd of
elephants bathing in a pool of water. They both
agree that they must take a photograph of this
sight so they drive the car closer to get a better
picture.

Both of them snap away happily, but when they
return to the car they see that it is stuck in the
mud. After several attempts, they realize that they
won't ever get the car unstuck, so they decide to
walk back to the entrance.

> They take their cameras and their suitcases and start trudging back. As they make the final turn in the road, they see a pride of lions laying in the road just ahead of them. The American starts shaking in his boots, but the Japanese business person sits down and starts putting on a pair of sneakers.
>
> The American looks at him as though he's crazy and says, "You can't outrun those lions!"
>
> "I don't have to," replies his Japanese companion. "I just have to stay one step ahead of you, the competition."

Competition is certainly an excellent impetus to get top management commitment for a supplier certification program. It is an undeniable fact that a company looks to its leaders for direction. Middle management is always ready to embrace a program if upper management is committed. People at lower levels in the company are ready to accept change, provided they are given the responsibility and authority to act and that there is direction from above. But, we need to overcome accepted practices which have conditioned top management to make all the decisions. A certification program requires suppliers and, in some cases, the suppliers' suppliers to work as a TEAM. We should point out that our book, **The World of Negotiation:** *Never Being a Loser* (PT Publications, Palm Beach Gardens, FL) complements the certification process. Negotiating with a supplier about changes necessary for a successful future partnership will require the win/win philosophy we advocate in our negotiation book.

A SUPPLIER PARTNERSHIP

As we have discussed throughout this book and have discovered in our work with clients (in industries such as electronics, automotive, food processing, cosmetics, pharmaceuticals, etc.) from around the world, there are eight objectives in the process of creating a partnership with suppliers:

- Move toward smaller lot sizes.
- Reduce set-up times.
- Develop inventory turn objectives.
- Increase frequency of deliveries.
- Eliminate waste in supplier's plant.
- Seek simplicity in solutions (EDI).
- Work for continuous improvement.
- Communicate results and make them visible.

This is the foundation upon which you will create a sense of teamwork. At a recent seminar, we came across a perfect example of a company trying to become certified in a Supplier Certification Program. We were pleasantly surprised to see the vice president of this company at our seminar on Supplier Certification. Most of the other participants were representatives of companies who wanted to implement a certification program. This vice president, however, represented a supplier who wanted to know what supplier certification was and, most importantly, how to work with a company requesting its suppliers to become certified.

The vice president agreed with the above objectives. He saw the value of working as a team with the company he was supplying. We cite this example because many companies believe that suppliers will automatically balk when asked to set the objectives above. They won't as long as both the supplier and the manufacturer work together. And, in most cases, suppliers fear for their jobs and will readily agree to participate.

At the same time these objectives are assimilated and become second nature through education and open discussion at the supplier, we should be setting objectives like the ones below at our own company and at our supplier's company:

THE TEN-STEP PLAN

1. Avoid studying or planning a project to death

2. Don't be satisfied with early successes

3. Don't get tangled up in techniques

4. Always strive for continuous improvements

5. Make problems, goals and accomplishments

   visible to all

6. Document all steps of your process

7. Believe in "small is beautiful" and frequent deliveries

8. Eliminate waste in your plant and supplier's plant

9. Seek simplicity in solutions

10. Develop inventory turn objectives, not stocking programs

Once these common objectives are established, both internally and externally, we are ready to begin implementation process.

THE TOTAL BUSINESS CONCEPT (TBC) APPROACH TO IMPLEMENTATION

In a certification program, it doesn't matter so much which suppliers start the process of implementation, only that we start. The key to the creation of a framework of continuous improvement is teamwork. The implementation and achievement of supplier certification consists of four activities:

1. Top Management Commitment

2. Team Administration

3. Training and Education

4. Interdepartmental Cooperation

Only minimal expenditures are needed to improve communication, to involve the workforce in problem-solving and decision-making, or to develop interdepartmental cooperation. And since direct labor will work with management on teams, there is an opportunity for both to learn how to work together. With this level of cooperation, learning curves are quickly diminished, thus lowering total cost.

In effect, the creation of a company culture fosters vision, responsibility, authority and accountability. We can think of the above activities as four pillars which support a roof. Take away one pillar and the structure crashes to the ground.

Thus, a certification program is really no more than a commitment to continuous improvement. To get there means taking what we call the Total Business Concept approach, a journey from exposure through orientation and education to program review and on-going support. The chart on the opposite page shows this approach.

The left side of the chart shows the preparation phase. It consists of three steps:

> **World Class Education** — communicate a consistent message about the program throughout the company.

> **Opportunities** — identify where opportunities exist and what benefits will ensue.

> **Action Plan** — develop a one-year plan (not a five-year plan which will be reviewed every six months) which shows the directions, objectives and goals for success.

Management's involvement in this phase is to provide guidance, vision and direction to the implementation teams.

The right side of the chart is the Implementation Process phase which consists of six steps. In step one, we form teams that are required to address issues in the process. The next step is to provide each team specific training in group dynamics and problem-solving. Next, we hold a supplier symposium to determine which suppliers are capable and willing to undergo the certification process which we then detail in the next step. In the fourth step, the individual teams decide on a course of action that is

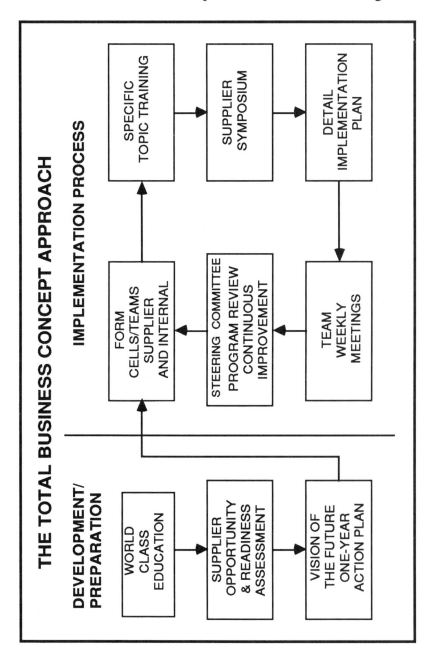

THE TOTAL BUSINESS CONCEPT APPROACH

IMPLEMENTATION PROCESS

SPECIFIC TOPIC TRAINING → SUPPLIER SYMPOSIUM → DETAIL IMPLEMENTATION PLAN

FORM CELLS/TEAMS SUPPLIER AND INTERNAL

STEERING COMMITTEE PROGRAM REVIEW CONTINUOUS IMPROVEMENT

TEAM WEEKLY MEETINGS

DEVELOPMENT/ PREPARATION

WORLD CLASS EDUCATION → SUPPLIER OPPORTUNITY & READINESS ASSESSMENT → VISION OF THE FUTURE ONE-YEAR ACTION PLAN required to meet the parameters set by a steering committee. The fifth step is to schedule weekly team meetings where problems are discussed and potential solutions are weighed. The results and activities of these meetings are then passed on to the steering committee which will direct the review activities.

The point of these six steps is to keep the process on-going, so that there is continuous improvement. This is the responsibility of the steering committee which should be comprised of the chairpeople of managerial staff. The steering committee should meet at least once a month. Its purpose is only to report on progress and to check that team efforts are on track. It does not meet to grant permission to teams so that they can start solving problems. The purpose of the Total Business Approach to implementation is to focus the whole program at the operator level. We must remind ourselves that these are the people who know best how to identify and solve production problems.

Many companies have developed progress charts like the ones below and on the opposite page to help them keep track of the steps

CERTIFIED SUPPLIERS		
Date	Supplier's Name	Letter Sent

SUPPLIER CERTIFICATION CANDIDATE CHART

Certification Candidate	Select Candidate	Committee Confirms	Start History	Notify Candidate	Suppl. Symposium	Team Participation	Commit Letter	Cand. Intro.	Survey	Team Meeting	Review Survey	Plans Established	Min. Requirement	Suppl. Plan Review	Corrective Action Plan	Track Corr. Action	Team Review	Phase I	Phase II	Phase III	Phase IV	Team Review	Team Assignments	Phase V
Supplier A	X	X	X	X	X	X	X	X	X	X	X													
Supplier B	X	X	X	X	X	X	X	X	X	X	X	X	X	X		due 1/30								
Supplier C	X	X	X	X	X	X	X	X	X			Should we certify?												
Supplier D	X	X	X	X	X	X	X	X	X	X	X	X	X	X		due 1/14								
Supplier E																								
Supplier F																								
Supplier G	X	X	X	X	X	X	X	X																
Supplier H	X	X	X	X	X	X	X	X	X	X	X	X	X		due 1/14									
Supplier I	X																							
Supplier J																								
Supplier K	X	X	X	X	X	X																		
Supplier L	X	X	X	X	X	X																		

Team Leader

each supplier has completed. Your charts may differ slightly, but the principle will be the same. The smaller of the two charts actually lists which suppliers have been certified and when and whether or not a letter has been sent out to apprise them of their newly won status.

EDUCATION AND TRAINING

Education, of course, is critical to the attainment of supplier certification. Our approach to education differs from the norm. We propose that top management spend more time in the education process than the rest of the plant as we have depicted in the educational pyramid below:

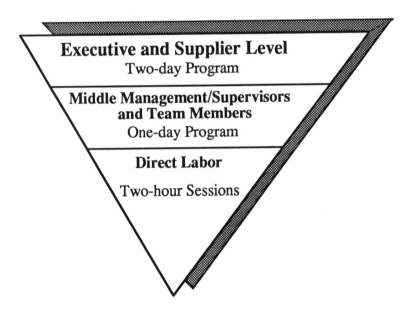

The inverted pyramid emphasizes that top management must be committed to education (learning the theory behind what you are doing) and to training (practicing what you have learned).

Although, education must occur at all levels of a company as well as in the supplier's plant, top management should receive more extensive education because without their understanding and commitment, the program will encounter difficulties. It is an undeniable fact that workers look to their leaders for direction. A middle manager is far more apt to embrace World Class/TQM if she sees a vice president genuinely committed to it.

Training is a tool to help business meet its objectives today and in the future. Our goal is to provide a positive atmosphere which will stimulate employees to discuss theory, practices and alternatives. We should base training on a competency model identifying each person or function needed as we explained in our book, **Just-In-Time Purchasing:** *In Pursuit of Excellence* (PT Publications, Palm Beach Gardens, FL). Training and education must become a way of life in our companies. Some companies, for example, always have structured activities for their workers to do whenever a line shuts down. We recommend that when a machine is down that the time be used to instruct employees in more problem-solving techniques.

SUMMARY OF THE IMPLEMENTATION PLAN

Before we move on to a discussion of teams and how they can be established and run, we want to summarize what we have said so far. Although your Supplier Certification plan may vary somewhat, the following steps are basic to every company's plan:

CONVINCING TOP MANAGEMENT

- **Educate top or key management in the tangible benefits and requirements of Supplier Certification. Pro-Tech, for instance, offers two-day education programs both publicly and in-house.**

- Conduct site visits to "best of the best" companies, where possible, to see Supplier Certification and partnerships in action.

THE STEERING COMMITTEE

- Form the steering committee to include the following functions: Purchasing, Quality Assurance, Engineering, Manufacturing, Sales, Marketing, Finance and a Union Representative (when applicable).

- Develop a company mission statement as it relates to Supplier Certification.

- Identify areas of opportunity related to Supplier Certification as part of your qualification process.

- Recommend resource allocations in order to take advantage of identified opportunities.

- Develop a one-year action plan for Supplier Certification implementation with a review and update every six months.

- Appoint and/or select the required Supplier Certification project team(s).

- Begin weekly team meetings and activities.

- Monitor team activities and progress on a monthly basis.

- Conduct specific Supplier Certification education sessions (two-day courses) with all project team members. Include key suppliers whenever possible.

- Conduct team activity training and problem solving sessions with each project team.

WHAT IS A TEAM?

A team is a group dedicated to a common goal, who rely on each other's strengths and fill in for each other's weaknesses.

The results of a team will be greater than the sum of efforts made by individuals. As we pointed out in our book, **Made In America: The Total Business Concept** (PT Publications, Palm Beach Gardens, FL), much of World Class/TQM has a gestalt, or holistic, effect. Even though a company is made up of autonomous parts, they add up to a whole. Teams are similar in that they are made up of individuals from a number of disciplines within a company and from its suppliers. Thus, when a team sets out to solve a problem, there are inputs from a number of areas, each of which states how possible solutions will effect them. Hypotheses and plans of action are made by a group process.

TEAM STRUCTURE AND MEMBER SELECTION

The first step in team-building is to form a steering committee. The steering committee should be an interdepartmental team consisting of 6-8 people from the areas of Engineering, Quality, Sales, Marketing, Production, Purchasing and Finance. It would also be wise to include a union person to impress upon members the importance and necessity of flexibility in a union environment. For nonunion plants, include a direct labor person.

The steering committee involves itself in the preparatory phase of the World Class journey:

---

1. Exposure to Supplier Certification and Supply Base Management through orientation and education.

2. Preparation of an opportunity and readiness assessment in terms of talent internal and external to your company.

3. Development of a future company vision and first year action plan through planning sessions.

The steering committee then discusses what teams should be formed in this implementation phase of the Total Business Approach. Project teams, as the name implies, coalesce around certain projects or commodities brought to attention by the steering committee. When starting a typical implementation project, we recommend four to five teams of 6-10 people to be established as a pilot.

The actual rules or plans of action are the job of a team working within the guidelines established by the steering committee. The steering committee is the catalyst. It defines what Supply Base Management means to the company, reviews projects, provides resources and guides the overall effort of continuous improvement. Another way to put this is to say that the steering committee creates the culture for change and maintains that environment.

If the steering committee is the strategy maker, then the team finds ways to implement that strategy. Any team, then, really has only one overall mandate — investigate symptoms, identify the causes (problems), identify the means to solve the problem and implement the lowest cost solution which eliminates the problem.

The composition of a Supplier Certification team should be 50% direct labor and 50% management from both the supplier and your company. Certainly, we need people on the team with expertise. We also need some people with little knowledge but with the ability to never be satisfied. There is something to say for "naive" members, the ones who ask all the "dumb" questions. For example: "Why do you do it this way?" We call this team process,

DSE, or Different Set of Eyes. Such a person has the ability to maintain an insight which is consistently fresh. That's the type of person we want on a team.

Selecting team members with fresh insight is one way to break down existing barriers in a company. Another way is to expose Supplier Certification teams to the full range of problems. The idea behind teamwork is to expand the base of experience, so that no one team, for example, becomes known as the team responsible for set-up reduction. Thus, we should make sure that set-up problems are identified on each team. The same holds true for other problems such as communication, morale, safety, preventive maintenance, quality, etc.

Besides the ability to question, team members must be given the proper decision-making authority and responsibility to make change happen. Since teams will ideally have both direct labor and management, we will have to demonstrate that we are working as a team. Giving direct labor equal representation is effective in encouraging participation, overcoming workers' fears and trusting management. In short, the same non-adversarial quality which determines supplier relationships should also determine the relationship between management and direct labor.

TEAM RULES AND OBJECTIVES

There are inherent problems with teams. Whenever a lot of cooks are stirring the broth, there will be arguments over what ingredients are best. How do you form and manage a team in which you reap the benefits of a diverse group while not stifling individual creativity? How can Purchasing sit down with Marketing, Engineering, Production and Quality and come up with integrated solutions? How do you create a team?

The answer comes in four parts. One, we need to establish ground rules, goals, objectives and a sense of direction. Two, we need to educate and train all levels of your company and your supplier in Supply Base Management techniques. Three, we must teach teams how to administer the formation and implementation of the action plans. Four, we must initiate program reviews and provide ongoing support. All of these four parts are done both internally and externally through the creation of a partnership with your suppliers and people.

One very effective way to keep a team under control is to keep accurate minutes of each team meeting. Not only do they document where you have gone, but they also list the action items to be taken before the next meeting. We can't stress the practice of taking good minutes enough. In fact, we spend a good deal of time with our clients' project teams teaching the scribe how to do this very necessary task. The first example below is of the minutes taken from a meeting of a Supplier Certification team at one of our clients. It is followed by an Interoffice Memorandum which is another effective tool to keep communication flowing between meetings.

MINUTES
OF THE
SUPPLIER CERTIFICATION
TEAM MEETING
April 16, 1999

1.0   The Supplier Certification team met Thursday morning, April 16.

2.0   Next Meeting —   Friday, May 15, 8:00 a.m.
                                      R&D Conference Room

MINUTES cont.

3.0 Meeting Minutes
We spent the meeting brainstorming on the kind of
Symposium we might have and the agenda for it.

3.1 Schedule
We decided that we will try and have a combined Supplier and Customer Symposium on
the same day. Maybe 8 a.m. to 4 p.m., including lunch.

And have an open bar from 4 p.m. to 6 p.m.
with hot hors d'oeuvres. Dinner will follow
the "attitude adjustment time."

We developed and signed up for Supplier
Symposium tasks:

> Develop a Supplier Certification
> Program presentation.
> Prepare briefing for symposium
> speakers.
> Develop a color brochure on our
> company.
> Invite Keynote speaker.
> Prepare a Quality Statement form.
> Develop guest list, suppliers and
> customers, for the symposium.
> Invite guests and monitor responses.
> Develop follow-up literature.
> Do follow-up mailings.
> Prepare Certification Implementation
> form.

MINUTES cont.

4.0 Action Items

Next week, as a team, we will develop an agenda for the Symposium. During this week, think about: how to arrange the day, should we do this over two days, what time should we start, exactly what do we want to cover.

5.0 Attachments — Sample Symposium Agendas

Agenda Sample #1

1. Who we are

2. Philosophy of Quality
   Partners in Quality

3. Certification Program
   Definition
   Goals
   What it will do for us
   What it will do for the supplier
   What we have done so far
   What we will be doing in the near future

4. Review of Symposium literature
   Quality Statement
   Certification Implementation Worksheet
   Review PT Publications' book:
   Supplier Certification II

MINUTES cont.

5. The Next Steps

6. Wrap-Up Statement by President

7. Keynote Speaker

8. Plant Tour

Agenda Sample #2

1. Introduction to the Company

2. Introduction to the Local Plant

3. Philosophy of Quality

4. Certification Program

5. What This Does for You — Supplier or Customer

6. Keynote Speaker

7. Review of Symposium literature

8. What's Next

9. Wrap-Up

10. Plant Tour

When utilizing outside assistance for implementation, it is extremely important to plan an agenda. The sample agendas we have provided are for your information.

INTEROFFICE MEMORANDUM

TO: World Class Teams
SUBJECT: Pro-Tech Visit/Team Meetings

For the upcoming Pro-Tech visit on November 19, 20, and 21, the following schedule has been established. If there are any conflicts, please try to resolve them with your team leader. Note: all meetings will be held in the Purchasing Conference Room.

November 19

8:00 a.m.	Commodity C Team Meeting
10:00 a.m.	Team Building Session
2:00 p.m.	Software Team Meeting
4:00 p.m.	Team Leader Meeting

November 20

9:00 a.m.	Inventory Team Meeting
10:00 a.m.	Commodity B Team Meeting
2:00 p.m.	Specification Team Meeting
3:30 p.m.	Steering Committee Meeting

November 21

10:00 a.m.	Survey Team Meeting
11:00 a.m.	Design for Producibility Meeting
1:30 p.m.	Information Systems Team Meeting
3:00 p.m.	Management Wrap-up Meeting

In addition, Pete Grieco will be available to meet with team members individually as necessary to help resolve any questions or problems.

PERFORMANCE MEASUREMENTS

During the certification process, the gathering and analyzing of performance data from your suppliers is essential. And it is also essential that the gathering and analysis is based upon the scientific method, that is, the unbiased evaluation of your supplier's actual capabilities and capacities. Your decision to certify should rely on nothing less than this. As we say to our clients: "In God we trust; everyone else must bring data!"

In many companies, you will find that the problem is not collecting data. Most organizations gather a wealth of data, but the bulk of it is never used in a scientific way. It is never used for problem identification and the development of corrective actions which continuously improve the process or product. Most of the data just sits on the shelf gathering dust. In the certification process, this performance data is used to identify the root causes of problems and then to identify the most cost-effective approach which will resolve the issue. That is the secret of continuous improvement and it relies on the collection of accurate data.

The gathering of accurate data requires a lot of hard work. The acquisition of data, its evaluation and the launching of the corrective action cycle is typically an eight to twelve month cycle. It has to be this long in order to insure that the supplier will be able to provide 100% quality, 100% count accuracy and 100% on-time delivery directly to work-in-process. The 100% level is only obtainable when all the required processes are under control and you and your supplier will know that only if you are measuring performance on a continuous basis.

How, then, will we know if we are succeeding? That is the question that must be addressed. We measure performance in order to be predictable, so that we know where we have been, where we are and where we are going. It is possible to measure the wrong areas as is pointed out in **Relevance Lost** (Harvard Business School Press) by H. Thomas Johnson and Robert S. Kaplan. Vice President Mel Pilachowski of Professionals for Technology Associates says that the problem with the old yardsticks of performance measurements is that they are not looking at total cost solutions. They look only at productivity levels and use a reactive, rather than a proactive approach.

Today, we must use new yardsticks which provide information to make decisions. Then, we will be able to compare actual data against predicted performance, giving us the opportunity to take corrective action. This is the definition of proactive: to measure the predictability of the outcomes of decision-making in real time.

This is best accomplished through a system of measurement that reflects a Total Business Concept. In general, the use of TBC measurements will show:

1. How close we are to having on-line, real-time information about both internal and external Manufacturing operations as well as Purchasing activities. Current information coupled with supplier involvement will provide a new approach.

2. How accurate our information is. We all know that a small mistake compounds over time. Unlike interest on your personal investments, this is not favorable. The surveyor who makes a mistake of one degree can cost you many valuable acres of land.

3. How much waste is present in Manufacturing and Supplier operations and Purchasing activities. Waste, today, is too often accepted as a given and

absorbed into overhead costs. This is truly a reactive way of thinking and must change as we compete in a world market.

4. How actual performance compares to the stated plan. Observing this variance is instrumental in making new plans which take corrective action. Those who don't learn from the mistakes of the past are doomed to repeat them.

These new yardsticks are based on total cost. In essence, Pilachowski points out, this is the same as measuring the performance of the whole company. Our principal thrust should be to emphasize a total cost-oriented, rather than a price-oriented, approach in financial measurements which attempts to gain financial control through cost improvement.

There are two principles behind cost improvement. One, we should not look at price alone in seeking to maximize profits, but also look at quality, quantity and delivery. Two, we should measure variances against cost, not price when evaluating our profitability. These two principles work in tandem with the basic principles of World Class companies, that is, building to demand and eliminating excess inventory and wasteful operations. This concept is a change from one of the present measurements of today, Purchase Price Variance, which is employed by many organizations.

As we streamline our plant through the reduction of costs, we find that Finance's job actually becomes easier as accountability is built into the process of manufacturing. For example, Finance's accounting of inventory becomes easier when we eliminate buffers, safety stocks, queues and lead-times. In the World Class environment, inventory can be accounted for merely by looking at prescribed levels of work-in-process. By giving up traditional manufacturing and accounting practices, we will have more control than before.

An overall measurement of the success of our certification program is the number of suppliers who are participating. The number of participants alone is not as important as how many part numbers are included. We should have a high percentage for those 25% of our suppliers that account for 90 to 95% of the process or part number. The goal is to achieve 100% of your suppliers shipping 100% quality components with 100% on-time delivery in accurate quantities 100% of the time.

THE SUPPLIER CERTIFICATION AUDIT

To help in the area of performance measurements, we have developed an audit procedure to assess the implementation of supplier certification. This audit is discussed at length in **Just-In-Time Purchasing:** *In Pursuit of Excellence* (PT Publications, Palm Beach Gardens, FL), but we list some here to give you an idea of what a TBC measurement is. There are, of course, no right or wrong answers to this audit. The point is to show that there is always room for improvement.

Throughput

What percentage of your total inventory has been sold? _____ %

Throughput measures the total amount of production which has been sold. If you bought enough material and components to build 100 products, built 80, have enough material to build 20 more in queue, and stored 10 units in finished goods inventory, your throughput percentage is 70%. Traditional methods would not detect the 30 units either in production or waiting to be sold. They may indicate that the throughput level is at 80, 90 or even 100%, since there is no material left in the storeroom. But, a TBC measurement makes no distinctions (as far as the bottom line goes) between material in a queue or in finished goods. The criteria here is simply how much did you sell. If you are overproducing, this measurement tells you so. It may indicate that you are not building to demand, that your company is still operating in a "push," rather than a "pull," environment.

Reduced Set-Up Times

By what percentage have your suppliers and plant reduced set-up times? ____ %

Set-up time is the amount of time it takes to change over a work center from the production of one item to another item. It is measured from the point where the last good product was produced for item #1 to the first good product of item #2 and should include the time it takes the operator to get the machine to full efficiency. Set-up time is one of the first areas to attack in reducing lead-times. It is also a highly visible area which can act as a great motivator to the implementation of further World Class/TQM practices. For example, we have a client who was able to reduce one set-up time from 35 minutes to 9 seconds. Recognition of that fact only serves to make people want to reduce the set-up times at their work centers by similar percentages.

It is quite evident that reduced set-up times increase the production rate and subsequently lower inventory levels as well as unlocking capacity which used to be wasted in excess and obsolete inventory. Another equally valid result is the ability now for production lines to be much more flexible and to reduce lot sizes.

This, in turn, allows you to come closer and closer to building products based on actual demand without storing excess inventory.

Ship-to-WIP vs. Ship-to-Stock

What percentage of your procured material is shipped directly to Work-In-Process? ____% To stock? ____%

This measurement presupposes that you first have excellent quality and on-time delivery to your receiving area. If you do not, refer to the next measurement described. Material delivered to WIP is ready to be consumed; it does not sit in storage or queues adding inventory carrying costs to your bottom line. Supplier Certification will contribute to achievements in this area.

On-Time Delivery

What percentage of supplier deliveries are on time? ____% How is on-time delivery measured to the delivery date? +/- __ hours +/- __ one day +/- __ five days __other (explain)

On-time delivery compares the actual receipt date to the supplier's committed delivery date based on shop need. This is obviously an important measurement since World Class/TQM manufacturing relies on just-in-time delivery from suppliers. Remember, however, that early delivery is just as costly as late delivery. If you're receiving parts two or three days ahead of schedule, inventory will rise. The higher the percentage of suppliers delivering on-time and the smaller your delivery window, the closer you come to being a World Class company. This is a measurement which needs to be calculated for delivery as a whole and for each individual supplier in order to gain improvement.

It is necessary for you to first determine what the on-time delivery baseline is. It could be: 1) the requested Purchase Order date, 2) the supplier's acknowledged date, 3) the supplier's lead-time translated into a delivery date, or 4) the supplier's ready date if the FOB point is the supplier's dock.

Whatever definition you choose, make sure that you and your supplier both have agreed to it and understand it. We recommend that you monitor both the acknowledged date as your baseline as well as your requested date for reference as depicted in the graph below. The difference between them is the lead-time. Then, both you and the supplier can work to reduce the lead-time in order to get true JIT delivery.

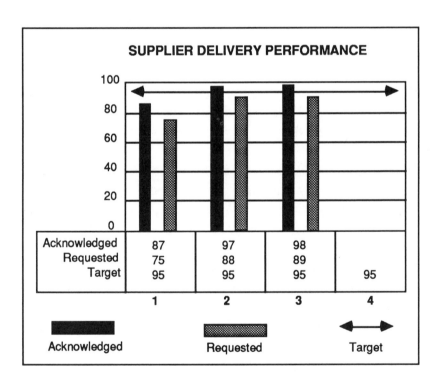

SUPPLIER DELIVERY PERFORMANCE

	1	2	3	4
Acknowledged	87	97	98	
Requested	75	88	89	
Target	95	95	95	95

Acknowledged   Requested   Target

We want to share a great story we were told by Denise Lester, a Supplier Certification team member from Brown & Williamson Tobacco. After all these years in consulting, we thought we had heard every excuse for poor delivery performance, but we hadn't. Denise and the team were preparing a supplier survey recently and according to their records, the supplier's delivery performance was sub-par. When they told the supplier, he informed them that they were wrong. His company, he said, was 100% on-time. He

---

Shipping Feedback Report

Receiver:

If you have any concerns with this shipment, please fill out this form as completely as possible, and fax to us at _____ or call us at_____.

Concern: _____

_____

Today's Date	Scheduled Dock Time/Date	Actual Dock Time/Date	Carrier	Truck/Trailer Identification

Comments by Carrier: _____

_____

Receiver's Name: _____
(Please print)

---

said that every lot of material was delivered with an attached form which stated that the material met specifications unless you filled out a form and returned it. Denise said she never even knew the form existed. It didn't take long before the form (which is shown here) was no longer used.

100% Count Accuracy

How accurate are the quantities for lots shipped from the supplier? ____ %

In the dark ages before Supplier Certification, everybody accepted the fact that an accurate count meant that the quantity could be ± 10%. If your supplier says that he cannot control processes close enough to guarantee 100% count accuracy, then he either doesn't fully understand Supplier Certification or he is counting on the overshipments to generate extra revenues. Surplus inventory in your facility, however, costs money, money that could be used for capital equipment, process improvements, personnel benefits, raises, etc. There is not enough room in anybody's budget to pay for inaccuracy. The best way we know of to improve accuracy and speed up the counting process at the same time is to use standardized packaging. The most common example is a carton of eggs. Nobody counts the number of eggs to see if there is a dozen. You look to see if there are any empty spaces. The same principle can apply to lot shipments from your suppliers. If a package has 100 slots and they are all filled, then there are 100 items. You don't have to count. A word of caution here: 100% accurate counts are not the same as 100% quality. These are two different areas that need to be worked on.

100% Defect-Free Products/Six Sigma

Does the supplier's product(s) conform to requirements 100% of the time? ___ Yes   ___ No

The first step in receiving defect-free products is to define your own requirements and specification clearly and completely. When you are sure, based on your definitions, that your supplier can make an acceptable product or render an acceptable service every time, then you and the supplier can begin determining the methods, techniques and equipment you will need so that the supplier can ship without going through an incoming inspection step. In other words, the goal of 100% defect-free products is to be able to ship directly to work-in-process. Some of the techniques we recommend are: Statistical random sampling plans, skip-lot techniques or on-site inspections. Once the data is collected, it should be analyzed for trends and defect isolation. It is also effective to measure the performance of one supplier against another or against agreed-upon requirements. We recommend that a chart similar to the one shown below be used to track a supplier's performance on a monthly or quarterly basis. We also tell clients to send the supplier a copy of this performance chart with an assessment of what corrective actions are necessary. If you put more than one supplier on the chart, use numbers to assure confidentiality. By including competitive comparisons, you indi-

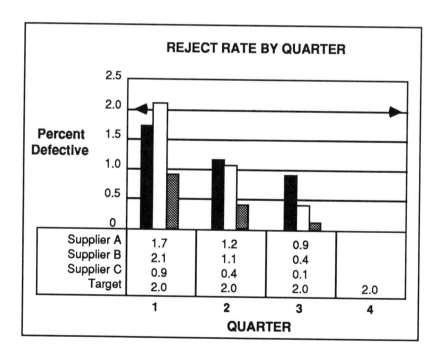

REJECT RATE BY QUARTER

	1	2	3	4
Supplier A	1.7	1.2	0.9	
Supplier B	2.1	1.1	0.4	
Supplier C	0.9	0.4	0.1	
Target	2.0	2.0	2.0	2.0

QUARTER

cate to the suppliers how each is performing against the goals and the competition. This will often spur even greater performance by all parties.

Inventory Turnover Ratio

How many inventory turns do you get a year? ___ #/yr

The inventory turnover ratio is the forecasted cost of goods sold over the next 12 months divided by the inventory investment.

$$\text{ITR} = \frac{\underline{\text{Forecasted Cost of Goods}}}{\text{Inventory Investment}}$$

In our book, **Made In America:** *The Total Business Concept* (PT Publications, Palm Beach Gardens, FL), we noted that the measurement of total inventory turns is perhaps the single best method for determining the progress of JIT/TQM implementation. Inventory turnovers are something like the Dow Jones Industrial Average in that both act as an overall indicator of the movements of many variables. In the case of the DJIA, these variables are 30 leading industrial companies. In the case of the ITR, these variables are associated with lot sizing, inventory management, line balancing and the Theory of One. We can increase inventory turns by planning for only as much material as a work station needs to make one product and by minimizing queues so that a work station has only enough material to make a product in its cycle time.

Most companies today are struggling to achieve three inventory turns a year. This means they carry four months of inventory. We have worked with companies that have raised the level to 14 turns, 26 turns, 36 turns, even 42 turns a year. Obviously, these companies have been able to coordinate many of the variables mentioned in the paragraph above. Purchasing, once again, can lead the way in the struggle to achieve a higher inventory turnover rate.

Other Purchasing Performance Measurements

The following seven performance measurements are used by the Purchasing department at International Totalizator Systems Inc. as part of their Supplier Certification program. As you can see, each of these graphs not only presents the data which has been collected but also shows how it has been analyzed and thus how

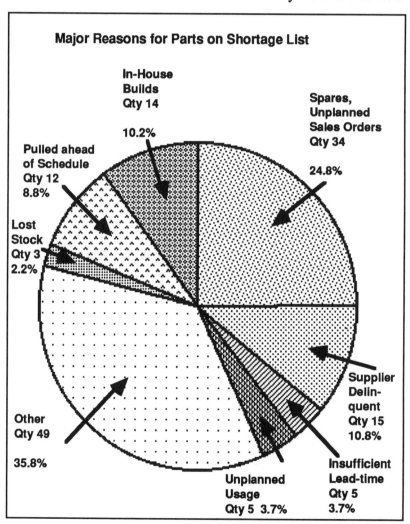

it can be used. The graph on the previous page, for example, shows the major reasons why components end up on the shortage list. Having that list divided into reasons makes it easier for ITS to identify where the problems are occurring and which areas to address first. At the same time, month to month measurements will show if improvement has been made and by how much.

Another important measurement is the number of open purchase orders which are past due. It will tell your company how well your suppliers are delivering products within the agreed upon lead-time. A high percentage means that delivery is suffering or that the supplier is not able to supply the quantities you require. This measurement can alert you to these types of supplier problems.

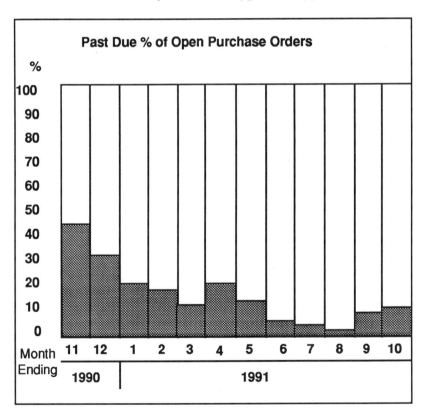

The next measurement, Purchase Order Changes, allows a company to track the number of changes to purchase orders and to analyze the reasons for the changes. This data can then be used to calculate the cost of making the changes in order to emphasize the

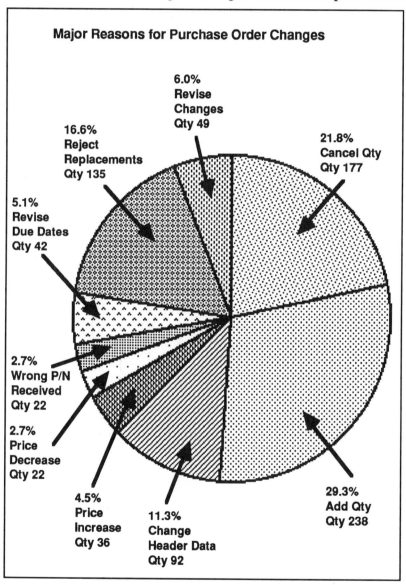

Major Reasons for Purchase Order Changes

6.0%
Revise
Changes
Qty 49

16.6%
Reject
Replacements
Qty 135

21.8%
Cancel Qty
Qty 177

5.1%
Revise
Due Dates
Qty 42

2.7%
Wrong P/N
Received
Qty 22

2.7%
Price
Decrease
Qty 22

4.5%
Price
Increase
Qty 36

11.3%
Change
Header Data
Qty 92

29.3%
Add Qty
Qty 238

need to improve. Although responsibility for this measurement often lies with the Purchasing department, your company will need to trace back the causes of the changes to the department or functional area making the requisition and the changes to the order. The graph on the previous page shows the areas where the most changes take place and thus where to start analysis to eliminate the problem.

Similar to the percentage of past due orders above, the measurement shown on this page is used to track the percentage of past due open purchase requisitions.

The next performance measurement tracks the lead-time re-

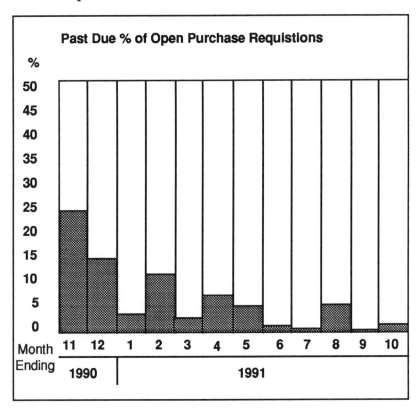

quested on purchase requisitions. Reduction of lead-time is, of course, a critical part of Supplier Certification as we have already discussed. This measurement should help your company make an effort in guaranteeing that stated lead-times conform to your requirements, an important goal in the achievement of World Class status in manufacturing.

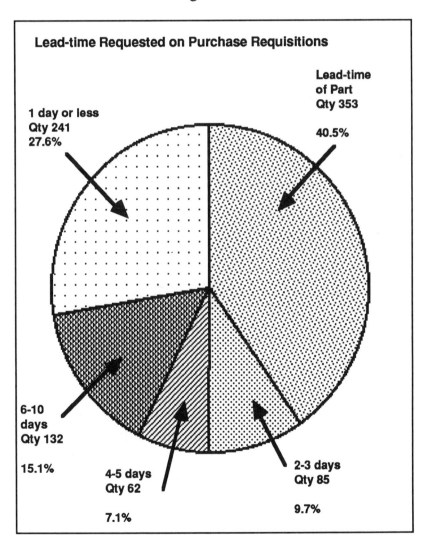

Lead-time Requested on Purchase Requisitions

Lead-time of Part
Qty 353
40.5%

1 day or less
Qty 241
27.6%

6-10 days
Qty 132
15.1%

4-5 days
Qty 62
7.1%

2-3 days
Qty 85
9.7%

The number of purchase change orders written on a monthly basis is a performance measurement which works in concert with the other purchase order measurements above. The overall effort of your company should be toward eliminating changes by making sure to communicate your requirements to the supplier.

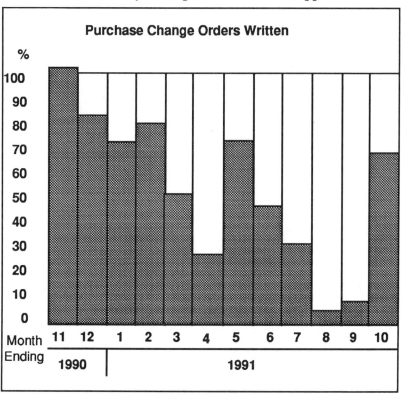

The last performance measurement, percent defectives by discrepancy type, is a quality measurement which is very useful to the Supplier Certification team. It helps to identify which areas are consistently having problems. Like the other performance measurements, this one points to problems and even points to solutions. But the real work of coming up with least total cost solutions and implementing them is still the responsibility of the team. Graphs and data are the tools they need to do their job well.

QUALITY YIELDS AND PERCENT DEFECTIVES BY DISCREPANCY TYPE

Item	9/30	10/7	10/14	10/21	10/28	11/4	11/11	11/18	11/25	12/2	12/9	12/16	12/23
Total Quantity	197	391	627	569	325	490	360	675	381	0	0	0	0
Quantity Rejected	30	45	43	62	52	36	31	37	27	0	0	0	0
Total Percent Accepted	84.8	88.5	93.1	89.1	84.0	92.7	91.4	94.5	92.9	NA	NA	NA	NA
Construction	23.3	19.6	15.9	34.8	28.3	22.2	6.5	21.6	11.1	0.0	0.0	0.0	0.0
Workmanship	30.0	17.4	54.5	42.4	54.7	33.3	19.4	32.4	55.6	0.0	0.0	0.0	0.0
Operate	3.3	32.6	0.0	1.5	3.8	11.1	19.4	5.4	0.0	0.0	0.0	0.0	0.0
Comp Fail 1	13.3	4.3	13.6	4.5	7.5	14.8	19.4	8.1	0.0	0.0	0.0	0.0	0.0
Comp Fail 2	10.0	13.0	9.1	0.0	3.8	3.7	3.2	10.8	14.8	0.0	0.0	0.0	0.0
Comp Fail 3	0.0	2.2	0.0	3.0	1.9	3.7	9.7	8.1	14.8	0.0	0.0	0.0	0.0
Comp Fail 4	6.7	10.9	4.5	12.1	0.0	11.1	19.4	10.8	3.7	0.0	0.0	0.0	0.0
Comp Fail 5	13.3	0.0	2.3	1.5	0.0	0.0	3.2	2.7	0.0	0.0	0.0	0.0	0.0

A COMPANY-WIDE PERSPECTIVE

If you have noted one dominant theme in our discussion on measurements, it must be the theme of interrelationship. By measuring one area in a World Class environment, you are in effect measuring how well the whole of your company is working. Quality, for example, is also measured by on-time delivery. You don't have an on-time delivery if there are defective parts in the shipment. As another example, let's consider the time it takes to process engineering change orders. Surely, this indicates how well your company is working as a team, but it also indicates how well your relationship with suppliers is working. Remember that earlier, we emphasized that engineering changes are as vital to your suppliers as it is to your production department. After all, suppliers are shipping the material from which you make your product.

REWARDS

How do we reward suppliers who are performing excellently? We recommend that you ask your suppliers and employees what they want as a realistic reward. Management often finds this topic difficult because it is hard to know what satisfies everybody. All the more reason, then, to involve the team in the process of selecting a reward system. With employees, rewards may come as money, recognition or both. With suppliers, it might be payment terms or cash for on-time delivery. Money may be a better reward than any plaque or certificate, but that is not to say that we should not recognize excellence with a more visible reward.

We have a client who placed an advertisement in the local newspaper of one of its suppliers. The piece praised the company for achieving supplier certification and for the high level of its quality and delivery.

The end product of a Supplier Certification team is to generate ideas or recommendations with accompanying action plans. And recognition must be more than unlocking a "suggestion box" and awarding one prize to the best idea while throwing the other ideas into the round file. The best run companies are willing to follow through on ideas which may end in failure. These companies are not afraid to include the word "failure" in their vocabulary.

Peter Grieco has said:

> **"A person needs the opportunity**
> **to fail**
> **in order to succeed."**

Thus, your company needs to create an environment where it is safe to make suggestions. No suggestion, no question, is unimportant. Toyota Motor Corp., for example, has developed a "creative suggestion system" in which its non-management 55,000-strong work force contributed over 2.649 million improvement proposals way back in 1986. The Mazda Co. in 1987 received 350,000 suggestions from its 800 employees. We wonder how many have been generated over the last few years. Obviously, it is safe to suggest changes in these companies. Besides having an open-minded attitude, these companies also act quickly on the given suggestions. Every idea is distributed to the appropriate team or department for action. In addition, we recommend taking "bad" suggestions (which may be suggestions which are not clearly described) and using them in training sessions where you teach company employees how to make more effective suggestions.

THE CHALLENGE

Progress toward the goal of a successful implementation begins with this assessment:

> **What are we doing**
> **and**
> **why are we doing it?**

Only when this question is constantly asked will a company be on its way to improvement. Top management commitment means building an environment where creative problem-solving is the norm. Furthermore, it means squarely confronting the most diffi-cult task of management — listening to people. This can be accomplished if management first establishes goals and objec-tives and exercises patience and persistence in working with people. It will require the development of trust with your people, suppliers and customers and the delegation of responsibility and authority to the lowest levels of the organization. You will know you are there when you can demonstrate the following actions:

- Establish an on-going training and education program.

- Adopt a no-waste attitude.

- Allocate/authorize financial support and measurements.

- Devote resources to project teams.

- Risk short-term operational results for long-term improvements.

- Foster interdepartmental communication and cooperation.

- Follow up, monitor, document and measure.

- Improve communications with suppliers and customers.

- Listen to the experts—your people.

- Correct processes, rather than rework parts.

- Foster a "no-waiver" environment in processes and specifications.

There is no question in our minds that Supplier Certification will work when this mind-set is employed. The next challenge will be to make all this fit into Computer Integrated Manufacturing (CIM). The complex problems which face us in the future cry out for more improvements and higher profits. Supplier certification is a step toward the goal of internal and external control. Don't get trapped into thinking that this is a supplier's problem. Many supplier's problems are ultimately caused by the customer (you)!

A supplier certification program requires commitment and time. Patience is important and so is doing it right the first time. In the next chapter are more examples of implementations with which we have been involved.

IMPLEMENTATION EXAMPLES

11

In this chapter, we want to provide you with examples of what some companies are doing to implement a Supplier Certification Program. Again, take note of the fact that all programs have the same framework. The differences lie in the requirements of various industries.

ABB INTERNATIONAL SUPPLY MANAGEMENT CONFERENCE
Zurich, Switzerland

During this conference, ABB (Asea Brown Boveri) invited its suppliers to an introduction of their Supplier Certification Program. We have included the agenda for Day 1 and ABB's written policy statements on quality as well as commitments and expectations. We would like to thank John Grossman, vice president of materials and Roland Andersson, vice president, for providing us with this material to share with our readers.

PROGRAM
ABB
INTERNATIONAL SUPPLY MANAGEMENT
CONFERENCE IN ZURICH

Wednesday

1:30 p.m.	Meet with John Gossman to discuss Keynote Address
2:00 p.m.	Meeting Opening Roland Andersson, Vice President Opening Comments Gerhard Schulmeyer, President
2:30 p.m.	ABB Executive's expectation on Supply Management Sune Karlsson, TPT
3:00 p.m.	The Supply Management Concept Peter L. Grieco, Pro-Tech
4:00 p.m	Coffee Break
4:15 p.m.	Cont'd — The Supply Management Concept Peter L. Grieco
5:00 p.m.	Results from the ABB/ATK Study Phase 1 Werner Kreuz, AT Kearney Scope Expansion ABB/ATK Study Phase 2 ATK/CS-PU
6:30 p.m.	End of Day 1
7:30 p.m.	Dinner

The statements which follow serve as a basis for introducing certification candidates to ABB's Supplier Certification program.

ABB POLICY STATEMENT
ABB Quality Policy

"The hallmark of ASEA BROWN BOVERI shall be quality." All of our commitments, actions and products must be recognized as an expression of quality. Our most important criteria of quality is the satisfaction of our customers. We must aim at maintaining their full confidence in ASEA BROWN BOVERI as a supplier. The demands and stipulations of the customer must be met by our commitments and products conforming to agreed terms. Each delivery should create a recommendation for further business.

The achievement of these quality goals and, consequently, our overriding goal to continue operating as a competitive and successful enterprise will both be determined by our resources, by our organization, by the dedication we show in our work and, above all, by our attitude to quality.

ABB Mission

ABB's Mission is to be the leader in delivering quality products and services for power generation, transmission and distribution, industrial processes, mass transit, and environmental control, that meet the needs and requirements of our customers and contribute to their success.

To ensure customer satisfaction, ABB provides value-added, integrated solutions that are driven by superior technology and performance. ABB's employees are committed to leadership standards in applying the Company's unique combination of experience and global resources to meeting societal goals for sustainable growth and clean energy.

ABB Goals

Through continuous improvement in quality, ABB makes these commitments to its major constituencies:

Customers — To become an organization that is measured by the contributions we make to our customers' success and satisfaction.

Shareholders — To achieve leadership results and competitive advantage in the areas of return on capital and order rate growth through the appropriate focus on management of risk and cash flow.

Employees — To create an environment of openness and trust in which employees take pride in the organization and feel responsible for its success.

Community — To assure good corporate citizenship by actively contributing to the welfare of the local communities where our employees live and work.

COMMITMENTS AND EXPECTATIONS
Statement of Commitment

ABB is proud of its history of providing customers with Quality products and of achieving a reputation of engineering excellence and exceeding customer requirements.

ABB is committed to maintaining and enhancing customer satisfaction throughout the 90's and beyond in order to meet competitive challenges head-on and be "The Supplier of Choice" for our products and services.

We will serve our customers with unequaled efficiency and

attention to detail, focusing on continuous improvement in exceeding their expectations and achieving excellence in all that we do. The Supplier Certification Program is an integral and necessary component of this effort.

ABB solicits input from its Suppliers on how ABB may become a better customer. The supplier certification process includes a two-way constructive discussion on how ABB and its suppliers can consistently meet or exceed ABB and its customer requirements and expectations the first time and every time. Suppliers who have served us well over the years will be afforded an opportunity to participate in our Supplier Certification Program. However, our intention is to reduce the supply base over time, with the objective to work with a number of highly qualified suppliers. We will also continue, through our world sourcing activities, to identify new suppliers who are able and willing to work with ABB and its divisions. Active participation in the Supplier Certification Program will help to build an environment of mutual trust and confidence between ABB and its suppliers. This process will provide continuous quality improvements and will result in benefits for our customers, our suppliers and ourselves.

Our ultimate goal is to establish and develop strategic alliances with key suppliers to continuously improve quality, technology, delivery performance and to reduce total costs through the integration of Core processes of ABB and its suppliers.

Supplier Certification Policy

ABB is committed to provide to its customers products and services which will meet or exceed customer requirements. ABB is further committed to be a highly competitive producer, provide superior service to our customers and maintain excellence in technology and quality. In order to achieve these goals, the goods and services that we purchase must consistently meet or exceed these criteria. Our suppliers are expected to:

- accept accountability for the quality of their facilities and equipment, and for the quality of the products and services which they provide.

- accept accountability for integrity of documentation, information and technical/design assistance which they provide.

- fully comprehend our expectations and requirements as defined in our inquiries and purchase orders and to take the initiative to obtain clarifications in the event of uncertainty.

- confirm that our expectations and requirements are within their capabilities and capacity before accepting or beginning work.

- provide fast and accurate responses to requests for quotations, update/status of orders in process, delivery of documentation, approval drawings and technical assistance.

- continuously work toward product and cost improvements through process analysis and cycle time reduction.

- demonstrate a commitment to quality that:

  A. accepts responsibility for the actions of their employees, sub-suppliers and subcontractors to furnish only equipment, products and services which conform to requirements as set forth in our purchase orders.

B. develops and sustains a proactive quality assurance effort to control their processes and procedures for prevention of nonconformances, rather than one which only reacts to defects after they occur.

C. communicates to ABB promptly any potentially adverse situations (strikes, material shortages, etc.) or impending changes to design, material construction, process, procedure or organization which could affect the quality or suitability of the equipment, facilities, products and/or services being offered or supplied.

Benefits of Certification

Supplier certification is ABB's recognition that the supplier has demonstrated a high level of performance and has appropriate process controls in place to ensure continued excellence. The benefits of supplier certification are as follows:

1. Strengthened relationships through certification seeks mutual gains in quality, cycle time, service and cost reduction.

2. For ABB, certification eliminates redundant testing, provides a guarantee of product quality and on-time delivery, and improves response time by reducing delays in production processes.

3. Suppliers who aggressively pursue, achieve and maintain certification of their products and processes will be given special consideration in supplier selection and evaluation.

INDUSTRIAL DRIVES
Radford, Virginia

The following agenda comes from a supplier symposium in which we participated. We have also included a few paragraphs explaining Industrial Drives' commitment to supplier certification and the goals it hopes to achieve.

AGENDA FOR I.D. SUPPLIER SYMPOSIUM

8:30   I.   Arrival of Suppliers — coffee and donuts

9:00   II.   Welcome and Introductory Remarks

9:10   III.   Opening Remarks and Review of Objectives by Charles C. Perry, President

9:30   IV.   Overview of Industrial Drives World Class Movement

9:50   V.   Quality Control, Inspection process and Rating System

10:10   VI.   Overview of Program — Peter Grieco, President and CEO of Pro-Tech
  A. Supplier Selection Criteria
  B. Supplier Selection Process
  C. Survey and Audit
  D. Supplier Quality Agreement
  E. History, Process and Program Review, Finalization, Certification, Audit and Maintenance
  F. Implementing the Program
  G. Continuous Improvement

12:00   VII.   Lunch

1:00   VIII.   Plant Tour

2:15   IX.   Concluding Remarks and General Agreement to Participate

---

The paragraphs which follow come from a booklet which was passed out to suppliers at the symposium. Entitled "A Partnership in Quality," the booklet also contains a complete supplier survey and an explanation of Industrial Drives' rating system in addition to what we have included below. The purpose of all this information is, of course, to introduce the supplier to the process of certification.

A PARTNERSHIP IN QUALITY
INDUSTRIAL DRIVES

Management Commitment

The markets that Industrial Drives services are truly global in scope. Competition for this business comes from around the world. To stay competitive in the future, Industrial Drives is committed to becoming a World Class Manufacturing facility. We will be using statistical process control, employee empowerment and Just-In-Time concepts to support this effort.

The supplier certification program, with its emphasis on quality, quantity and on-time delivery, gives us the vehicle to tie our quality and process improvements to our supplier community. Working together to form close partnerships will allow both companies to benefit from these quality and process improvements. These improvements will lead to Industrial Drives being able to satisfy our customers' needs with on-time, quality products at a competitive price. Our commitment to Supplier Certification is an integral part of Industrial Drives' commitment to achieve total customer satisfaction.

Partnership Goals

100% Quality. 100% Quantity. 100% On-Time. We agree to continuously strive to reduce cost and improve quality.

Certification

The Industrial Drives Certification Plan is part of an ongoing drive for quality improvement and a competitive advantage. Our goal is to have all our suppliers reach certification through a multi-level process. The percentage of business awarded will be determined by certification status and demonstrated performance levels. It is important to recognize this is a "process," that it is an ongoing drive for improvement and will not stop at some point in time, but continue to strive for improvement. This multi-level process is outlined as follows:

I.   LEVEL 1 ACCEPTABLE SUPPLIER LIST - ASL
     This is comprised of current suppliers that have demon-strated acceptable levels of performance and a desire to become certified.

II. LEVEL 2 QUALIFIED SUPPLIER LIST - QSL
     These suppliers have successfully completed a Supplier Survey, a minimum score of 60 points, a source audit by Industrial Drives personnel, and have demonstrated a good level of performance in quality areas of the product they supply.

III. LEVEL 3 SUPPLIER QUALITY AGREEMENT - SQA
     In order to have a true partnership, each side must be committed to meeting certain responsibilities. This agree-ment becomes the statement of purpose, scope and objec-tives to guarantee that these responsibilities are maintained. Care must be taken at this level to define the details of the responsibilities by both parties.

IV. LEVEL 4 CERTIFIED SUPPLIER
     A supplier, who has accomplished the objectives of the

supplier agreement, demonstrated his performance outlined in the Supplier Rating System by maintaining a minimum score of 95, shall be designated a Certified Supplier to Industrial Drives. This certification will be reevaluated every month by their supplier rating score.

SUPPLIER BENEFITS
AND REWARDS

Industrial Drives recognizes that for a supplier to attain certified status, they must achieve and sustain a high level of outstanding effort, performance and reliability. We encourage suppliers to share their thoughts and concerns on any ideas regarding Supplier Benefits and Rewards. Suppliers must ultimately embrace the concepts of JIT/TQM to become efficient Certified Suppliers. We believe our supplier's ability to compete in their own markets will be enhanced through the improvements and benefits of Supplier Certification.

Other benefits include:

- Sharing in the growth and success of Industrial Drives.

- Certified Suppliers will receive more of Industrial Drives' business.

- Opportunity to participate in new products and business ventures.

- Certified Suppliers will have preference over other suppliers in early payment terms and elimination of invoices.

- Industrial Drives and our Certified Suppliers will share in the benefits of cost reduction efforts.

DYNACHEM
Tustin, California

After LeAnn Zunich first attended Pro-Tech's seminar on Supplier Certification and we conducted a few internal programs for the corporation, the Supplier Certification team developed documentation which they have agreed to share with all of us. Their Supplier Certification Program is reprinted here in full. It is an excellent example of a document which is written to be understood by all people, not just by people already well-versed in Supplier Certification. Today, they continue their hard work which has paid off in innumerable ways.

You will notice that the Dynachem process is similar to the implementation program we introduced in the first edition of this book and which we have discussed in our public seminar program. Another excellent tool in developing your program is our VideoEducation Series for self-managed programs. We believe that each and everyone of you can implement a successful process today.

DYNACHEM ELECTRONIC MATERIALS
SUPPLIER CERTIFICATION IMPLEMENTATION
PROCESS

1. Goals
2. Resource Requirements
3. STEP 1. Goals of Supplier Certification
4. STEP 2. Developing Supplier Selection Criteria
5. STEP 3. The Supplier and Customer Symposium
6. STEP 4. Certification Candidate Selection
7. STEP 5. The Certification Program
          a. Documentation History

GOALS

Supplier Certification is a process, not an event.
Why certify suppliers? To eliminate waste in everything we
do. To satisfy the customer.

GOALS:

1. **100% Quality**. Certify all suppliers, products and
    services.

2. **Total Quality Management**. To be able to ensure
    that our entire manufacturing cycle, from product
    development through customer receipt, meets our
    quality standards.

3. Receiving the **Lowest Possible Number of Lots**. To
    receive the fewest number of lots possible, given the
    supplier's manufacturing capability.

4. Developing **Supplier Partnerships**. Relationships
    with suppliers are critical to the achievement of our

goal. The partnership will foster increased profitability for our suppliers and us.

5. **Controlling and Simplifying Logistics.** We must control and simplify the movement of material between functions or activities.

6. **Eliminate Waste.** Waste is anything other than the absolute minimum resources of material, machines and manpower required to add value to our product.

7. **Satisfy the Customer.** Everything we do must be geared toward providing the Customer with products that meet their specifications every time.

RESOURCE REQUIREMENTS

1. **Culture Changes.**

    The environment for Supplier Certification requires that the attitudes be changed to reflect a partnership relationship with each supplier that is involved in the program.

2. **Total Cost Approach.**

    The total cost should be based on the financial analysis, the analysis of the cost of quality, and delivery cost impacts, cost of inventory, and the cost data required for decisions.

3. **Lot-for-Lot Rule.**

    We want our supplier to produce the fewest possible

number of lots, given its manufacturing capability. We want to deal with the fewest number of lots internally, too. For instance, we want to make only what is sold, produce the quantity scheduled, and have on the floor only one pallet of material, etc.

4. Generalist, Not Specialist.

It is better to be a generalist in order to see the entire picture than to concentrate on just one aspect of the problem, project or activity.

5. Simplistic Control Techniques.

The more easily something can be explained, the better the chance of success.

6. Small Work Cells.

The groups which are the smallest, yet most committed achieve the most. Larger groups of people, in most instances, cannot be effective.

STEP 1: GOALS OF SUPPLIER CERTIFICATION

Task: Create a Supplier Certification Team that includes: Quality, R&D, Finance, Manufacturing, Traffic, Planning, Purchasing, Marketing and Distribution.

Why: Eliminating waste and inspection are the premier goals of Supplier Certification.

What is good for our customer is good for us and is good for our supplier.

What we expect from our supplier, we expect from ourselves and our customers expect from us.

What has to change and what will be affected:

1.   **Preventive Maintenance**

What is the preventive maintenance program and what is its effect on manufacturing?

In order for Supplier Certification to work, we and our suppliers must have preventive maintenance programs in effect.

2.   **Training**

Education and training require top management commitment. The time and the funds must be available to educate personnel.

3.   **Impact of Engineering Design**

Engineering cannot be limited to product design. The producibility of the product is equally important.

R&D and Process Engineering must be involved in determining customer need and designing to that specification. The objective is to simplify and reduce the cost of product through design.

4.   Discipline

Discipline is required to make changes in a timely fashion. Not only formulation and product design changes, but process and organization changes at our plant and at our suppliers' plants are required.

Discipline creates an environment where people have a clear picture of their responsibilities, and management can clearly articulate their responsibilities.

5.   Product Life Cycles

Product life cycles must be considered in the planning of manufacturing activities. Important considerations are length of production runs, integration of existing products, and supplier availability.

6.   Design Integration

Design must integrate functional groups in the product life cycle: Marketing, Manufacturing, QA, R&D, Purchasing, Planning, Suppliers, Finance, and the Customer.

7.   Specification/Requirement Testing

Testing must be part of the design process so that our suppliers know how to test a product to achieve the desired results.

We cannot demand zero-defect material from a supplier, if we don't know how to test for it ourselves.

8.   Coordination of Activities

There must be coordination and trust between the supplier and us.

We must correlate our testing methods and our requirements with our suppliers in order to facilitate the manufacture of raw materials.

9.   Changing the Culture

The environment for Supplier Certification requires a culture change — a new set of attitudes which reflect a potential partnership with each supplier.

This is accomplished by implementing program requirements at the supplier's plant as well as our own.

Part of the culture change is the adoption of the Least Total Cost approach. We can no longer be dependent upon price analysis as the major criterion for determining product cost.

10.   Lot Sizing

We want our supplier to provide the fewest number of lots, given its manufacturing capability.

We want to produce only what is sold, produce only the quantity scheduled, and store only enough to provide the customer with its desired level of service.

A Supplier Certification program has to work

toward ensuring the delivery of the right material in the right quantity at the right time.

11.   Human Resources

We need generalists, not specialists.

A generalist is better able to see the entire picture, a quality which is almost mandatory.

12.   Control and Application Techniques

True awareness of an entire company's policies, procedures, and operations is not possible without a movement toward simple control techniques.

The easier it is to explain something, the better its chance of success.

13.   Will it Work?

Success begins with the commitment of our top management and our suppliers' top management to the process of continuous improvement.

Top management must be committed to the creation of a company culture which fosters responsibility, authority, vision (company-wide), and accountability.

STEP 2: DEVELOPING SUPPLIER SELECTION CRITERIA

Task:

A. Develop a description of qualities and abilities we want our suppliers to have.

    1. Develop a list of the attributes we would like all of our suppliers to have.

    2. Rank those things in descending order of importance.

    3. Send a copy of this list to every person who might select a supplier: the president, vice president, laboratory person, etc.

    Include a cover letter that says: "Cross off what you don't like and add what you do like."

    Note: This is the first "hook" in getting everyone in the company committed.

    4. Follow up with the non-respondents.

    5. Reorganize the list of criteria, adding the new inputs.

    6. Reorder the list to reflect the company's top priorities.

B. Publish the list of criteria for all employees to read.

    1. The president must publish a memo to all Dynachem employees stating that this is our Selection Criteria for new suppliers.

Note: This is an important step and the second "hook." People will all agree to standards for new suppliers; it doesn't threaten any relationships they have with current suppliers. Only after the program is in place (the memo has been published) do we start applying them to the current base of suppliers.

C.   Determine the relative value, to Dynachem, of the criteria.

     1.   Within the Supplier Certification Committee, after the criteria have been selected, split the criteria into major functional categories. For instance, quality, administration, technical, etc.

     2.   Assign a value to each criterion, developed in A above, and weigh each area relative to the others. This value is the relative worth of that attribute when we are selecting a supplier.

         a.   Make the value of all the criteria equal 100.
         b.   Determine "critical" criteria; those which every supplier must meet.
         c.   Determine what will be the minimum number to get orders. Maybe 70 on a scale of 100.

D.   Rank our suppliers.

     1.   Create a hard copy listing of all our suppliers.

     2.   Using a worksheet with our criteria and the

ranking developed in **C** above, rank all of our suppliers.

3. Separate the list of suppliers:

    a. One list of suppliers that meet our minimum criteria standards as developed in **C.2** above, and
    b. A second list of all other suppliers.

E. Quantify the supplier listing.

1. Create four lists:

    a. **Certified Suppliers.** Those that are certified through this program.

    b. **Qualified Suppliers.** Those that get a rating of 70 or higher.

    c. **Restricted Suppliers.** Those that get a rating of 69 or lower.

    d. **New Suppliers.** Those that have not been rated yet.

F. Determine how many suppliers we need.

1. List the broad categories of items we purchase, i.e. corrugated, plastic bottles, caps, monomers, etc.

2. Determine how many suppliers we have for each category.

3. Look at the list of Qualified Suppliers. How many of each kind of supplier is qualified?

4. As a team, determine how many suppliers of each item we need.

5. Reviewing the numbers developed above, list how many suppliers we need to add (or subtract) for each purchase category.

6. The number of suppliers we need to add (or subtract) is the goal for our supplier base over the coming 24 months.

7. Draft a plan, using the 80/20 rule, to determine which supplier to certify first.

STEP 3: THE SUPPLIER SYMPOSIUM

Task:

A.　　Prepare for a Supplier (and Customer) Symposium.

1. Invite all suppliers to a symposium, at site(s) of our choosing, to explain our Supplier Certification process, what our standards are, and what they will be expected to do to be a certified supplier.

   a. Option: Hold a program in the afternoon for our customers to explain the program to them.

2. Supplier salespeople are not the target audience of the symposium. The goal is to get decision-making officers to attend.

B. Symposium Preparation Overview.

1. Write Supplier Certification Program handout.
2. Develop Dynachem brochure.
3. Prepare Quality Statement Form.
4. Prepare Certification Form.
5. Develop Guest List.
6. Decide where to hold the meeting(s).
7. Plan Symposium Day.
8. Brief speakers.
9. Invite guests.
10. Hold Symposium.
11. Follow-up.

C. Symposium Preparation Details.

1. Develop a Supplier Certification presentation for a Supplier Symposium.

   a. Introduce Dynachem and our product lines.
   b. Set out certification goals.
   c. Explain our requirements.
   d. Set out our supplier selection criteria.
   e. Explain how certification time line will be developed.

2. Develop a color brochure on Dynachem.

3. Prepare a Commitment Letter.

   a. Statement of Dynachem's goal in certification.

    b. Suppliers will sign up to work toward certification.

    c. Supplier's President is to sign.

4. Prepare a Certification Implementation Form.

    a. Form will list major components in Dynachem's Certification Program.

    b. Form will provide space to fill in dates to achieve each step.

    c. Form will have space to fill in when each step is completed.

    d. The form will be introduced at the Symposium, and completed during the certification process.

5. Develop a guest list for Symposium.

    a. Determine President of each supplier: name, title, address.

6. Decide where to hold meetings.

    a. Tustin, Moss Point, Woburn, Elmhurst.

    b. Determine whether to have at plant or off-site.

7. Develop follow-up literature.

    a. Thank-you letters.

    b. Survey of effectiveness.

8. Plan Symposium Day.

    a. Schedule speakers.

    b. Schedule food.

9. Brief Symposium speakers.

   a. Our president should do the welcome to attendees, introduce Morton International, and Dynachem.
   b. Speaker to introduce the benefits of certification to Dynachem and to our suppliers.
   c. Speaker to talk about what the quality department expects from suppliers.
   d. Speaker to discuss Dynachem's manufacturing and our efforts to become a World Class manufacturer.
   e. Speaker to discuss the criteria the company will use to select suppliers and the process for certifying them.
   f. All Certification Team members will introduce details of the certification process.

10. Invite guests.

    a. Send letters.
    b. Monitor responses.

11. Hold Symposium.

12. Do follow-up mailings.

STEP 4: CERTIFICATION CANDIDATE SELECTION

Task: Select Suppliers to Certify.

A. Identify potential certification candidates.

    1. Each person on the team should pick at least two, but no more than four, suppliers to certify.

        a. Each person should always have two suppliers in the certification process.

    2. Identify potential certification candidates using any logical criteria:

        a. The best suppliers we have.
           1) Subjectively (gut feeling).
           2) Objectively (performance data).

        b. The most important products we buy.

        c. Our highest dollar volume supplier(s).

        d. Our highest dollar volume item(s).

        e. Pareto's law — 20% of our suppliers provide 80% of our product.

        f. The fewest number of suppliers required to meet our business requirements.

    3. The Team, as a whole, makes certification candidate selections at the suggestion of Team members.

        a. Each Team member, when making a certification candidate suggestion, should discuss the selection and the reasons why with the entire Team.

b. The Team member should have a comparison of his/her certification candidate with the Supplier Needs matrix developed in Step 2, Sect. F.

    1) How many suppliers do we need for a category?

    2) How many Qualified suppliers do we have in this category?

    3) Do we need to find more suppliers or reduce the number of suppliers for the category?

    4) Will the certification candidate meet the needs of the category?

c. The Team should be prepared to question each supplier proposed:

    1) How important is this supplier to us?

    2) How much business do we do with this supplier?

    3) Can we all use this supplier? (If not, how many do we need nationwide?)

    4) What other suppliers provide this product/service, and are we willing to let them go?

        a) What will be the status of other suppliers of the same product/service?

    5) What was this supplier's initial rating?

4. When the Team agrees to a certification candidate, a "Small Team" is formed — two or three Dynachem people who will guide the certification process.

5. Prepare a certification data file for each supplier candidate; include for each product:

    a. Copy of Quality Specification.
    b. Copy of Inspection process(es).
    c. Documentation History.
    d. Process documentation.
    e. Program documentation.
    f. Post-Certification Standards.

6. The Small Team leader notifies the certification candidate of our intent to start the certification process.

    a. Usually by telephone, but can be written or followed up with a letter.

    b. Identify Dynachem Certification Team to supplier, probably a buyer and a quality rep or buyer and sales rep.

    c. Ask supplier to identify an in-house team to work with our team.

STEP 5: THE CERTIFICATION PROCESS

Task: Develop certification requirements for each candidate and begin certification process.

A. Begin the certification process.

1. Obtain commitment letter from supplier, if they haven't already provided one.

2. The Small Team leader learns who is on the supplier's team.

3. The Small Team leader asks the supplier to rate itself, using the Rating Worksheet.

4. The Small Team leader sets up a meeting/teleconference with the suppliers' team to review the Rating Worksheet together.

5. The Small Team meets to discuss strategy and requirements for the certification of the candidate and agree on:

    a. Specifications, inspection requirements, and testing.
    b. Certification time period.
    c. Documentation requirements.
    d. Tracking method(s) to be used.
    e. Who will collect and maintain paperwork.

6. Dynachem Small Team needs to review rating completed on supplier.

7. Dynachem Small Team needs to decide what inspection will be done, how it will be decreased if the supplier is certified.

8. Dynachem Small Team should meet with supplier team and convey requirements of certification.

    a. Supplier team must agree to all requirements.

b. There may have to be further technical meetings to agree upon specs, etc.

9. Dynachem Small Team and supplier team should go through a new rating form together.

10. All deficiencies should be recorded and a corrective action plan developed and tracked.

11. All incoming product and documentation will be tracked for the certification period.

12. Indicate where information is lacking/missing in certification file. Obtain documentation/info.

13. If a supplier has not been audited in the last 36 months, consider an on-site supplier audit. See Step 6.

STEP 6: SUPPLIER SURVEYS

Task:

A. Visit suppliers for an on-site Certification Review whenever possible.

1. It is not practical to visit all suppliers targeted for certification.

2. Those suppliers that can be visited by a team member, during other business trips, will be reviewed.

B.   The Certification Review.

> Note: The Certification Review is not a Quality Audit. The Implementation Worksheet is used to review operations.

1. The responsible team member contacts the supplier and schedules a visit.

2. The team member visits the supplier.

   a. Questions, based on the Implementation Worksheet, are asked.
   b. Documentation supporting supplier claims of programs may be requested.

3. The team member reviews his/her findings with the supplier while on site.

   a. The team member creates a corrective action plan, when necessary, for deficiencies.

4. The Small Team tracks implementation of the corrective action plan.

STEP 7: TRACKING FOR CERTIFICATION

Task:

A.   Continue doing 100% inspection of all incoming product, tracking their documentation to our results.

B.   If there are differences, do necessary correlation studies. If there is a difference, correct and restart tracking period.

C.   Measure track for length of time determined in Step 5.

STEP 8: CERTIFICATION

Task: Certify suppliers.

A.   Develop a process to certify suppliers.

> Note: When supplier has achieved a 90% or more on the Implementation Worksheet and has delivered 100% zero-defect product for the length of time required, it is recommended for certification.

1.   The Small Team collects data on inspection results, Worksheet rating, and compliance with documentation requirements.

2.   At a regular Certification Team meeting, the Small Team leader reviews all documentation and scoring with the team.

3.   Recommends certification.

4.   The Certification Team may:

   a. Request additional data.
   b. Suggest further corrective actions.
   c. Comment on the recommendation in any other way.

5. If there are benefits to the supplier with certification, those benefits will be shared with the team at the time the decision to certify is made.

   a. For example, if the supplier of a production material will no longer be subject to 100% inspection of all incoming lots, that information will be made available to the team prior to certification.

6. With the agreement of the entire team, the supplier is certified, or required to perform/ provide additional information.

   a. If the supplier is asked to provide/perform additional information, the Small Team leader will present the supplier again for certification at a later meeting.

7. A Certification Announcement letter, signed by our president, is sent to the supplier.

8. The supplier's name is posted on the Certified Supplier plaque in the company lobby.

STEP 9: AUDIT AND MAINTENANCE

Task:

A. Determine how often we will audit product.

   1. 3 of 10 lots, 1 of 10 lots, etc.

B.   Conduct regular spot checks of incoming products.

C.   Develop documentation review schedules.

D.   Develop plans for:

     1. Decertification.
     2. Re-Certification.
     3. Disqualification.

STEP 10: IDENTIFYING PARTNERS

Task:

A.   Develop partnerships with key certified supplier.

     1.   A partner should be audited in-person once a year.

B.   Identify partnership candidates.

C.   Develop partner definitions.

D.   Develop partner guidelines.

E.   Do ceremonial award to partners honoring their input.

STEP 11: CONTINUOUS IMPROVEMENT

Task:

A.   With certified suppliers, develop tasks to foster improvements in the process.

B.   Develop enhancements to certification program.

PURPOSES OF CERTIFICATION

Make purchases from only good suppliers.

As a byproduct, shrink the supplier base to a reasonable number with which we can work efficiently.

Educate suppliers about Supplier Certification.

Survey suppliers once a year on a regular basis.

NOTES

The goal is to use only World Class suppliers.

In the process of developing and using only World Class suppliers, the supplier base will probably shrink and probably become more efficient to work with.

Make the QSL out of the RSL, using what we know today. Don't do resurveys of suppliers; don't dig out history.

Out of the CSL will come partnerships. We should visit all partners once a year. We cannot develop a partnership with the salesperson; we need to go out and meet the manufacturing people.

An idea for Dynachem: 12 partners — production, non-production, and transportation. That way we can survey and visit one partner a month each year.

Develop a form for R&D to deviate from preferred suppliers, along the lines of the Directed Source form used for single sources.

OTHER

Corrective Action Forms: First you send them out, then you get back the plan to correct the problem.

We don't want to give supplier more business, but more profit.

To implement: By product you ship to a customer, so a certified package goes out as a unit. Product, bottle, cap, box.

What do we want out of certification? An item to come in with no inspection required, ever.

We want our certified supplier to have a process quality control system.

> The goal of Supplier Certification is to eliminate incoming inspection. This is only possible when we can be sure that the supplier not only has quality and process controls in place, but a system which maintains those controls.

A potential certified supplier must share our quality and customer service philosophy and goals.

> Dynachem wants its suppliers to have a quality control system in place which subscribes to the same zero-defect goals and processes as we do.

> What is good for our customer is good for us and is good for our supplier. What we expect from our supplier, we expect from ourselves and our customers.

A Supplier Certification program is a long-term commitment. Continuous improvement takes time. A culture change is required at all levels of the suppliers' and customers' plants.

ADDITIONAL FORMS

The forms which follow on Pages 431 to 435 are discussed in the document above and can be used by your company in the Supplier Certification process.

DYNACHEM
SUPPLIER CERTIFICATION
COMMITMENT

- **Production Requirements**
  - **Non-Production Requirements**
    - **Transportation Requirements**
      - **Warehousing Requirements**

Dynachem's Supplier Criteria for Production, Non-Production, Transportation and Warehousing Requirements have been defined to our satisfaction. As a supplier of materials and/or services, we acknowledge and agree to comply with the listed criteria.

Criteria _____ Company _____

Approved By _____ Title _____

Date_____

SUPPLIER CERTIFICATION IMPLEMENTATION WORKSHEET

Production

Supplier:
Representative:
Date:

All candidates for certification must complete these nine steps.

	Completion Date
1. **Attend Symposium**	
2. **Commitment Agreement** A copy of Dynachem's Commitment Agreement, signed by an officer of the company, must be on file at Dynachem.	
3. **Initial Inspection** Dynachem will do 100% inspection of a specified number of lots. Compliance will be documented with a letter on file at Dynachem.	
4. **Certify to Specifications** Candidate Certificate of Analysis must certify to all Dynachem specifications.	
5. **100% Certification of Analysis** Certificate of Analysis must be supplied for all materials.	
6. **On-Time, Complete Delivery** Dynachem will track deliveries. On-Time means ± 1 working day. Complete means meeting individual order requirements.	
7. **Complete Documentation** Candidate must provide complete documentation as called for by Dynachem including (but not limited to) insurance requirements, invoices, bills of lading, etc.	
8. **SPC Program** Candidate must have an active program of SPC as evidenced by supplier documentation.	
9. **Supplier Rating** The candidate must receive a rating of 90% or more on the Supplier Selection and Measurement Criteria Worksheet. Any deficiency will require a corrective action plan and will be reevaluated when the corrective action plan has been implemented.	

SUPPLIER CERTIFICATION IMPLEMENTATION WORKSHEET

Non-Production

Supplier:
Representative:
Date:

All candidates for certification must complete these eight steps.

		Completion Date
1.	**Attend Symposium**	
2.	**Commitment Agreement** A copy of Dynachem's Commitment Agreement, signed by an officer of the company, must be on file at Dynachem.	
3.	**Initial Inspection** Dynachem will do 100% inspection of a specified number of deliveries/orders. Compliance will be documented with a letter on file at Dynachem.	
4.	**Certify to Dynachem Requirements** Candidate must certify to all Dynachem requirements. This is documented with a letter on file at Dynachem.	
5.	**On-Time, Complete Delivery** Dynachem will track deliveries. On-Time means ± 1 working day. Complete means meeting individual order requirements.	
6.	**Complete Documentation** Candidate must provide complete documentation as called for by Dynachem including (but not limited to) insurance requirements, invoices, bills of lading, etc.	
7.	**Total Quality Improvement Program** Candidate must have a method of measuring performance against Dynachem standards. Candidate and Dynachem will work together to improve performance.	
8.	**Supplier Rating** The candidate must receive a rating of 90% or more on the Supplier Selection and Measurement Criteria Worksheet. Any deficiency will require a corrective action plan and will be reevaluated when the corrective action plan has been implemented.	

SUPPLIER CERTIFICATION IMPLEMENTATION WORKSHEET

Transportation

Supplier:
Representative:
Date:

All candidates for certification must complete these eight steps.

	Completion Date
1. **Attend Symposium**	
2. **Commitment Agreement** A copy of Dynachem's Commitment Agreement, signed by an officer of the company, must be on file at Dynachem.	
3. **Initial Inspection** Dynachem will do 100% inspection of a specified number of deliveries/orders. Compliance will be documented with a letter on file at Dynachem.	
4. **Certify to Dynachem Requirements** Candidate must certify to all Dynachem requirements. This is documented with a letter on file at Dynachem.	
5. **On-Time, Complete Delivery** Dynachem will track deliveries. On-Time means meeting agreed-upon or contract delivery schedules. Complete means meeting individual order requirements.	
6. **Complete Documentation** Candidate must provide complete documentation as called for by Dynachem including (but not limited to) insurance requirements, invoices, bills of lading, etc.	
7. **Total Quality Improvement Program** Candidate must have a method of measuring performance against Dynachem standards. Candidate and Dynachem will work together to improve performance.	
8. **Supplier Rating** The candidate must receive a rating of 90% or more on the Supplier Selection and Measurement Criteria Worksheet. Any deficiency will require a corrective action plan and will be reevaluated when the corrective action plan has been implemented.	

SUPPLIER CERTIFICATION
IMPLEMENTATION
WORKSHEET

Warehousing

Supplier:
Representative:
Date:

All candidates for certification must complete these eight steps.

Completion
Date

1. **Attend Symposium**
2. **Commitment Agreement**
   A copy of Dynachem's Commitment Agreement, signed by
   an officer of the company, must be on file at Dynachem.
3. **Initial Inspection**
   Dynachem will do 100% inspection of a specified number of
   deliveries/orders. Compliance will be documented with a
   letter on file at Dynachem.
4. **Certify to Dynachem Requirements**
   Candidate must certify to all Dynachem requirements. This is
   documented with a letter on file at Dynachem.
5. **On-Time, Accurate Order Completion**
   Dynachem will track order completion times. On-Time means
   same-day order pull and shipment within one working day.
   Accurate means orders accurate to ±2 percent per month and
   documentation accurate to one keystroke per page.
6. **Complete Documentation**
   Candidate must provide complete documentation as called for
   by Dynachem including (but not limited to) insurance
   requirements, invoices, bills of lading, etc.
7. **Total Quality Improvement Program**
   Candidate must have a method of measuring performance
   against Dynachem standards. Candidate and Dynachem will
   work together to improve performance.
8. **Supplier Rating**
   The candidate must receive a rating of 90% or more on the
   Supplier Selection and Measurement Criteria Worksheet. Any
   deficiency will require a corrective action plan and will be
   reevaluated when the corrective action plan has been
   implemented.

INDUSTRY, GOVERNMENT, and INTERNATIONAL STANDARDS

12

The procurement problems at the Pentagon are only the tip of the government's problem in obtaining quality material at the lowest cost. The entire process of selecting suppliers and ensuring quality is riddled with outdated, inefficient and costly procedures. By focusing on products, such as hammers which cost $600, critics of government programs are falling into the same trap as the government. It is not the price and quality of products that the government should be concerned about, but the quality and control of processes at their suppliers' plants. Supplier certification is the only way the government can begin to address these issues as we point out in our VideoEducation Series, *Supplier Certification: The Path to Excellence*. In fact, the government would be wise to observe those companies which have embraced the new orientation toward certifying the supplier's process, rather than inspecting finished goods.

The first obstacle for the government to overcome is the entrenched bureaucracy present in most of its departments and agencies. Somebody in the executive branch, perhaps the President himself, has to take charge and make a commitment to ridding our government's procurement system of traditional and inefficient procedures. Once that commitment has been made, it is then necessary to educate and train an overworked and inadequately trained staff in the philosophy and application of supplier certification. This commitment to revamping procurement practices should pertain to all departments and agencies which purchase material for the government. In other words, there shouldn't be one system for the Department of Defense and another for the Food and Drug Administration. Part of the problem has been a sort of Tower of Babel approach to procurement by our government. Everybody speaks a different language. When a supplier to the government needs several "interpreters" to understand the mass of governmental regulations, then it should come as no surprise that costs escalate.

Anybody who has looked at government manuals issued to suppliers is aware of a plethora of paragraphs and sub-paragraphs stating procedures and specifications which must be adhered to. You would think by the sheer mass of information that the government is doing a good job of controlling every detail. By fixing their attention on the details, however, they have seen the trees, but missed the forest. These manuals fail to achieve quality at the supplier's plant because they emphasize picayune procedures over the control of processes. The government has constructed a system which guarantees that suppliers will produce excellent paperwork *and* faulty components.

The government makes two mistakes when it formulates specifications for products. First, it draws up specifications for the inspection of finished products, rather than designing specifications for controlling a process. Second, it overspecifies. Specifications are not determined by customer need. The government wrongly believes that by tightening specifications, it is insuring quality. Quite the opposite is true. In a supplier certification environment, specifications conform to customer requirements. It seems, for example, that a soldier could get by with a $20 hammer off the shelf as well as he could with one costing 30 times more. There are, of course, some products that the government buys which require the most technically feasible specifications possible. Parts for the space shuttle, for example. In other words, conformance to customer requirements varies according to the

criticality of the part or material being purchased. Supplier certification recognizes this need and assures us of the highest quality
and safety when this is truly the demand of the customer. The same
criteria used for buying space shuttle parts, for example, need not
be the same criteria we use to buy hammers or toilet seats.

These manuals, especially the MIL standards put out by the
Department of Defense, are also oriented toward an Acceptable
Quality Level (AQL) rather than a Certified Quality Level (CQL).
As we have noted before, an AQL approach allows defects. In fact,
a 2% AQL says that two parts out of every 100 will be bad. Total
Quality Control does not accept anything less than 100% quality
and achieves that level by being statistically driven. There must be
more emphasis in government documents of Statistical Process
Control (SPC), a cornerstone of supplier certification. With SPC,
the emphasis is on controlling the supplier's process and making
them responsible for producing quality parts. If machines are so
well maintained and controlled that they never produce bad parts,
then 100% quality becomes a far easier goal to achieve as it
eliminates wasteful paperwork and red tape. In fact, the government would find that far more suppliers would be willing to do
work for the government if they did not have to jump through so
many hoops.

EXAMPLES OF GOVERNMENT REGULATIONS

MIL-STD-45662

In the Department of Defense's MIL-STD-45662 for calibration
systems requirements, there is no mention of using statistical
methods to control the accuracy of measuring and test equipment.
Here is a perfect example of what we just mentioned. Furthermore, the emphasis on merely defining standards instead of
process control is vague. It leaves the determination of how to

control accuracy to the individual supplier. Thus, the government must send in inspectors to determine if the job is being done correctly. And, of course, every supplier will be different which makes the government's role even more difficult. This emphasis on inspection should be replaced by one program which applies to every supplier. That program utilizes statistical control and puts the responsibility for quality at the supplier's door.

It may be nitpicking, but the fact that there is a spelling mistake in this document does set a tone. At the top of the third page, in capital letters, is the word "FORWARD." Obviously, what they meant to put was "FOREWORD." It makes one wonder about the level of quality control in their own department. Remember: what you demand from a supplier, you must also demand of yourself.

MIL-Q-9858A

This document on quality program requirements states in section 3.5 (Corrective Action) that "the quality program shall detect promptly and correct assignable conditions adverse to quality." That sounds reasonable upon first reading, but a closer reading reveals some problems. Again, it merely states the desired result without mentioning how the process of corrective action should be controlled. Later in the section, it does mention the need to analyze trends in processes. Nowhere, however, does it mention that the purpose of corrective action is not to treat a symptom, but to find and cure the problems which cause the symptoms to appear.

Section 6.1 (Materials and Materials Control) says that all "supplier's materials and products shall be subjected to inspection ..." This is unnecessary in a supplier certification environment. At the end of the paragraph, it states that "evidence of suppliers' satisfactory control of quality may be used to adjust the amount and kind of receiving inspection." Here is evidence, we think, of the government's reliance on an AQL approach to quality. The answer is not to use less final inspection as a reward, but to eliminate final inspection by controlling the process.

In section 6.6 (Statistical Quality Control and Analysis), the document states that statistical methods "may be utilized whenever such procedures are suitable to maintain the required control of quality." In our opinion, this is a rather weak endorsement of the engine that drives supplier certification and the achievement of 100% quality.

Contractor System Status Review Guide

What can you say about a document over 180 pages long which presents a very complete picture of how to audit a supplier? We have seen documents from our clients that cover the same material at the same depth in less than a fifth of the number of pages the government requires. We also wonder how often this document is actually used and how well trained the people are who conduct the audit? Is this just another instance of overspecification?

GOOD MANUFACTURING PRACTICES
Food and Drug Administration (FDA)

In contrast to the above document, there is an 11-page paper issued by the FDA entitled "Good Manufacturing Practices." Here is what it covers:

Organization and Personnel	**Buildings**
Control of Raw Materials	**Equipment**
Packaging and Label Control	**Product Evaluation**
Holding and Distribution	**Records**
Production and Process Controls	

In those 11 pages, this document gets across more about the principles which underlie supplier certification than most other government publications. It emphasizes housekeeping and preventive maintenance, education and training, calibration scheduling, SPC and conformance to customer requirements. The FDA, on the basis of this document, seems to be more process oriented than product oriented in its approach to quality. Perhaps this is so because the agency deals with items which are critical to the lives and health of human beings. It goes to show that high levels of quality are achievable if the effort is made.

THE BALDRIGE AWARD

The purpose of the Malcolm Baldrige National Quality Award, in the words of a 1988 winner, is to help "American companies become world class." We couldn't agree more with this statement which was made by John C. Marous, Chairman and Chief Executive Officer of Westinghouse Electric Corp., whose subsidiary, Westinghouse Commercial Nuclear Fuels Division, won the award in the manufacturing category.

The award, which contains a medal bearing the legend "The Quest for Excellence," is the United States' equivalent of Japan's Deming Prize for Quality. The Baldrige Award is the highest accolade for quality that an American company can receive. It was created by Congress in 1987 and named in honor of Secretary of Commerce Malcolm Baldrige who died that year in a rodeo accident. Currently, the award is administered and funded by a group of private companies and is managed by the Commerce Department's National Institute of Standards and Technology.

Why the Award was Established

Besides administering the granting of the award and providing feedback to applicants, the Baldrige Award was also established, according to the **1992 Award Criteria** booklet, to:

- "Help elevate quality standards and expectations.

- Facilitate communication and sharing among and within organizations of all types based upon common understanding of key quality requirements.

- Serve as a working tool for planning, training assessment and other uses."

As you can see, the Baldrige Award was designed to increase the World Class awareness of the whole country and to publicize companies that have achieved World Class Status. It is hoped that their efforts will be emulated by other companies in the United States.

Responding to some suggestions in the past couple of years, the Baldrige Award has placed a new emphasis on dual results-oriented goals. While striving to maximize "the overall productivity and effectiveness" of the company, it also seeks to continuously improve the delivery of value, service and product to the customer of that company. It is becoming more and more clear that quality improvement works best when the company has the customer in mind. That is why Supplier Certification is so important. Without defect-free parts and materials, the satisfaction of customer requirements will fall short.

Core Values and Concepts

Award examiners consider a number of core values and concepts in each category of the award. These values and concepts are designed, according to the **Award Criteria** booklet, to "address and integrate the overall customer and company performance requirements." Again, the emphasis is on customer satisfaction and quality performance. Below we have listed the values and concepts (with brief descriptions) which the Baldrige examiners use to build the Award Criteria used in the evaluation process. They are an excellent guide to the development of a company culture in which quality is a way of life. Not surprisingly, they read like the core concepts of a successful Supplier Certification program.

- **Customer-Driven Quality** — The Baldrige Award defines this area as a strategic concept to gain market share and retain customers. Besides meeting customer requirements and reducing defects and errors, customer-driven quality also demands a company which is aware of developments in the industry and flexible enough to meet an ever-changing customer demand.

- **Leadership** — This as described as senior management's success in creating and sustaining a quality culture. True leadership comes from the men and women who actively participate and articulate their vision and their goals. Leaders are people who are capable of making other people into leaders of their own individual areas.

- **Continuous Improvement** — The Baldrige Award says that only companies with a "well-defined and well-executed approach to continuous improvement" can achieve the highest levels of quality. We extend this a bit more to say that the same goals are necessary for your suppliers as well. The World Class company is as interested in the continuous improvement process at their suppliers' facilities as they are in their own.

- **Full Participation** — The emphasis here is on educating and training your work force to be personally and actively involved in eliminating waste from all the activities in your company. A new book, co-authored by Pro-Tech vice president Wayne L. Douchkoff, **People Empowerment:** *Achieving Success from Involvement* (PT Publications, Palm Beach Gardens, FL), explores this area in detail.

- **Fast Response** — In essence, this area is a subset of Customer-Driven Quality. The aim here is to reduce the response time to customer demands, requirements and specifications. Work in this area often involves simplifying work processes and designs and thus has clear ramifications in the quality and productivity areas.

- **Design Quality and Prevention** — Another concept closely related to quality, improving design quality seeks to build quality into a product and the processes by which it is produced. This is another area where Supplier Certification figures prominently. Design quality relies, of course, on well-designed parts and components. This will mean that you will need to communicate at length and early with your suppliers when designing any new product or making changes to a current one.

- **Long-Range Outlook** — This is a cornerstone of Supplier Certification as well. The goal is to establish long-term relationships with both your customers by providing them with a quality product and with your suppliers by helping them achieve the high levels of quality needed to survive in today's global marketplace.

- **Management by Fact** — Again, just like Supplier Certification, the emphasis is on using reliable data, including statistical data, and analyzing it for continuous improvement. The feedback cycle which takes data and uses it to improve performance is the engine which drives the whole quality movement.

- **Partnership Development** — Partnerships are very similar to Full Participation. We cover this area in **JIT Purchasing** and in **The World of Negotiations** (both by PT Publications, Palm Beach Gardens, FL) as well. It is our view at Pro-Tech that the company of the future is the company capable of forming long-term commitments in a win/win environment.

- **Public Responsibility** — The Baldrige Award also realizes that a World Class company is also a good citizen. Quality is not possible without protecting health, safety and the environment. Quality planning must take into account the full life cycle of a product. That means waste disposal and the development of products which do not have avoidable adverse effects.

Customer Satisfaction

A recent issue of the magazine, *Electronic Business*, was devoted entirely to a discussion of quality in the electronics industry. One of the principal themes in all of the articles was customer satisfaction. Many authors noted that 300 of a possible 1,000 points in last year's Baldrige Award was allotted to the category of customer satisfaction. That's twice as many points as any other category. Deservedly so, we say. The customer is ultimately the reason you are in business. Sometimes, however, it is difficult for a company to know who their customer is. One maker of electrical products asked whether their customer was the purchasing manager at the customer's company, the manufacturing department, or the end user, the person who buys and uses the customer's product. In a certain sense, they all are, but they all have different needs. Supplier Certification helps you put these needs into perspective. Remember, as we explained in the first chapter, we are all suppliers and we are all customers. Once we realize that, we can then move toward the implementation of total solutions. By that, we mean solutions that go beyond meeting specifications. We need to look toward working on solutions that anticipate the needs of tomorrow.

The Application Process

To win the Baldrige Award, a company must complete up to 75 pages of criteria and answer over 133 questions about quality. Those who pass this tier are then subject to a three-day, on-site examination. The criteria are very rigorous and emphasize both quality achievements and systems for quality improvement.

Your company is eligible to vie for this award if it is incorporated and located in the United States. The company can be either public or private. The Baldrige Award is given in three categories: 1) Large manufacturing companies or subsidiaries, 2) Large service companies and 3) Smaller companies (independently owned and under 500 full-time employees) either in manufacturing or service. The rules today allow for up to two winners in each category. We feel, however, that there should be as many winners as there are companies which meet the criteria. Let's showcase our companies against the world's competition.

After the application is submitted by a company, the Board of Examiners selects members to review and evaluate an application. Companies which score high are then eligible for on-site visits by one or more teams of examiners which are comprised of experts in quality from universities, industry and professional/ trade associations.

As we stated, the on-site visit lasts two or three days. Its purpose is to verify the application's contents. While visiting a company's departments, records are reviewed and corporate officials are interviewed with the idea of getting up-to-date information about the company. Most important, however, is the examiners assessment of the adoption of company culture focused on quality and customer satisfaction.

The examining teams then write up a report which they submit to a panel of nine judges. These judges are entrusted with the task of recommending award recipients to the National Institute of Standards and Technology and the Secretary of Commerce.

For further information about the Baldrige Award and the application process, write to:

> Malcolm Baldrige National Quality Award
> National Institute of Standards and Technology
> Gaithersburg, MD 20899.

ISO 9000 SERIES OF STANDARDS AND ANSI/ASQC Q90

From the outset of this discussion, we want to point out that registration with the International Organization for Standardization (ISO) as outlined in the ISO 9000 Series of Standards is not the same as certification as we describe it in this book. ISO registration is more general in nature and requires less "proof" of performance sustainability. Rather, the focus is on documentation. However, certification to the standard will be required to ship into European communities. The ISO was formed to develop and promote international standards in a number of areas. The ISO 9000 Series of Standards deals specifically with five international standards for quality management and quality assurance. The standards are designed not for any specific product or industry. It is expected that companies will develop and implement quality management systems which follow these standards, but which use whatever technology and techniques are appropriate to the company. The ISO 9000 series is also, word for word, the standards adopted by the United States as the ANSI/ASQC Q90 Series.

The five standards mentioned above which are part of the ISO 9000/Q90 Series are:

- **ISO 9000/Q90** — This standard is a guide to the other standards in the series. It defines key terms and concepts.

- **ISO 9001/Q91** — Specifies a quality system model for use when two companies require a demonstration of a supplier's ability to design, produce, install and service a product.

- **ISO 9002/Q92** — Specifies a quality system model for quality assurance in production and installation.

- **ISO 9003/Q93** — Specifies a quality system model for quality assurance in final inspection and testing.

- **ISO 9004/Q94** — Provides guidelines for the development and implementation of a quality system and for quality management.

The ISO 9000 series was developed to bring some order to an increasingly confused situation in which various organizations and European countries were each developing quality system standards. Although many of the standards were very close, it was felt that standardization was needed at an international level. The result is the ISO 9000 series of quality management and quality assurance standards which are reviewed on a five-year cycle to keep them abreast of the latest developments.

The ISO 9001/Q91 model, as described above, is a quality system assessment which is similar, but not as extensive as the supplier audits described in this book. The ISO audit covers the following areas:

- **Management Responsibility**
- **Quality System**
- **Contract Review**
- **Design Control**
- **Document Control**
- **Purchasing**
- **Purchaser Supplied Product**
- **Product Identification Traceability**
- **Process Control**
- **Inspection and Testing**
- **Inspection, Measuring and Test Equipment**
- **Inspection and Test Status**
- **Control of Nonconforming Product**
- **Corrective Action**
- **Handling, Storage, Packaging and Delivery**
- **Quality Records**
- **Internal Quality Audits**
- **Training**
- **Servicing**
- **Statistical Techniques**

It should be noted that any company which is doing business or plans to do business with the European Economic Community should be aware of these standards. Adherence to these standards is not a requirement for all products. At present, you would be best advised to obtain more information about your specific products.

SUPPLIER CERTIFICATION AS THE TOOL

We believe it is clear that the government should adopt a supplier certification program as a way of life. Such a program will undoubtedly result in more bang for the taxpayer's buck. Right now, you and I are supporting waste with our hard-earned dollars. Supplier certification will also assure us of quality products and do much in eliminating defense projects which don't work, disasters such as the Challenger and nuclear plants which pollute our environment. It will take hard work and an unrelenting commitment, but it's not impossible.

Recently, for instance, Hughes Aircraft Co. was authorized by the Department of Defense to deliver tactical display systems without government inspection. Hughes was the first major contractor ever to be given this status. Prior to this certification, Hughes had to submit its final products to the Navy for inspection and approval. Now, having obtained a Certificate of Conformance from the government, the company is able to deliver products based on its own quality certification. We, at Pro-Tech, are proud to say as well that Hughes has made the reading of our book mandatory.

Hughes achieved this level by improving its own quality control and its suppliers'. A supplier certification program called Partnership in Excellence (PIE) was started. Top management support was solicited from Hughes' major suppliers and the program was based on detecting defects in the process using statistical methods. Hughes made a commitment to determine the causes of problems, rather than treating symptoms. And, as in the program we have explained in this book, workers were given responsibility and authority for quality. They were also involved in problem-solving.

In the case of Hughes Aircraft, we believe that the government is moving in the right direction. But let's not stop here. Remember that supplier certification is also a program of continuous improvement. We want to see *America* keep moving ahead.

QUESTIONS FREQUENTLY ASKED ABOUT SUPPLIER CERTIFICATION

13

The following questions and answers are all derived from actual work done at clients of Professionals for Technology Associates, Inc. (Pro-Tech), an international management counseling and education firm, and from discussions with people knowledgeable in the area of supplier certification. We have attempted to select companies like yours to whom we could pose questions which are uppermost in the minds of company managers. These are questions about real situations, questions we think you would want answered.

Take a careful look at the following questions. There may be some you haven't thought of and some that you want to ask of your suppliers and customers. Refer back to the indicated chapter or pages for a detailed answer. All of these questions are also addressed in our VideoEducation series, *"Supplier Certification: The Path to Excellence,"* available from PT Publications, Palm Beach Gardens, FL.

1. **What should be the make-up of the steering committee?**
   The steering committee should consist of representatives from Marketing, Quality Assurance, Manufacturing, Engineering, Purchasing or Materials Management and Finance. See Chapter 10.

2. **How do we improve communication between plants and suppliers?**
   The best method of improving communication is to begin to listen. Team presentations using fishbone diagrams are also very effective. See Chapter 3.

3. **How can the plants supply better input/data into the Supplier Certification process?**
   Plants can improve their input/data by using control charts and the performance measurements described in Chapter 10.

4. **What is the importance of documentation?**
   Documentation establishes a baseline for improvement, uncovers opportunities for improvement and pinpoints problem areas. See Chapter 2 and Chapter 10.

5. **Who will do all the work?**
   This is our favorite question. The short answer is simple
   — everybody. See Chapter 1.

6. **What is Corporate's expectation and involvement in the process?**
   The corporate level of company should show its involvement by being totally committed to Supplier Certification and by granting authority and responsibility to the
   team. See Chapter 10.

7. **How can we keep the plants apprised of who is on the approved, qualified, and certified supplier list?**
   This is easily done under Supplier Certification, since
   the team is the only entity which can put suppliers on the
   appropriate lists. See Chapter 3.

8. **What is a certified supplier?**
   A certified supplier is a company which can deliver
   100% quality, 100% of the time, 100% on-time, with
   100% accurate counts. See Chapter 1.

9. **How does certification fit into our policies and proce-dures?**
   We need to write a formal procedure for Supplier Certi-
   fication in the policies and procedures manual. See
   Chapter 10.

10. **How do we address human resource and personnel policies?**
    Like all issues and questions, human resource and

personnel policies should be handled by the Supplier
Certification team. See Chapter 10.

11. **What will this process look like in three years?**
It will be a company-wide process which will strive for
continuous improvement. See Chapter 1.

12. **What's in it for the supplier?**
The supplier stands to gain more business and increase
its profits. See Chapter 1.

13. **Has certification worked for other companies? Suppliers?**
Absolutely yes! See the case studies throughout this
book.

14. **What are the financial benefits of a certification program?**
The principal financial benefit is the elimination of
waste. See Chapter 1.

15. **Are expectations the same for all the plants?**
Yes, the Supplier Certification program must be consistent throughout the corporation. See Chapter 1.

16. **How are minority supplier programs incorporated into a Supplier Certification program?**
Minority supplier programs are handled in the same
manner as any other supplier. See Chapter 1.

17. **How does Corporate gather data from the plants on quality, delivery and quantity performance?**
Corporate gathers data through the use of performance
measurements as described in Chapter 10.

18. **How do we ensure confidentiality of supplier data?**
    We can assure confidentiality by signing an agreement
    as part of the Supplier Certification program. See Chap-
    ter 7.

19. **What competitive advantage does Supplier Certifica-
    tion offer?**
    The competitive advantages are numerous. Some of the
    more important are higher quality, on-time delivery and
    accurate counts. See Chapter 7.

20. **What benefits does the program offer in process
    improvements, productivity, efficiency, utilization,
    etc.?**
    Supplier Certification offers all of the benefits above and
    more. Benefits are only limited by the amount of com-
    mitment brought to the project. See Chapter 11.

21. **How do we certify a supplier whose processes are not
    under control?**
    Another easy question — you don't. Start them on a
    program like SPC which will help them get their pro-
    cesses under control. See Chapter 9.

22. **What testing and auditing programs should be
    incorporated into the process?**
    Use testing and auditing programs like those described
    in the surveys which appear in Chapter 4, Chapter 5 and
    Chapter 9.

23. **How do we ensure that our specifications are accu-
    rate so that our suppliers have a chance?**
    You can assure that specifications are accurate by having

the team work on gathering one set of complete and accurate specifications.

24. **Who should be on the Supplier Certification team?**
The team should consist of representatives from direct labor, management and from suppliers. See Chapter 2.

25. **How do we get financial commitment from top management for the program?**
We can get financial commitment by explaining the benefits and payoffs — larger market share, increased profits, improved productivity, etc. See Chapter 10.

26. **How do we quantify our survey and audit issues?**
The best method to quantify survey and audit issues is to select ones that can be quantified. Stay away from fuzzy or "feel-good" categories. See Chapter 4.

27. **How does Supplier Certification tie into TQM? Or does it?**
TQM is an integral part of any Supplier Certification program. See Chapter 6.

28. **Can Supplier Certification be applied to MRO?**
Yes, see the Dynachem forms and approach in Chapter 11.

The case studies which follow are the answers we received to a survey that we conducted of our own clients. All point to the importance of supplier certification in their goal to become World Class companies. All the case studies also provide you with valuable information about how you can start and maintain your own program.

E.I. DuPont de Nemours, Inc.
Imaging Systems Dept.
Towanda, PA

QUESTIONS: How has this DuPont plant designed its supplier certification program? In particular, how has it coordinated internal and external requirements?

ANSWERS: The Towanda plant of DuPont has a supplier certification program in place which subscribes to the first and foremost rule of such programs — recognition of the fact that supplier certification has both an internal and external component. The people responsible for this plant's program have set clearly defined goals and have made considerable progress in achieving those goals.

The internal component of the program begins with a set of beliefs. Although drawn up for the Towanda plant, keep in mind that these are also principles to which suppliers should adhere:

1. World class status provides a competitive advantage for the Towanda plant and the businesses it serves.

2. World class status is attained by unleashing the potential for innovative thinking residing in the plant's people.

3. Unity of purpose is the result of open, fair and caring treatment of people.

4. A competitive, high-performance organization relies on output-driven, customer-focused, self-managed teams.

5. Safety is a prerequisite for achieving functional excellence.

6. A total quality approach which emphasizes "doing it right the first time" and "fixing problems at their source" is required to achieve functional and competitive excellence.

7. Continual improvement is the path to long-term economic and global viability. This is attained by upgrading and improving people's skills while implementing state-of-the-art technologies in product, equipment and organizational processes.

8. Setting benchmarks will accelerate our advancement towards world class manufacturing.

The Towanda plant has also based its progress towards world class status on the four pillars of Just-In-Time, Total Quality Control, Employee Involvement and Total Reliability. The company has recognized that a certification program works only when its internal organization is equipped to handle the just-in-time delivery of zero-defect parts from its suppliers. To further this end, they have adopted the following principles for each area:

JUST-IN-TIME

1. We will only pursue "value-added" activity and eliminate "cost-added" activity.

2. We will audit each process step activity and work to cut:

> Work-In-Process.
> Flow times.

Set-up and change-over times.
Flow distances and floor space requirements.
Testing.
Cycle interval time.
Product scale-up time.

3. We will release only defect-free material to the next work station.

4. We will promote teamwork between manufacturing operations and all business departments and functional groups.

5. We will promote JIT through education and communication.

6. We will be guided by world class manufacturing concepts in how we plan, design, implement, automate and operate facilities.

TOTAL QUALITY CONTROL

1. We will develop quality performance expectations and goals to measure our ability to meet customer needs.

2. We will treat the problem, not the symptom.

3. We will only ship conforming product.

4. We will provide feedback and assistance to our suppliers regarding quality.

5. We will consistently provide product within specification to the next operation in the process chain.

EMPLOYEE INVOLVEMENT

1. Each employee will accept responsibility and accountability for responding to internal and external requests.

2. Each employee will seek to continually improve his ability to identify and solve problems.

TOTAL RELIABILITY

1. We will understand the cause of failure (statistics or preventive measurement) and take action to prevent problems.

2. We will provide frequent and regular scheduling for preventive maintenance.

As for the suppliers, the Towanda plant expects them to meet or exceed DuPont specification requirements. These expectations are no more than what DuPont demands of itself. For example, suppliers are asked to continually improve product quality and reliability through total and statistical quality control techniques. They are asked to be responsive to corrective action requests and to provide advance notice of any major process and product changes.

This is precisely the partnership we have discussed earlier in this book. The actual phases of the certification program also follow the basic five steps we demonstrated earlier as well. The Towanda plant has successfully brought the internal and external components of supplier certification together into a synergistic whole.

PENTON LEARNING SYSTEMS
New York, NY

DATA: Penton Learning Systems and Quality Alert Institute (QAI) present seminars across the country on topics of interest to business professionals.

QUESTIONS: 1) How popular are supplier certification programs?

2) What are the reasons people attend?

3) Is any one group particularly interested? Or, does participation cut across all departments, management levels, industries and company sizes?

ANSWERS: President Rick Worden says that Supplier Certification has consistently been one of Penton's most successful seminars since its inception. He believes that is because people want a "nuts-and-bolts" understanding of how to tackle poor quality at its source, that is, with the supplier. He also believes that companies see the advantage of revamping their own quality systems in order to work with suppliers who will be delivering 100% quality, on-time. Companies also see how Supplier Certification seminars can help them in their quest to be better suppliers to their own customers. It's a "multiple benefit seminar," Worden says. He adds that most of the participants are mid- to senior management and come principally from purchasing and operations, but that it would be wrong to see Supplier Certification as just for these areas alone. Certainly, however, they can be the ones who will introduce Supplier Certification to the other functions back at their plant.

THE CLOROX COMPANY
Pleasanton, CA

QUESTIONS: 1) What are the goals and objectives of Corporate Quality Assurance?

2) How did your company implement its supplier certification?

3) How did the suppliers react?

4) How were project teams implemented? Who served on them? How were meetings conducted?

5) How was the program implemented?

ANSWERS: 1) The primary goal of Corporate Quality Assurance (CQA) is to consistently provide top quality consumer products through the concept of Total Quality Management. This is in line with our company goal of providing the customer with only needed, quality products. The plan is to develop within each of the five divisions of Clorox:

> - The necessary statistical tools to measure the production and/or processes.
> - A documented process of transferring products efficiently from R&D to Manufacturing.
> - An ongoing quality program that relies on quality built into the process and only an audit of production.
> - Support production with supplier certification, where applicable, that can move to JIT iteration if needed.

Supplier certification has been driven by CQA based on a need identified at the design stage of our new detergent plant in Dyersburg, TN. It resulted from the obvious conclusion that traditional "toll gate" quality control testing could not be used to release product at the contemplated production rates.

From this, CQA developed a policy based on in-house experience and knowledge of current quality thinking (e.g. Statistical Process Control or SPC). The policy was applied to the Dyersburg plant as a pilot program which we saw as having a high potential for success. Raw material suppliers to the project were already identified and were, therefore, approached directly for their interest in supplier certification. Teams were formed and our policy shared with the supplier and implemented.

2) The suppliers reacted very positively. They liked our policy approach, understanding that it was a dynamic process that could be adjusted if needed. They also liked the statistical measuring steps that allowed everyone to follow the success of the project and the emphasis to work out the actual certification step at the plant production level. It was interesting to note that most suppliers were at our level of SPC expertise or below. In some cases they had committed to SPC, but had not implemented it. One supplier took our Dyersburg project as its pilot program for SPC implementation and now wants to introduce its suppliers to the concepts contained in our supplier certification policy.

3) CQA requested, as a minimum, that each supplier provide representatives from Quality, Manufacturing, and Sales to the team. Clorox was to provide a similar group made up of Purchasing (the primary contact for all meeting matters), CQA (for all test method and SPC), Manufacturing, and Division QC. Representatives from process and product development departments were

also included. The concept was to have a fluid team membership that would change as the certification process progressed.

Initial meetings are held at the Technical Center. Subsequent meetings, as needed, are at the supplier's technical and/or production facilities or at the Dyersburg plant. The idea is to create a team that will meet where it is most appropriate (e.g. in the middle of Wyoming, 1/4 mile below the surface in a soda ash mine on one occasion). To emphasize the team concept, the host company organizes the meeting and leads the discussions.

4) CQA has been responsible for implementing the first two parts of our policy: Test Method Alignment (which includes the mutual agreement on key variables to be measured) and Feasibility (a preliminary statistical evaluation of supplier historical data).

Division QC and the actual production location (i.e. Dyersburg) will drive the final capability phase with the supplier. CQA remains on the team as a resource. We have currently introduced 10 of our Dyersburg suppliers to our certification policy. Three of these should be certified by January 1989, and the others by March 1989. We have contacted three other suppliers and expect to have initial meetings with them in November.

COSMAIR, INC.
Piscataway, NJ

QUESTIONS: How do you rate suppliers? How do you define defect?

ANSWER: Since Cosmair is a complex entity of focused business units, it was necessary to create one system of rating suppliers. This system was based on Cosmair's commitment to the establishment of consistent methods of procurement, improvement in quality standards, and the development of a partnership with every supplier. Thus, suppliers were rated to determine how far each was progressing toward the goal of "Best in Class."

All suppliers currently doing business with Cosmair were rated in the following areas:

Quality of goods	**40% of rating**
JIT/Service commitment	**30% of rating**
Cost competitiveness	**20% of rating**
Technical abilities	**10% of rating**

Quality of goods rates each delivery of a component, WIP or finished product from a supplier on a scale from 10 to 0. A "10" means that there are zero defects in the shipment. A "0" means that all shipments were rejected. A score of "1" to "9" is given according to the number of defects present and the acceptable levels. Ratings are then averaged on a monthly basis for each supplier.

JIT/Service commitment consists of three items:

- Commitment to cycle time reduction.
- Respect of lead-times and delivery commitments.
- Policy of inventory reduction.

Cost competitiveness requirements are:

- Commitment to becoming certified suppliers by reducing all non value-added wastes.
- Value analysis programs to reduce costs.
- Breakdown of cost elements (material, labor, overhead, profit).

Technical abilities of suppliers should demonstrate:

- State-wide processes and facilities.
- Technical innovation/creativity in design.
- Control of secondary operations.

Furthermore, Cosmair came up with a standard definition for each of three classes of defects. They are:

Critical Defects A defect which can:
- Cause harm to the consumer.
- Render the item useless.

Major Defects A defect which can:
- Reduce to a major degree the commercial value.
- Reduce the usable/salable of the item.
- Hinder normal use on line or by the consumer.
- Be defined by limits as aesthetic.

Minor Defects A defect which:
- Has minimal impact on the commercial value.
- Is not likely to reduce usable or function.
- Exceeds aesthetic limit standards.

With the standardization of ratings and defect definitions, Cosmair and its suppliers speak a common language. That makes it easier to create a partnership and to maintain it.

RICOH CORPORATION
San Jose, California

QUESTIONS: 1) What kind of foundation is necessary to begin a Supplier Certification program? 2) What does a Total Quality Management Charter contain?

ANSWERS: 1) In one sense, Jim Kvek, manager of the Total Quality Management Department at Ricoh (an electronic equipment manufacturer), is trying to work himself out of a job. Kvek says that when his company first began to consider a certification program, they quickly realized that they were "putting the cart before the horse."

"You can't begin a program in the middle," he adds, "so we went back to the beginning. We began by reviewing our quality assurance procedures and by implementing an internal program of Total Quality Management. We aimed for total involvement from everybody in the company. My job is to transfer the responsibility for quality from the TQM Department to the whole company." Kvek says that he effects this transference by communicating goals through pamphlets to employees and new hirees and through committees composed of people from different levels of the organization.

"I am not here to give presentations, " Kvek says. "I am here to assist project teams and provide them with the tools they need to understand and solve problems. Of course, training and education is one of the most valuable tools I can provide."

All of Ricoh's efforts at establishing a foundation for Supplier Certification have been greatly aided by the complete support of top management. Much of the California plant's top management worked at Ricoh in Japan when the company won the prestigious Deming Prize for quality control, the top award in Japan and arguably the world. Kvek points out that there was no need to "go through a convincing process."

2) Much of the company's effort revolves around a Total Quality Management Charter. It defines TQM as:

"... an environment in which all of us accept the responsibility of our customers as that of our own; a customer is any internal or external individual affected by our actions."

Furthermore, the definition states that TQM is an "attitude reflecting teamwork, integrity, honesty and a commitment to satisfy all customer needs." It also states that TQM is "involved in all aspects of company activities."

The adopted philosophy is that each step in a process is the previous step's customer.

As for the goals of the TQM Charter, they can be summed up as achieving the acceptance and practice of TQM by the entire company as well as the recognition that it is everybody's responsibility to contribute ideas, effort, time and service in support of these objectives. More specifically, the charter contains the following goals:

BUSINESS GOALS

Schedules being met
Improved quality
Reduction in rework
Attainment of optimum product cost
Lower inventory
Supplier certification program
Improved customer satisfaction

PERSONAL GOALS

Improved employee morale
Lower turnover rate
Fewer absentees

INTERNAL GOALS
Improved profitability
Meeting Sector goals

This charter also outlines the responsibilities of the TQM Department. As Kvek stated earlier, one of the principal responsibilities of his department is to provide training in Total Quality Management. The document also cites another responsibility as finding a consultant whose "ideology is compatible" with that of the company. Ricoh selected Professionals for Technology (Pro-Tech) in Palm Beach Gardens, FL, because their skill base was compatible with the company, particularly Pro-Tech's knowledge of both American and Pacific Rim companies. The duty of this consultant is to organize all the training courses about TQM.

The charter includes the means by which Project Teams or employees are to be recognized for outstanding contributions to the TQM project. This is important, the charter says, because it "provides a continuous, company-wide forum for recognizing and publicly thanking employees for their extraordinary perception, dedication and action in responding to the business needs of our customers, both internal and external."

It is clear that Ricoh has recognized as well that Supplier Certification not only rests on a foundation of Total Quality Management, but also on a base of respect and open communication with their people. Kvek wants the people at Ricoh to build quality into their work. He hopes that project teams eventually become second nature at the company. Then he will know he has done his job right. As a footnote to this story, Ricoh has also set a corporate goal of winning the Baldridge Award for quality excellence.

AWD Ltd.
Dunstable, England

QUESTIONS: 1) What questions do you ask a potential supplier? 2) What kind of format do you use for a supplier appraisal? 3) What are some of the requirements of supplier certification and a supplier agreement?

ANSWERS: AWD, Ltd., a truck and bus manufacturer, has woven together a comprehensive Supplier Certification program.

The supplier questionnaire, says Senior Purchase Engineer I.W. Burgess, is the form sent to potential suppliers in order to assess whether they meet AWD's requirements. The form shown here gives some of the questions which the company deems important:

AWD LTD.
SUPPLIER QUESTIONNAIRE

1. NAME OF COMPANY: ....
   ADDRESS: ....
   ....
   ....
   TELEPHONE NO: ....
2. COMPANY PERSONNEL
   (Please include organization charts)

3. DETAILS OF FINANCIAL STRUCTURE AND AFFILIA-
   TIONS WITH OTHER COMPANIES. (Please include copy
   of latest Annual Report)

4. ANNUAL TURNOVER: ....
5. DATE COMPANY ESTABLISHED: ....
6. SIZE OF PLANT IN SQUARE FEET: ....
7. PLANT LIST:...
   ....
8. TOTAL NUMBER OF EMPLOYEES: ....
9. ANNUAL LABOR TURNOVER:
10. HAVE YOU:
    (A) A SEPARATE QUALITY CONTROL DEPT.?
    (B) A LABORATORY?
    (C) ADEQUATE FACILITIES FOR TESTING TO
        MEET OUR SPECIFICATIONS?
11. HAVE YOU:
    (A) YOUR OWN TOOL ROOM?
    (B) TOOL DESIGN FACILITIES?
    (C) TOOL TRYOUT FACILITIES?
    (D) WHAT PERCENTAGE OF YOUR TOOLING
        IS SUB-CONTRACTED?

2) Providing that the received information from the supplier satisfies AWD's critical requirements, a full appraisal visit is then scheduled at the supplier's plant. The appraisal team consists of a representative from Purchasing Engineering, S.Q.A. and Laboratory departments. This team completes a Supplier Appraisal form. The example shown below is a partial listing of its components:

<u>**AWD LTD.**</u>
<u>**SUPPLIER APPRAISAL**</u>

SUPPLIER: ....

ADDRESS: ....

....

TEL NO: ....

DATE OF VISIT: ....

PERSONNEL INTERVIEWED: ....

....

....

....

PERSONNEL AWD: ....

....

....

....

RECOMMENDATION: ....

....

....

....

	FULL APPROVAL	PARTIAL APPROVAL	NIL
Purch. engineering	[ ]	[ ]	[ ]
S.Q.A.	[ ]	[ ]	[ ]
Engineering	[ ]	[ ]	[ ]
Laboratory	[ ]	[ ]	[ ]

Suppliers which meet the following requirements are designated as "Certification Approved":

- Minimum Category 4 compliance to S.Q.A. general quality standards for purchased material.

- Have proven sample and bulk performance ascertained from existing quality documentation.

3) The supplier must then submit a "Certificate of Bulk Conformity" each month to cover all conforming parts delivered during the preceding month. At the discretion of a Certification Committee, a supplier who demonstrates satisfactory performance over a 12-month period will only be required to sign an agreement confirming that AWD's quality requirements will be met. The "Certificate of Bulk Conformity" contains the following paragraph:

> **We hereby certify that the above mentioned parts/material have been manufactured, tested and inspected in accordance with the requirements of the drawing, documents and specifications current at the time of manufacture, issued by AWD LTD. We certify that the said parts/material were found to be in conformity herewith.**

The Certification Committee is responsible for controlling the list of participating suppliers. It is comprised of Materials Management and Quality Control representatives. A full list of "Certification Approved" sources is retained and updated by Purchase Engineering. This list is then made available to Purchasing Groups, S.Q.A., Laboratory, Product Engineering and Material departments.

A supplier can be removed from the certification system for the following reasons:

- S.Q.A. appraisal at source.
- Quality Assurance and/or Laboratory rejections.
- Initial sample rejections.
- Machining/Assembly/Processing rejections.

All rejections are then investigated by S.Q.A./Laboratory. When a supplier is removed from the program, the Purchase Manager will notify the supplier in writing, giving full reasons for the removal. To be reinstated, a supplier must demonstrate a satisfactory performance over a six-month period. The S.Q.A./Supplier contact group will then resurvey the supplier. Prior to any reinstatement, a meeting is set up between AWD and the supplier by Purchasing. The purpose is to restate the principles of the certification program and obtain the supplier's assurance in writing that it will comply with AWD's requirements.

BAXTER HEALTHCARE INTERNATIONAL
Paramax Systems Division
Irvine, CA

QUESTIONS: 1) Why is Supplier Certification important to a manufacturer of healthcare products? 2) How has the Paramax Division handled the implementation phase?

ANSWERS: 1) Bob Wielenga, past Director of Materials at the Paramax Systems Division of Baxter Healthcare International manufacturing facility, pointed out that the healthcare industry is certainly one area where it is clear that 100% quality is absolutely necessary. The division manufactures a blood chemistry analyzer and the supporting products.

"Quality means conformance to requirements. In the healthcare industry, quality and service to the customer is essential," Wielenga said. "Baxter's products are used in making critical decisions. For that reason alone, we think Supplier Certification is essential."

Wielenga cited the increasing costs incurred by healthcare providers as another reason for a certification program. As hospitals and doctors, for example, find it more expensive to provide medical care, suppliers, such as Paramax, must develop ways to reduce costs without sacrificing quality.

In order to lower these costs, however, the supplier must receive quality goods from their suppliers with zero-defects, on time, and in the right quantity. Again, there can be no sacrifice in quality. Supplier Certification, Wielenga found, is the means whereby all the links in the supply chain of healthcare can work with each other in the improvement of quality and service.

"The partnership developed through Supplier Certification allows us to continually improve our requirements and to reduce costs," Wielenga said. "It builds long-term relationships in which we can improve quality. Quality in this sense extends beyond meeting print specifications and also includes delivery, quantity, and standard packaging requirements."

2.) Implementation at the Paramax Systems Division has been governed by an internal/external philosophy. Two groups have been formed to work on both of these components. The first group is concerned with internal documentation, process control and paperwork. In other words, those items needed to get a Supplier Certification program off the ground.

The second group works on the supplier side, acquainting them with the foundations of Statistical Process Control, Just-In-Time and Total Quality Control. Paramax firmly believes, however, that no company should attempt to teach these techniques and philosophies to suppliers unless they are using them at their own company.

Together, the two groups are placing the cornerstone for what Steve Barbato, Vice President of Manufacturing, says will be a "world-class manufacturing organization."

"You cannot achieve this type of an organization," he adds, "without certified suppliers."

CASE STUDIES, APPLICATIONS AND NEWSLETTERS

14

KRAFT DAIRY GROUP
Supplier Certification Program

Recognizing that the quality of raw materials and packaging received from suppliers significantly impacts the quality of Kraft's finished products, the company began a Supplier Certification program to take advantage of supplier in-house quality tests and to emphasize the importance of 100% quality. Right from the beginning, Kraft also had its own customers in mind. The company wanted to significantly reduce consumer complaints about their finished products.

The program itself is run out of the Philadelphia General Office Purchasing Function which has the responsibility of communicating the program to suppliers through a letter. This letter describes Kraft Dairy Group's quality needs and introduces a plan for a mutually acceptable quality test program. The next step is to establish a more detailed and regular level of communication in which the quality control program is more thoroughly described and to provide product specifications, incorporate quality tests currently being performed by the supplier, conduct a plant inspection under the auspices of Kraft's Quality Control department and establish a start-up date for the Supplier Certification program.

One of the key elements in Kraft's Supplier Certification program is the "certificate of analysis." The certificate shows what series of quality inspections were conducted by the supplier before shipping the material to the Kraft Dairy Group. Basically, it indicates that the supplier is performing quality control tests and SPC (for those who have such a program) in order to keep the product within Kraft's specification standards. A certificate must accompany each shipment and any variances are duly noted and sent back to the supplier for explanation. Any product that does not meet specifications is put on hold until the supplier has corrected the process.

All of the program is maintained by regular evaluations of the supplier's performance. Items such as quality, delivery and service are carefully monitored and will be supplemented by on-site plant inspection by a team from Kraft. The plant inspection will review the performance to specifications, housekeeping and sanitary procedures, utilization of SPC in the process, and general in-house quality control programs. All results are documented in order to provide reports to the supplier and to the affected plants in the Kraft Dairy Group.

LORAN CASSETTES AND AUDIO PRODUCTS
Supplier Assistance Team Certification Manual

Rob Loranger
President

Loran, a Ford Q1 Supplier, has published a 28-page manual to familiarize companies with the way the audiocassette manufacturer expects to do business with suppliers. The Supplier Assistance Team (SAT) was created to assist suppliers in achieving 100% good product, delivered on time, at a competitive cost, with demonstrated process control which assures product capability to specifications while providing a vehicle for continuous improvement. The overall mission, as with all good Supplier Certification programs, is to help the manufacturer evolve into a World Class company by building a win/win partnership with suppliers.

After the introductory material, the manual goes on to explain what requirements a company must meet in order to become certified. These requirements focus on process control, continuous improvement and performing to specifications. The requirements section also lists the advantages of being a partner:

- **Forecast of orders.**
- **Commitment to forecast.**
- **Elimination of waste and, thus, reduction of total cost.**
- **Special payment terms.**
- **Long-term agreement for continued business.**

The section even quite plainly lists the disadvantage of being a non-certified supplier:

> • **Alternate sources will be investigated.**

Next, the manual points out the responsibilities and purpose of the Quality Assurance department. Principally, their role is to establish the standards of quality which reflect the requirements of Loran and, equally importantly, Loran's customers. QA also has the responsibility of ensuring that each supplier is using the proper statistical controls and/or inspection testing and auditing techniques are in effect and being used in the proper manner. QA, itself, in the following section restates its firm commitment to quality and customer satisfaction while providing a leadership role in the development of new ideas. The same level of commitment is also reserved for the development of a continuous improvement program for products, processes and systems.

The overall steps in Loran's Supplier Certification program is described next before going into more detail about the procedure for inspection and the procedure for conducting the supplier Quality System Survey. The inspection procedure describes how a supplier progresses from 100% inspection to skip-lot inspection and finally to certification. The Quality System Survey describes what the team from Loran will be reviewing while visiting the supplier's facility and the purpose of such a survey.

An excellent summation of a supplier analysis/qualification visit is given in the manual as well and bears printing in full:

> Plant visits and evaluations are one of the most
> effective ways of evaluating prospective suppliers.
> The trained mind and the experienced eye can iden-
> tify many aspects of a new supplier's operation which

reveal its capabilities and weaknesses. The adequacy of equipment; the effectiveness of production, quality and cost control; the competence of technical and managerial personnel, the morale of the work force; and past performance all represent important indicators of a supplier's capability. A properly conducted visit will also reveal the willingness of the supplier's key Quality, Manufacturing and Engineering personnel to accept the orders and cooperate with counterparts in its own company in order to fulfill them satisfactorily.

In order to derive the maximum benefit from plant visits, whether for the purpose of appraising a potential supplier, resolving a problem with an existing supplier or becoming better acquainted with a supplier's operations and personnel, these visits must be well planned. This means careful selection of who makes the visits, careful formulation of the type of questions which should be asked, and careful thought as to whom these questions should be addressed.

A good supplier is a company which is at all times honest and fair in its dealings with customers and employees; which has adequate plant facilities and know-how so as to provide materials which meet all the customer's specifications, in the quantities required and in the time promised; whose financial position is sound; whose prices are reasonable both to the customer and itself; whose management policies are progressive; who is alert to the need for continued improvement in both its products and manufacturing processes; and who realizes that, in the last analysis, its own interests are best served when it best serves its customers.

PREPLAN YOUR VISIT: The planning stages for a supplier plant visitation is the most important issue. **BE PREPARED.** An agenda will be prepared and distributed to the people who will make the visit. The agenda will then be sent to the supplier one week before the visit with any samples that will assist in the meeting. The agenda should include the following issues: When is the visit to take place, who will attend and who is needed to attend from the supplier's staff, what are the issues, what articles or items are needed to assist in making an agreeable action plan or corrective action, what items or areas are proprietary information or processes and what is needed to approve the viewing of these items or areas.

As you can readily see, the above explanation is just as useful to the company planning to make the visit. The manual then ends with a brief overview of the Quality System Survey and how it is scored. It is similar to the surveys found earlier in this book. A company must budget for Supplier Certification.

MASCO CORPORATION
Taylor, Michigan

Robert W. Carr
Director of Purchasing

MASCO recently held a purchasing conference to which all division purchasing professionals were invited. The purpose of this meeting was to communicate the concepts and techniques of Supply Base Management which would be required for the company to compete successfully in the future (Target 2000). In both the presentation by Vice President, Technology and Support

Services John Ullrich and the one by Bob Carr, the theme was to delineate the changes which will be necessary for purchasing executives to face. Pete Grieco's keynote address on Supplier Certification was included to pull together all the concepts which purchasing faces today in order to prosper tomorrow.

One of the slides Bob used in his presentation summarizes the company's view of suppliers:

"We can look at our suppliers as being internal suppliers, one department to another, or we can look at suppliers as outsiders. Most frequently, we look at suppliers as outsiders. Supplier networking means that we must recognize that the real benefits of the new supplier relationship comes from non-price issues. We need to recognize that the cooperative effort that you and I share has the same goals, that you as the supplier and me as the customer will both benefit. These benefits may or may not be in equal proportions. We must, however, both recognize that the cooperative relationship generates the lowest total cost, not necessarily the lowest price."

Bob then goes on to explain just what the difference between lowest total cost and lowest price really is:

"An investigation of MASCO's sources of steel revealed that twelve suppliers were being used as well as several offshore producers. Although prices were similar, there were significant differences between the suppliers. Deliveries were inconsistent and often over a week late. Freight rates varied considerably. Quality varied by division and from source to source. Supplier relationships were, at best, adversarial. In other words, a fairly typical picture which many of you can relate to.

During the timeframe of our contracts, the entire steel industry was undergoing some major changes in this country. U.S. producers were becoming smaller in size and fewer in numbers. Fifteen years ago, for example, U.S. producers had 150 million tons of capacity. Today, it is only 100 million with more reductions in capacity expected. In fact, in March of 1992, Bethlehem Steel Corp. announced that it had decided to get out of the bar, rod and wire business. In effect, they would idle two plants and part of a third.

Not all the news is bad. Less foreign steel was being purchased inside the continental U.S. at the same time that capital improvements were being directed to reduce costs and improve quality in American steelmaking companies. The result was that U.S. producers became more competitive than world producers. In fact, now, steel is one of the lowest cost raw materials. Although one might expect that prices to rise with fewer suppliers and more limited capacities, the total cost has not if we look at other factors.

When MASCO embarked on a program to consolidate sources, we were not driven only by price. We looked long-term at who we thought would be around and who was making an investment in the future. We made frequent visits to supplier's plants as well as inviting them to our plants. In essence, we began sharing infor-mation with each other and establishing partnerships. One by one, we began to eliminate sources who weren't able to join in this kind of relationship.

In 1991, we purchased 86% of our steel from four suppliers. Our largest supplier had less than 15% of our steel requirement. Today, that same supplier has 40%. In 1992, MASCO decided that they should change the entire process of selecting and awarding their steel business. The team's decision was made to stop competitive bidding. It was agreed that we should work toward long-term contracts with our suppliers. After several discussions and meetings, it was agreed that we would enter into a three-year contract with four suppliers.

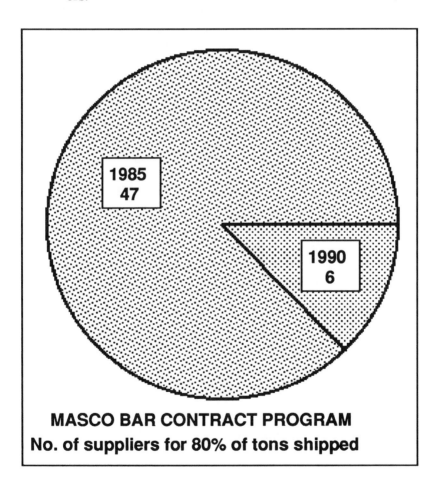

MASCO BAR CONTRACT PROGRAM
No. of suppliers for 80% of tons shipped

These agreements differed sharply from previous contracts. The terms called for a substantial reduction in product/operating costs over the three-year term. The agreements state that we will share cost savings with our partners and that they can enter our respective plants and review all operations by jobs.

This openness is a first and required the approval of confidentiality agreements by both sides. Until 1992, steel suppliers were not allowed in MASCO plants' operating areas except to view a specific problem. The new contract require us to share equally and develop a sense of trust. We have to extend our engineering and technical expertise to each other. To accomplish this task, we assigned a coordinator at each of our facilities to a team that worked with suppliers. We needed to develop, for example, methods of tracking suggestions and developing cost systems which we could rely on.

Lake Erie Screw, for instance, recently request Republic Engineered Steel to do an in-depth study of a bolt used in an automotive application. The cost implication was dramatic. The new screw eliminated several costly manufacturing steps and the total cost was significantly lower even though the price per pound for the steel to make the screw increased between 30 and 50 percent."

MASCO has aggressively extended its program of partnership into several more areas:

Natural Gas —	35 locations, 17 utilities in 10 states.
Tool Steel —	1986 supply base = 15.
	1992 supply base = 7.
Powder Coating —	11 divisions participating.
	Smaller supply base.
	25% savings.

The program in the future has plans to tackle total cost and partnership issues in the following areas:

> **Office Supplies**
> **Oils and Lubricants**
> **Corrugated Packaging**
> **Stretch and Shrink Film**
> **Waste Disposal**
> **Maintenance Chemicals and Supplies**
> **Transportation**
> **Steel Contracts**

As you can see, MASCO has started to meet the challenge of the future. We support their activity and wish to thank them for allowing us to share this information with our readers.

BROWN & WILLIAMSON TOBACCO CORP.
Macon, Georgia

C. Denise Lester
Procurement

Brown & Williamson, a Pro-Tech client, is in the early stages of Supplier Certification. Denise Lester, who has been instrumental to their program, has shared some of her insights with us about the program. In addition, Claudia McGill has been instrumental in initiating a program for all the MRO suppliers to Brown & Williamson. The following statement indicates some of the preliminary steps that the company took when first implementing the program:

> Brown & Williamson (B&W) organized a team of
> representatives from purchasing, quality, R&D,

manufacturing and finance to initiate supplier certification with our suppliers. The first task was to divide all the materials into categories. Next, we began the long, arduous process of determining and defining the criteria most important to B&W. It took months to finish that process. Then, we tackled a scoring method as well as qualification, certification and decertification requirements. At that point, the initial groups of teams and the materials for which they were responsible were selected. A one-day team training session was provided by Pro-Tech during which we realized that additional training was needed for all team members. Input from all team members also indicated that we needed to add notes to our questions to aid team members who were not part of the original team when assessing a supplier with our criteria. A second training session was then scheduled for all the team members — a two-day Supplier Certification workshop.

A month later, a supplier symposium was held for 70 suppliers from 20 different companies. Once commitment letters were signed and returned to the Director of Purchasing, we then scheduled visits to the suppliers' plants.

We learned many lessons during the process. One is to make sure that the right people are on the certification team and to fill in with expertise from other areas as required. It is also a good idea to develop a plan early in the process, sell the plan to all involved and get commitment for the resources required to make the plan successful. Since there is a logical flow to the planning and implementation process, it is important that direction be clear from the start and continue to be understandable until everyone who is involved becomes comfortable with their role.

Getting all team members comfortable with their role is a difficult task. We started by having meetings and talking through experiences that the certification team had during its first few visits to supplier. We also decided to send an experienced person with anyone who had not previously made a visit.

The B&W supplier evaluation criteria is similar to most of the examples we have already included in this book. However, their Finance section does bear showing to our readers.

FINANCE

1. **Percent of Business** — The goods and services purchased by B&W from any supplier should be less than 50% of the total value of goods and services sold by that supplier.

    a. Is the percentage of goods and services sold to B&W within the above stated policy?

2. **Financial Condition** — Preference will be given to suppliers who can demonstrate that they are financially secure and are effectively using assets to generate profits within the division servicing B&W.

    a. What is the financial stability of the supplier as determined by evaluation of following financial ratios and associated analysis of financial statements and accounting policies?

Liquidity Ratios
    Current Ratio: Current Assets/Current Liabilities
    Acid Test Ratio: (Cash + Marketable Securities +
                                     Net Receivables)/Current Liabilities

Activity Ratios
    Receivable Turnover: Net Sales/Average Net Receivables
    Inventory Turnover: Cost of Goods Sold/Average
                                     Inventory
    Asset Turnover: Net Sales/Average Total Assets

Profitability Ratios
    Profit Margin on Sales: Net Income/Net Sales
    Rate of Return on Assets: Net Income/Average Total Assets
    Rate of Return on
      Common Stock Equity: (Net Income - Preferred Dividends)/
                                     Average Common Stockholders'Equity
    Earnings per Share: (Net Income - Preferred Dividends)/
                                     Weighted Shares Outstanding
    Price Earnings Ratio: Stock's Market Price/Earnings per
                                     Share

Coverage Ratios
    Debt to Total Assets: Debt/Total Assets or Equities
    Times Interest Earned: Income before Taxes and Interest
                                     Charges/Interest Charges
    Book Value per Share: Common Stockholders' Equity/
                                       Outstanding Shares

Annual Report, 10K Report (or equivalents)
    Must include Income Statement, Balance Sheet, Cash Flow
    Statement and related notes and accounting policies.

3. **Cost Control** — The supplier should be actively involved in cost control programs and should be able to demonstrate results of these activities:

   a. To what degree can the supplier demonstrate that they are actively involved in programs to control and reduce costs in the areas of waste reduction, supplier cost control, productivity improvement, efficiency improvement, and technological advancement?

   b. To what extent does the supplier set cost standards against which operations can be meaningfully and usefully measured and to what extent do they mirror the usage, efficiency, productivity and other quality and control measures utilized in the production process?

   c. To what extent are standard and other costs allocated appropriately to the supplier's product purchased by B&W?

   d. To what extent does the supplier's Accounting staff interact with Operating staff? Is reporting of results frequent and useful?

   e. To what extent is the supplier familiar with the cost of quality?

   f. To what degree do the supplier's customers benefit from the results of cost control measures?

   g. To what extent does the supplier control lead-time costs?

    h. To what extent does the supplier effectively control raw material, intermediate material and finished goods inventories?

4. Cost Information Sharing — Cost information sharing provides mutual benefits through commitment to long term supplier relationships which protect supplier profitability while assuring B&W of acceptable costs.

    a. To what extent is the supplier willing and able to provide the components of cost?

The Supplier Certification team was responsible for developing another excellent tool in their program of continuous improvement. It is a work sheet with crib notes for the survey team to use. Below is a sample which covers compliance with government regulations at suppliers' plants:

MANAGEMENT POLICY
Compliance with Government Regulations

Compliance with Government Regulations — The supplier should be able to demonstrate that they are in compliance with all appropriate federal, state and local regulations.

    a. To what extent can the supplier demonstrate knowledge of and responsibility and accountability for federal, state and local regulations to which they are subject (Equal Employment Opportunity, Fair Labor Standards, Federal Wage and Hour Laws, American Disability Act).

Crib Notes:

1. **Affirmative Action Plan** — If a company employs more than 50 people, they must have a plan. If less than 50 people are employed, but they are a federal contractor (i.e., sell to the government), they must also have a plan. Ask to see the most recent Affirmative Action Plan (which is prepared annually). Key items to ask to see in the plan are:

   • Scope and purpose of the plan.
   • Workforce analysis (lists by job level, the makeup of workforce of minorities).
   • Goals and timetables for minority hiring.
   • Must have a statement regarding company policy relative to sexual harassment.

2. **Posting of disclosures for employees** — The employer must post several notices regarding federal policies which detail employee rights. They must be posted prominently in places where all employees would pass by them:

   • Statement of Age Discrimination.
   • Federal Wage and Hour Law.
   • Veteran Rights Poster.
   • Policy signed by plant manager or company president indicating company does not discriminate based on race, creed, religion, sex, national origin (Equal Employment Opportunity).
   • Nondiscrimination against Americans with Disabilities (effective 7/26/92).

Ask supplier to show you where these are at their facility.

3. Based on the above, evaluate degree to which supplier appears to be committed to employee rights and equal opportunity.

b. Has the supplier ever been cited for noncompliance with any regulations? If so, when and for what? Is the supplier currently in compliance?

Crib Notes:

1. Identify individuals responsible for compliance. Is this adequate?

2. Have there been any employee complaints or actions related to EEOC, Fair Labor Standards, Affirmative Action, Sexual Harassment, etc.? If yes, what was resolution?

3. What are the supplier's procedures for handling employee complaints? Are they addressed in a timely fashion?

4. Has the company ever been found at fault or cited for noncompliance with regulations?

As for the area of MRO, the team started with over 3,500 suppliers as of December 31, 1991. Six months later, the supply base had been reduced to 444. The year-end goal is to have only 300 suppliers. Congratulations are due for Claudia and her team. Chuck Dawson, Director of Purchasing, recently appointed Fred Banks as the full-time Supplier Quality Manager. In this new capacity, Fred has begun to accelerate the program even faster.

MOTOROLA, INC.
Schaumburg, Illinois

We at Pro-Tech are proud to be associated with Motorola's supply base program. As faculty members of Motorola University, we are presenting state-of-the-art purchasing and supply practices. Motorola's aggressive plan for supply base management is an excellent example for other companies to follow.

The program began in 1988 when Motorola's Chairman Bob Galvin visited both large and small suppliers of the company. He was looking for what suppliers thought about Motorola's purchasing operation and input on what they would like to see change. Most of all, he wanted to understand how to improve the company's relationship with suppliers. An article in *Industry Week* had this to say about what he saw on his trips:

> "Virtually all of our buyers are demonstrating a keen interest in, if not a total support of, the principles of partnership, and are acting as peers and partners with suppliers — and no longer acting as if the position of buyer was that of being like a god."

Such statements have made Motorola a World Class leader with an acute awareness of how to manage the supply base. Their win/win approach is widely accepted and copied and being copied is the best flattery you can receive. Today, Motorola offers a thorough program of education and training for it employees, suppliers and customers via its "university." It forms the basis for a drive that began in 1981 when Motorola set a goal of a ten-fold improvement in quality. Likewise, a six sigma mandate for both internal and external activities helped them regain the top spot in the U.S. semiconductor market. And finally, in 1991, Motorola won the Purchasing Magazine Medal of Professional Excellence Award. The reasons for their success include the following areas:

> - **Improved supply base.**
> - **Best in class practices.**
> - **Benchmarking.**
> - **Sharing information with suppliers.**
> - **Aggressive goals.**
> - **Assessing supplier performance.**
> - **Quality System Review (QSR).**

APPLICATIONS

The following section shows how the Waukesha Engine Division of Dresser Industries, Inc. and the Pepsi-Cola General Bottlers, Inc. used our services, books or videotape series to develop and implement Supplier Certification programs. We have elected to show you the brochures and pamphlets they put together for their own employees and for their suppliers' management. We want to thank the numerous other companies who also submitted brochures to us, but, due to space considerations, we elected to share the following two. We think that the quality of work and design which went into these high quality brochures is a testament to each company's commitment and understanding.

Both the Pepsi-Cola and Waukesha brochures depict a powerful demonstration, both in words and photographs, of the need for a quality partnership in order to make Supplier Certification work. It shows their determination *not* to do business as it has always been done, but to head toward a more profitable future with the company's suppliers. A key factor depicted in these brochures which cannot be overlooked is education and training. Continuous improvement is not possible without them. Those who don't keep learning will stand still and eventually wither away.

Waukesha's
Commitment To Total Quality

TO OUR VALUED SUPPLIERS:

Competition in today's world-class marketplace forces each of us to re-evaluate our respective organizations from our customers' perspectives. In our customers' opinions, do we provide quality products and services? Do our products meet or exceed our customers' requirements and expectations at a price which is competitive with other world-class manufacturers? Do our organizational cultures internally foster a commitment to Total Quality which is consistent with the expectations of our customers?

Today, more than ever before, our customers base their procurement decisions on the quality and value of the products and services available in the marketplace. Thus, our efforts must continuously focus on the customer and his perception of value. Customer satisfaction requires us to provide a value-to-price ratio for each of our products which is equal or superior to that of our world-class competition. At the same time, our stockholders require us to produce products with an above-average value-to-cost ratio, to achieve superior financial performance. To meet these challenges, the management of Waukesha Engine has rededicated itself to a consistent management strategy of TOTAL QUALITY MANAGEMENT which creates value - for our customers, our employees, and our stockholders.

In today's highly competitive, global markets, the imperative for a value creation is managing our operations to achieve Total Quality in everything we do. Traditionally, Total Quality has been defined as "meeting requirements without error". This approach, often called Zero Defects or Error-Free Performance, can be paraphrased as "Doing Things Right The First Time". From Waukesha's perspective, however, Total Quality has taken on a broader definition: "Total Quality Is Performance Leadership In Meeting Customer Requirements By Doing The Right Things Right The First Time". In other words, concentration on the fundamentals of manufacturing and procuring quality components and materials with which to produce our products. It's that basic.

This booklet has been developed with that concept in mind. It explains Waukesha's outlook on quality, and what we expect of our suppliers relative to same. Hopefully, it will answer many of the questions you may have regarding Waukesha's Total Quality Management System and Supplier Certification Program. We recognize that our success depends heavily on the relationship we share with each of our suppliers. Our program have, therefore, been structured to enable our suppliers to share in the benefits realized by reducing the risks, costs, and problems associated with poor quality and late delivery.

We look forward to the challenges and opportunities facing us in the world market, and to the rewards to be gained for Waukesha and its suppliers, our partners in quality.

Peter C. Trombley, President
Waukesha Engine Division
Dresser Industries, Inc.

A Supplier's Guide To Doing Business With Waukesha Engine

INTRODUCTION

Products change. Markets change. Industries change. As the world markets expand, new demands and challenges force us to re-evaluate the way we manage our operations. Our products must offer our customers the maximum value available at a competitive cost. Quality has become the standard. No longer will the customer accept less than excellence in products or services.

To meet those challenges, WAUKESHA ENGINE, a world-class manufacturer of industrial engine systems, has adopted a system of TOTAL QUALITY MANAGEMENT. This booklet explains that system and the requirements it places on Waukesha Engine and its suppliers.

As partners in quality, we share a common goal... To enhance the value of our products and, thereby, ensure our place in the global markets of tomorrow.

3

Waukesha Engine – From A Machine Shop To A Modern Production Facility

1906 – THE COMPANY WAS FOUNDED

In 1906, the Waukesha Motor Co. was started in a small garage making boat engines for use on nearby resort lakes. The reputation of those engines for reliability and performance spread rapidly, creating demand for the product in other applications. By 1911, business had expanded to the point where additional manufacturing space was needed. The company was thus moved to a new site located where the present plant now stands.

THE EARLY 1900'S

The early 1900's saw the growth and expansion of the company into air compressor drives, engines for portable hoists, excavating equipment, and pumps. With the onslaught of World War I, Waukesha entered into the production of army transport truck and farm tractor engines. Later, Waukesha engines were used for construction equipment, oil rigs and big timber operations, both domestically and abroad.

THE 1930'S

In 1936, the Company introduced the Refrigerator Division, later changed to the Railway Division. They also started building engine-driven air conditioning units for railway passenger cars. Before long, these and Waukesha engine-driven electric generating units, were in use on most major railway lines.

THE 1940'S

In World War II, Waukesha Motor Company production was again mobilized for the country's Armed Services. Waukesha engines were put to work in every part of the world.

This rugged service accelerated the development of new design features, fields of application and proved, again, the reliability and long life of Waukesha-built engines and power units.

WAUKESHA – TODAY

From the experience gained in the 1930's and 1940's, Waukesha engineers developed their first big-bore methane engine, the forerunner of today's VHP. Since then, Waukesha has steadily advanced the state of gas engine technology.

Today, Waukesha's large spark-ignited engines are the most cost effective and environmentally compatible drivers for a variety of petroleum, municipal and power generation/cogeneration applications requiring continuous duty output from 30 to 3500kW.

4

Waukesha's Supplier Selection Criteria

Our emphasis is on selecting suppliers who have both the CAPABILITY and the INTEREST to become certified suppliers for Waukesha. This means the supplier must be dedicated to the principle of CONTINUOUS QUALITY IMPROVEMENT. Selection of the Division's suppliers is based upon the following criteria:

CAPABILITIES
1. Type, age, condition, and suitability of equipment to Waukesha products.
2. Available capacity vs booked business.
3. Long-term vs short-term interest in Waukesha business.
4. Industries and customers currently served... References.
5. Source of supply of raw materials and under what terms.
6. Process controls (SPC) for parts and tooling.
7. Inspection equipment and procedures (documented).
8. Material handling equipment and methods.
9. Packaging equipment and methods.

FINANCIALS
1. Length of time company has been in business.
2. Financial stability... Asset ratio, debt ratio (long and short term), cash flow, profitability.

MANAGEMENT COMMITMENT
1. Preventive maintenance program in place (documented).
2. Quality program in place (documented).
3. Company quality statement.
4. Employee involvement programs.
5. Business plan (one to five years).
6. SPC program... Active/documented/understood by employees.
7. Cost reduction programs/value analysis.
8. Subcontracting policy and environmental policy/controls (i.e., EPA compliance, hazardous waste disposal, etc.).
9. ETHICS

LABOR CONDITIONS
1. Union or non-union operation.
2. Contract expiration date.
3. History of labor disputes.
4. Employee training programs used.
5. Management's philosophy regarding employees.

DEDICATION TO QUALITY
1. Formal quality system in place (documented).
2. Employees aware of company's position regarding quality (a written policy statement exist and is posted for employees and customers to review).
3. Experience as a certified supplier for other customers (who and under what terms/ measurement criteria).
4. Essence of company's supplier certification program (criteria used and how they are measured).

6

Waukesha's Purchasing Department - Your Primary Contact

Waukesha's Purchasing Department, and the buyer you deal with regularly, will be your primary contact regarding purchase order releases, payment of invoices, and quality issues. Your buyer will introduce you to the appropriate people within Waukesha and will act as your guide to ensure that your business dealings are handled to your satisfaction.

In today's competitive business environment, the timely flow of accurate information is essential. As a valued member of the "Waukesha Team", you can expect to receive all relevant information necessary to assist you in meeting the quality, delivery, and pricing requirements placed on you by Waukesha. The Purchasing Department has been organized by commodity to assist you in accessing the appropriate buyer quickly to obtain answers to your questions.

In the event you are unfamiliar with Waukesha Engine, and have questions regarding our procurement requirements, please direct your initial call to the main department number: 414-549-2845. Your call will then be forwarded to the appropriate buyer.

Waukesha's Supplier Quality Assurance Department - There To Assist You

THE ORGANIZATION

Waukesha's Supplier Quality Assurance Department reports to the Division's Quality Assurance Manager. Structured to provide the maximum supplier support, department personnel are assigned to one of three specific industry segments, thereby providing specific expertise to the resolution of problems encountered by each of the Division's suppliers. The goal of Waukesha's Quality Engineers is to provide assistance to the Division's suppliers regarding quality and supplier certification, quality planning, and clarification of product and print requirements.

PRIMARY RESPONSIBILITIES

* Provide technical support to the Division's suppliers.
* Conduct supplier surveys.
* Conduct quality audits.
* Evaluate and report supplier quality performance and recommend certification.
* Assist the Division's suppliers in their quality planning.
* Assist the Division's suppliers in their corrective action planning.

5

Waukesha's
Supplier Certification Criteria

The adoption of our Total Quality Management System has forced us to critically analyze how we manage our business, our internal manufacturing operations and the requirements we place upon our suppliers. As you read through this section, you will notice that the certification criteria (incoming quality level, on-time delivery, count accuracy, and competitive pricing) become increasingly stringent over the course of the next five years. Our objective is to achieve a level of Total Quality consistent with the criteria established for the much-coveted Malcolm Baldridge Award for world class quality... Zero defects, 100 percent on-time delivery, and 100 percent count accuracy. The attainment of that objective will require a program of continuous improvement from our employees and our suppliers. It is only through such a program that we can assure our competitive edge in a global market, today and in the future.

QUALITY

Without quality, there is no market for the products we sell. Quality is, therefore, the primary criterion used by Waukesha in the selection and certification of our suppliers.

As shown by the chart at the top of page 9, on a quarterly basis we tabulate the total number of rejects from a given supplier versus the total quantity of parts received from that supplier in said period. The reject rate is then derived and graphed for presentation to the applicable supplier. To become certified, a supplier must achieve and maintain an incoming acceptance rate equivalent to that illustrated by the chart on the bottom of page 9. In addition, we require all of our suppliers to complete our Quality System Survey, and to update same should a change in their operations occur. We require outgoing inspection certification on each lot of material shipped to Waukesha, and we require a Corrective Action Sheet covering the actions taken should a defect occur.

Material received from our Certified Suppliers will be coded "no inspection", but will be audited annually for compliance. We expect our suppliers to provide defect-free products to Waukesha, just as our customers look to us for defect-free engines and parts.

Supplier Quality Assurance
System Survey Report

8

PRICING

1. Delivered cost compared to other suppliers' pricing for the same product/service.
2. Supplier's previous pricing history/policy.
3. Commitment to price reductions/value analysis/cost savings over a defined period.
4. Supplier's position relative to long-term price agreements/consignment programs/JIT deliveries/quantity pricing.

LOGISTICS

1. Ready access to primary transportation arteries (air/truck/rail/port).
2. Availability of an in-house fleet.
3. Typical mode of delivery and typical timing.

SUPPORT

1. Knowledge of supplier's sales representative relative to Waukesha-type products and requirements.
2. Competency of supplier's technical staff and availability to assist Waukesha manufacturing.
3. Supplier's responsiveness to requests for information and/or assistance (at all levels within the operation).

AFTERMARKET PHILOSOPHY

1. Receptiveness to a non-compete contract which guarantees Waukesha Engine's exclusive right to market its products to aftermarket customers and distribution channels.

Waukesha's
Purchases By Product Class

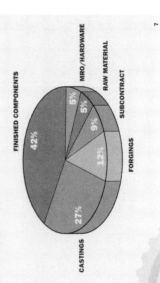

- FINISHED COMPONENTS 42%
- CASTINGS 27%
- FORGINGS 12%
- SUBCONTRACT 9%
- RAW MATERIAL 5%
- MRO/HARDWARE 5%

7

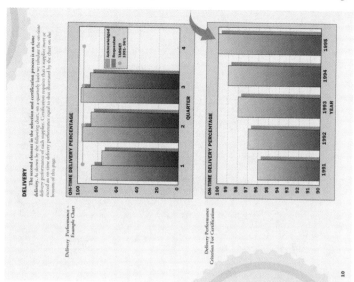

DELIVERY

The second element in the selection and certification process is on-time delivery. As shown by the following chart, on a quarterly basis we tabulate the on-time delivery performance of each supplier. Certification requires that a supplier meet or exceed an on-time delivery performance equal to that illustrated by the chart on the bottom of this page.

Delivery Performance – Example Chart

Delivery Performance Criterion For Certification

10

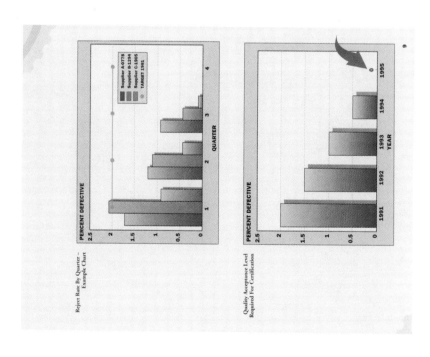

Reject Rate By Quarter – Example Chart

Quality Acceptance Level Required For Certification

9

Our thanks to each of you, our valued suppliers, for your support, assistance, and dedication to the principles of total quality management. With your help, our future as a world-class manufacturer of industrial engine systems will be ensured.

The Employees and Management
Waukesha Engine Division
Dresser Industries, Inc.

Waukesha **DRESSER**

This publication has been entirely printed on recycled paper.

In making the calculation, we consider the supplier's established lead-times. Obviously, we cannot and do not expect our suppliers to respond to short lead-time orders with the same level of performance as those given with adequate notification. We do, however, expect our suppliers to meet or better the delivery dates they acknowledge. It is against those acknowledged delivery schedules that we measure our suppliers.

Unless otherwise specified, the delivery date designated on Waukesha's purchase orders reflects the requested date of delivery at Waukesha, NOT the requested ship date of the product. It is incumbent upon each of our suppliers to ensure that delivery commitment is met. It is also incumbent upon each of our suppliers to hold their published lead-times to a minimum to keep our joint inventory investment small.

PRICE

Competitive pricing of Waukesha products to and through the distribution channel is a key element to our future success. In order to meet that criterion, it is essential that we maintain stringent controls over our product cost. To do so, we must control our internal manufacturing costs, overhead, and the cost of the materials and components we purchase directly from our suppliers.

We look to our suppliers to provide products that meet or exceed Waukesha's design specifications at prices which are competitive. We recognize, however, that design and tolerances do impact cost. As such, we are always open to suggestions regarding how we might alter the design to reduce the cost without sacrificing design integrity. Relative to same, we invite our suppliers to take part in our design review process to assist us in the classification of design characteristics. We rely on the supplier's expertise in their respective industries and welcome their valued input as we embark upon the design of new products and enhancements to existing components.

In Summary

A certified supplier for Waukesha Engine is one who:

1. Provides defect free products.
2. Provides those quality products on time, every time.
3. Provides complete accuracy in quantity.
4. Offers competitive pricing.

Quality, on-time delivery, count accuracy and competitive pricing...all are key ingredients in the formulation and maintenance of a successful supplier certification program. They are also the cornerstones of Waukesha's TOTAL QUALITY MANAGEMENT SYSTEM.

We invite you to join us in our PARTNERSHIP IN EXCELLENCE.

11

Our Commitment to Excellence

MISSION STATEMENT

It is the goal of Pepsi-Cola General Bottlers to achieve the status of being the premier soft drink company in every market in which we do business. We will accomplish this by:

- providing the finest soft drink products and services to our customers,

- embracing the concept of continuous improvement

    - and most importantly -

- involving all of our employees and suppliers in these efforts.

Partners in Quality

Pepsi-Cola General Bottlers, Inc.

A Whitman Company

PEPSI

Pepsi-Cola General Bottlers and strives to continually improve upon that quality over the duration of our relationship.

It is our aim to provide you with feedback on your products and to support your efforts to continuously improve.

We expect the fostering of open communications between PCGB and our independent suppliers will yield mutual benefits in the form of cost savings, increased profits and the development of long-term relationships.

As you will see, this Supplier Certification Program is an integral part of our company wide quality effort. The following pages describe how the program works.

"In the race for quality, there is no finish line."

If the eighties was the decade when America became quality conscious, then the nineties must prove to be the decade when American business makes continuous quality improvement a way of life. No company is exempt. No department within any company can sit this one out. It's going to mean changes, but those already involved in the quality revolution are finding this new mission stimulating, positive and exciting.

At Pepsi-Cola General Bottlers (PCGB), we're proud to be among the first major soft drink producers to launch a comprehensive, company-wide quality initiative. This initiative will reach out to include our business *partners*, the suppliers who provide products and services to our company, as well as all of our employees.

Beginning in 1989, we started sending every member of our management team to *Continuous Improvement* courses and *Total Quality Management* seminars. Today, these training programs continue, reaching out to PCGB employees.

They're exposed to the basic concepts of continuous improvement, total quality management, teamwork, brainstorming, and statistical process control (SPC). Like quality improvement itself, this kind of training is never ending.

Some of our current suppliers have already joined us in our mission to pursue excellence. They have agreed to cooperate with us in the perpetual process of improving quality. In the future, we expect all of our suppliers to become certified. It's a meaningful process that will help everyone involved.

To launch the supplier certification program, our Quality Steering Committee has drafted the following statement of purpose:

Pepsi-Cola General Bottlers has embarked upon a quality initiative in order to achieve the status of a best-in-class producer and distributor of soft drink products through the efforts of all its employees and suppliers.

This quality initiative is nothing short of a total commitment by our management and all our employees to total customer satisfaction through training and continuous improvement in all areas of our business.

To underscore our commitment, the company has established a Quality Council consisting of top management, including the President, to insure that the company does not lose sight of its mission. In addition, continuous training in the concepts of Total Quality Management will be given to all PCGB employees. Training and education of all our employees are the cornerstones of Total Quality.

A new era and partnership between you, our suppliers, and Pepsi-Cola General Bottlers has begun. The company realizes that our suppliers contribute significantly to the quality of our products and services. Therefore, our goal is to be selective in choosing only outstanding suppliers.

Our decisions will be based on quality of product and service as well as cost. The partnership that develops will be built on mutual respect, courtesy and fairness.

As a supplier, your goal is to provide a level of quality that meets the needs and expectations of

Supplier Certification Program: Becoming Certified

Performance Expectations. For suppliers to be certified under this program, they must meet or exceed expectations established by Pepsi-Cola General Bottlers for specific characteristics. These criteria were developed over time based on our own experiences as well as lengthy discussions with our current suppliers.

Although we're confident that these expectations are achievable, we frankly hope that they're not *easy* to meet. Remember, our objective is to be the best.

Survey and Evaluation. Each supplier must receive a favorable Supplier Visit Report completed by Pepsi-Cola General Bottlers personnel as well as favorable subsequent performance evaluations.

Neither the first visit nor the subsequent return visits will be "surprise inspections." Our goal is to foster a feeling of *partnership* between our suppliers and ourselves. So we'll announce, in advance, when we're coming, who's coming, what we're looking for and with whom we'd like to meet.

Quality Certification Checklist:

☐ Must meet minimum PCGB quality expectations.

☐ Must receive favorable initial evaluation.

☐ Must receive favorable subsequent evaluations (where appropriate).

Supplier Certification Program: Working Together

Supplier Quality Plan. All suppliers should be familiar with the principles of statistical process control and be able to document their efforts thoroughly. When we evaluate our suppliers, we will be observing whether they've developed a flow chart of the production process showing all quality-related procedures. We will also observe whether they identify each operation selected for SPC data collection and analysis.

SPC records must be maintained on every lot, run or batch produced. We expect our suppliers to review this data constantly, always searching for trends and indicators that might help them learn more about their process, always alert to identify new ways of improving quality.

Naturally, we expect our suppliers to maintain a system for eliminating out-of-control or out-of-specification products.

Documentation. For our quality initiative to succeed, each supplier must maintain statistical data for a minimum of two years and be willing to provide these records to Pepsi-Cola General Bottlers upon request.

Quality Certification Checklist:

☐ Provide a production flowchart showing quality procedures.
☐ Maintain SPC records for a minimum of two years.
☐ Constantly review SPC data looking for ways to improve.
☐ Provide PCGB with historical data upon request.

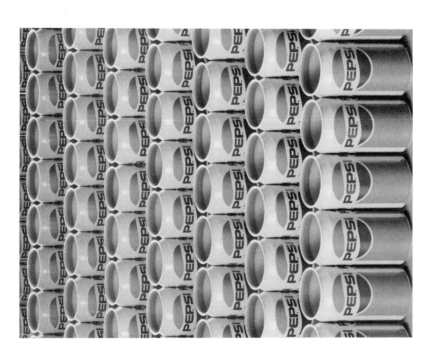

Supplier Certification Program: Our Future Together

After Certification Is Established. We'll come to the supplier's location and make a formal presentation of certification. Some suppliers will want to take photos of the event for their own public relations purposes, and that's fine with us.

We hope you'll agree that this program is both positive and exciting. It holds out the hope of cost savings and increased profits for both of us. What's more, it should encourage and promote continuous improvements in quality, innovation and creativity.

Yet the biggest reason for launching a program like this is perhaps the simplest motive of all. Everyone in the business world, whether a manager or an employee *or the consumer who buys our product*, finds personal satisfaction in the simple old-fashioned notion of a job well done.

Quality Certification Checklist:

☐ Formal presentation will be made.
☐ Philosophy of continuous improvement is at the heart of the program.
☐ Personal satisfaction for everyone involved.

A Quality *Partnership*

No company can achieve the goal of producing a quality product entirely on its own. At Pepsi-Cola General Bottlers, we're not afraid to admit that we need the help of every company with which we do business. We rely upon our suppliers to give us the best possible quality.

We're determined to create a feeling of *partnership* between ourselves and our suppliers by getting rid of, as much as possible, any feeling that we're working on different teams. Already, we've formed several PCGB quality advisory teams with members who are *not* on our payroll. They're employed by our suppliers, but provide us with invaluable input concerning ways we can improve our performance.

To further enhance the spirit of a quality *partnership*, we're designating all of our certified suppliers as *Quality Partners*. We will award them plaques and other items bearing the *Quality Partner* identification. We will conduct seminars at their place of business to help their employees better understand issues which are important to PCGB. And yes, we hope we'll be invited to sit on some of *their* quality teams, too.

For many employees, at both PCGB and the companies who supply us with necessary goods and services, this is a new way of doing business. But we're confident that it will help us all to realize our goals more efficiently. After all, quality products come from quality *partnerships*.

Pepsi-Cola General Bottlers, Inc.
3501 Algonquin Road
Rolling Meadows, IL 60008

© 1991

A Message from the President

There's a lot of talk these days about the awakening of American business to the need for a quality revolution. But the fact is, in a country that was once admired throughout the world marketplace for the quality of its goods and services, many people never lost their dedication to the concepts of excellence. It's just that their voices got drowned out by the raucous clamor for some of the less important, short term and short-sighted goals of business.

Thankfully, that era is coming to an end. Even the most success-driven businesses are recognizing that the best way to achieve a healthy bottom line is to focus on higher ideals. Improving quality is the best way to cut costs. It's the most dramatic way to increase profits. And it's the easiest way to increase sales. Suddenly, the voices of those who preach quality are once again being heard in the board rooms of business, much to the delight of the ultimate determiner of our economic health – the consumer.

At Pepsi-Cola General Bottlers, we're delighted at this turn of events, because we see it as an opportunity to more fully accomplish the goals we've held high for years. And now, with our new *Quality Initiative*, a momentum has developed that's unstoppable. You've read about it in our mission statement. Hopefully this brochure has clarified some of the details of how our suppliers will help us to accomplish it. In *partnership* with all of our employees and every one of our suppliers, we're going to succeed in our goal "to achieve the status of being the premier soft drink company in every market in which we do business."

Sincerely,

G. A. McGuire
President

NEWSLETTERS

Newsletters are an important concept in Supplier Certification programs. In this section, we have included some of our client's internal newsletters. The articles deal with Supplier Certification programs or with programs in support of the certification process. They are a good indication of what the people at these companies think and how the program is implemented. Lastly, they are also excellent examples of how the company can communicate with its people through informative discussions of events happening around the facility.

KRAFT GENERAL FOODS
Dover, Delaware

The Ingredient Line

Q. U. E. S. T.

You've heard about Q.U.E.S.T. ...
You've seen Q.U.E.S.T. signs ...
You've even seen co-workers attend
                    Q.U.E.S.T. meetings ...

                but

What is Q.U.E.S.T.??
How is Q.U.E.S.T.??
When is Q.U.E.S.T.??
Where is Q.U.E.S.T.??
Why Q.U.E.S.T.??
Who is Q.U.E.S.T.??

Q.U.E.S.T. is a process by which you involve the entire workforce to continually reduce waste.

Q.U.E.S.T. utilizes teams to solve the problems that prevent us from doing our jobs right the first time.

Q.U.E.S.T. is every day. Each day we must try to solve one problem. Each small step leads us further up the road to success.

Q.U.E.S.T. is everywhere. The opportunity for improvements is all around us.

Q.U.E.S.T. is important because you know your job and the opportunities for improvement better than anyone. Your ideas are important to our success.

Q.U.E.S.T. is you and Q.U.E.S.T. is me. We each have a responsibility to make this plant a better place.

Watch for improvement opportunities. Share your ideas. Become involved. We all have a responsibility to ourselves and those around us ... to "QUEST" to be the best ... that we can be.

"Supply Chain Fever" spreads in Dover

A new word for the new year — "Supply Chain" has been added to the growing vocabulary at the Dover Plant. What is this "Supply Chain" and how does it work?

Supply Chain is the culmination of JIT, Q.U.E.S.T. and Total Quality Management. Supply Chain is an intensive study into the business unit — from the accuracy of a sales forecast to proper and efficient manufacturing processes and finally moving the right product to the right place at the right time.

Dover's focus in the Supply Chain study is manufacturing. We are studying the causes of line downtime, and taking corrective action to increase uptime. We need to increase line efficiencies and line reliability — which is producing the product when it is scheduled. All of these pieces, when put together, will make the department and the plant a world class manufacturer.

The Supply Chain began in Stove Top and now covers most of the product lines in the plant. Most recently, Supply Chain has begun in Rice and Desserts. It is our plan that the entire plant will someday be operating this way. Look for Supply Chain to begin in a department near you soon!

GERBER PRODUCTS COMPANY
Fort Smith, Indiana

Bridges: Quality for Tomorrow Created Today

Supplier Certification an Important Ingredient for Product Quality

by Greg Winters, training coordinator/facilitator

Finished product quality at Gerber is dependent on four things:

- **a well-educated, top-notch workforce;**
- **clean, well-maintained, efficient equipment;**
- **high-quality ingredients;**
- **well-documented manufacturing and processing methods.**

All four of these items are important. If any one of these pieces is missing, our product quality suffers.

All of these items are controllable in-house, except for the ingredients. That is why the Fort Smith plant is getting involved with Supplier Certification. In order to understand Supplier Certification, we must first understand what quality means. Quality is getting what you need, in the quantities you need, when you need it, at a cost that is agreeable and profitable to both sides.

So, a Certified Supplier is the supplier who *can* provide us what we need, when we need it, at a profitable price. In other words, it is the supplier who provides us with quality ingredients — whether it's fiber or a bag of flour. All ingredients must be fit for our use when they arrive — without inspection.

It is, indeed, a monumental task to find such a supplier who meets our requirements, but it is a task we cannot afford *not* to do.

We began our Supplier Certification program in March 1991 when a supplier certification consultant from Pro-Tech, visited the Fort Smith plant for two days.

Fort Smith Team Selects First Contacts for Supplier Certification

by Greg Winters, training coordinator/facilitator

The quest for constant quality improvement continues at Gerber. In March, the Fort Smith Supplier Certification program began. Four suppliers were selected as the first contacts. They were a fiber supplier, a cereal carton supplier, a label supplier, and a yogurt supplier.

Four corresponding commodity teams were formed to work with the selected suppliers through the new certification program. Consisting of both salaried and hourly employees, the teams are:

THE FIBER TEAM
THE LABEL TEAM
THE CEREAL CARTON TEAM
THE YOGURT TEAM

These teams will be involved in extensive education. The certification process will not happen quickly. True trust and open communication between supplier and the teams will take time. The rewards of Supplier Certification will be a better relationship between our suppliers and us, quality in all our ingredients, employee involvement, and empowerment! GOOD LUCK, TEAMS!!!

BARR LABORATORIES, INC.
Barr News Capsule: The Employee's Newsletter

WORLD CLASS MANUFACTURING (WCM)
What is the Future for Barr ...

About 25 years ago, Toyota Motor of Japan began a program of continuous improvement of its company. The plan was to have every employee make daily improvements in the way things were done. It began with *housekeeping!* For many years, they worked on having a place for everything, and everything in its place. Once housekeeping was under control, they began to branch out into what are today the major areas of World Class Manufacturing (WCM).

WCM has been described different ways, depending on the company, but our definition at Barr Laboratories is as follows:

---

1. **Employee Involvement** — Teams of employees working on problems in their areas of expertise.

2. **Total Quality Control** — Supplier Certification and Statistical Process Control.

3. **Just-In-Time** — Certain techniques of managing the manufacturing process such as KANBAN, ANDON, pull system vs. push, etc.

Supplier Certification II

Employee Involvement

It is our goal to have every Barr employee on a team working to solve problems in their work area. One year ago, we had no employees on such a team. Today, we have approximately 90 people involved in teams. Some of their work is now being implemented with great results. The new look of this newspaper, for example, comes from one of the teams.

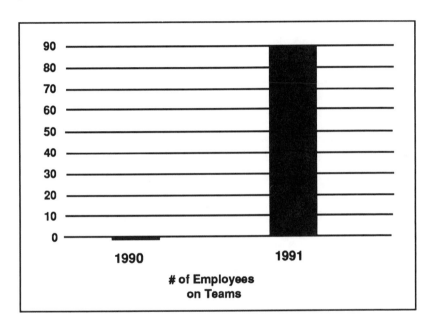

# of Employees on Teams

Total Quality Control

Total Quality Control is a bit more difficult. It has to do with the notion of zero defects. We want to increase our ability to make things absolutely correct the first time. This requires an enormous effort. First, we must study our processes to see why they vary. A small team of 10 people has begun this work.

Second, we must study our raw materials and with that the processes of our suppliers. This part of the WCM program is called **Supplier Certification.** We will eventually certify that each supplier can produce our raw material according to our specifications.

Our major measurement for this effort will be *the number of batches passed first time*. This means nothing has to be done; no retests, resampling, etc. The data for this measurement has been completed and looks like this:

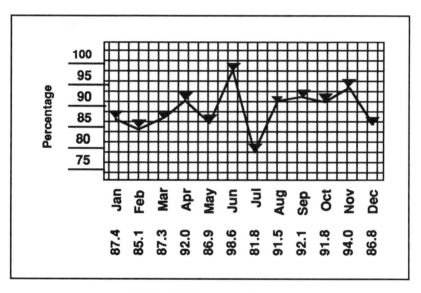

FIRST TEST RELEASE

Just-In-Time

Just-In-Time is a phrase used to describe a different method of manufacturing using small lots produced only when needed. We are used to the concept of producing the largest lot or the longest run. This concept of long runs had to do with amortizing the set-up cost over a larger number of units. Today, as our Barr teams work to reduce set-up times (52% reduction on Machine 16, for example), the length of the run can be reduced because the changeover is getting shorter and easier. For each reduction of one-half in the lot size, the average inventory required to keep the same service levels drops by one-half. To do more lots, however, means we have to improve the quality so there are no rejects and we have to become very efficient in the laboratory or we will be swamped by more testing.

When we analyze the basic elements of World Class Manufacturing, what we find, at its very heart, are our people. Do we have the people at Barr to support such an enormous effort? The answer is an unqualified *yes!* Will we become, if we are successful at WCM, the best pharmaceutical manufacturer in the world? The answer is an unqualified *yes!*

COSMAIR, INC.
Piscataway, NJ

Liaison de Lancôme

DEPARTMENT UPDATE

BY: Les Horowitz
JIT Purchasing

JIT Purchasing involves everyone in Piscataway, including the purchasing group, accounting, engineering, quality control and the line operators, says Pat Cafaro, Piscataway's Director of Purchasing.

With a team that consists of people from Purchasing, Traffic, and Supplier Certification, Pat's group is responsible for bringing JIT to the purchasing function. The most important part to any JIT program is to make sure we get top quality from our suppliers.

"Once we get quality," says Pat, "we can concentrate on the other aspects of JIT such as smaller delivery quantities and reducing inventory."

A good example of this is the work being done with Bridgeport Metal Goods, including different size caps in the same carton and bottles that were decorated poorly.

A group from Piscataway, that included operators and members of the Quality Team, met with Bridgeport representatives and hashed out all of the problems we had been having, plus, how we were being affected by these problems. Once Bridgeport understood our problems, they worked with us to correct these defects.

Pat says Bridgeport is not perfect and they are not a certified supplier yet, but there is enough improvement so that we can go on to other aspects of JIT. By the end of the first quarter we should be on JIT with the Immencil line. The intention is to bring in enough components for one week's production. There should be nothing stored in the Warehouse. Details still to be worked out include finding a trucker that can stick to this delivery schedule and deciding how, and where, to unload the truck (will it be the dock or directly in the Makeup garage?) Once this program is established, the other Makeup lines will be on a JIT basis, "always with an eye on quality," states Pat.

Treatment has also started on a JIT program that consists of supplier Make and Hold. The supplier keeps a certain amount of component inventory and releases it as it is needed in Piscataway.

Pat believes that JIT will be achieved in Piscataway because of the dedication of the people here.

"It takes a lot of teamwork and all areas of the plant have been very cooperative. Our suppliers have been very impressed with our World Class Manufacturing efforts," states Pat.

"A key term to remember," says Pat, "is continuous improvement. Look where we are now and what has been accomplished in the last 6-12 months. There will always be problems, but today we are doing a better job of solving them."

BAXTER HEALTHCARE CORPORATION
Irvine, California

Quality Leader

Paramax Introduces
Zone Manufacturing Concept

The Zone system for production was one of the most significant improvements for the Paramax Systems Division (PSD) in the past year. The principles of Quality Leadership enabled management and production employees to tackle the challenges that faced them as they began the awesome task of changing the entire manufacturing layout.

Zone Concept Explained

A Zone is an independent, self-managed team, that is responsible for completing specific Paramax manufacturing processes.

Each Zone team is composed of representatives from various departments whose primary purpose is to achieve conformance to requirements in all customer/supplier relationships.

Zone Prototype

The Planning Team played a key role in the implementation of the Zone concept. This team consisted of representatives from each functional area that would be included on a Zone team. Their charter was to develop the requirements and the timetable for implementation. They ensured consistency between Zones and worked on Zone-to-Zone issues such as the overall floor layout, bill of material configuration, measurements, and the device history record.

In the meantime, the Planning Team took the Transport Plant, one of the most complex assemblies, and developed a prototype of the Flow Manufacturing Process, with the help of a consulting group — Professionals for Technology Associates, Inc. (Pro-Tech).

As the planning evolved, one Zone team was created to work on the detail and was identified as the model for other teams. As Vice President of Manufacturing Steve Barbato recalled, "We used the first evolution of Zone One to see what the issues, dynamics, and concerns were."

To be certain they were on the right track, the team used the services of Peter Grieco of Pro-Tech to make the plans feasible. Pro-Tech helped the teams work out the dynamics of the people working together on the floor by identifying problems and by helping each team manage its business segments.

Improving Internal Customer-Supplier Relationships

The Zones were established with the vision that each Zone would operate as both a customer and supplier to the other Zones, and have control of all components that make up those subassemblies. This autonomy put the Zone team in a better position to identify the real problems.

Any problem with a subassembly could now be focused to a particular Zone. The Zone would then be involved and would help assess and resolve the problem as shown in the figure on the opposite page.

Having the responsibility for one complete subassembly revealed some interesting situations that existed with the old method of assembly. Vice President Steve Barbato recalled, "In one incident, we found different requirements for one subassembly. The requirements where we built the subassembly were different than the requirements needed to functionally test Analyzers. The subassembly was built to tight tolerances in one Zone, but then dismantled for testing and reassembled to different requirements in another Zone." This led to the recognition of a need to improve internal Customer/Supplier relationships.

While Paramax management was implementing the Supplier

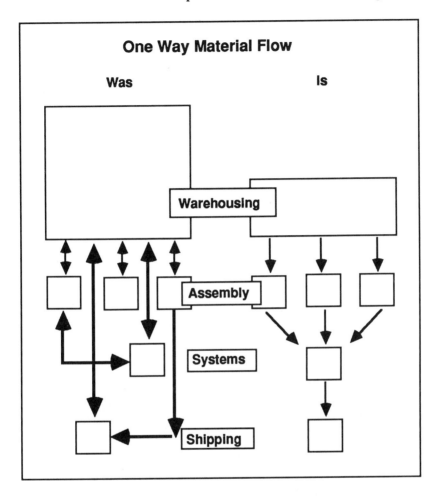

Certification Program to their external suppliers, recalled
former Director of Materials, Bob Wielenga, "we were trying
to foster that same relationship between the Zones on the
manufacturing floor. Each Zone has customers and they are
also suppliers. We should be operating the same way we expect
our suppliers to operate. In fact, we should be the model of
how we expect our suppliers to operate."

AGI INCORPORATED
Chicago, Illinois

Continuous Improvement Focus

The purpose of this publication is to provide you with a report of the activities and accomplishments of AGI's Continuous Improvement Program.

Almost two years ago, we began our involvement in this program by providing training in Statistical Process Control to over 100 of our employees. Any of our activities can be defined as a process. We start with input such as raw materials; we perform an operation such as printing; and we end up with output such as a printed sheet. Statistical Process Control (SPC) measures our output against a predefined standard (specification) and identifies variation in our process. Then it is up to us to find and correct the source of that variation. SPC can be used in any of our departments: sheeting, printing, die cutting, accounting, sales, etc. But SPC is only one element of our program here at AGI.

Our theme and our program's identification is Continuous Improvement. This means that what we are doing today, we can do better tomorrow. By working toward this end we will be able to sustain our growth by being a better supplier to our customers. This will enable us to compete more effectively in our markets and attract more business. In turn this creates a more secure future for us all, more opportunities for individual advancement, working capital for investment in state of the art equipment and facilities, and money for wage and salary increases.

Continuous Improvement at AGI is measured by:

---

1) The attainment of 100% quality.

2) An improvement in overall efficiency.

3) A substantial reduction in waste.

4) An increase in Customer Satisfaction.

Our aim is to be the best supplier in the world to the markets we serve. Make no mistake about it — AGI is a top quality supplier of packaging now. But we can be even better!

Note: AGI is a certified supplier to numerous customers.

INTERNATIONAL TOTALIZATOR SYSTEMS, INC.
Carlsbad, CA

ITS BARCODE READER

Just-In-Time

As you are probably aware, the company has retained the services of Pro-Tech to train our employees in the application of Just-In-Time (JIT) manufacturing techniques. This program begins with the establishment of work teams that are then tasked with various business problems. The teams meet and, utilizing the brainstorming and problem-solving techniques taught by Pro-Tech instructors, set out to solve a variety of problems. The process is expected to yield both short and long range benefits for ITS, not the least of which is a heightened sense of employee participation and an enriched working experience for all those involved. The company anticipates that the time and energy invested in the JIT program will prove to be a sound business decision and will return our investment many times over. Let's all keep the level of enthusiasm high for JIT.

MILLER ELECTRIC MANUFACTURING COMPANY
Appleton, Wisconsin

A FIRST:
MILLER SUPPLIER CERTIFICATION AWARDED TO FURNAS

In ceremonies at Osceola, Iowa on September 13, the Furnas Electric Company became the first firm to receive the Miller Supplier Certification award.

All 300 employees were in attendance. Officials and certification team members of Miller Electric and Furnas Electric participated in the program.

In presenting the plaque, Ken Booher, Miller Chief Operating Officer, said, "One of the most important aspects of Total

Miller Quality, or TMQ, is working closely with our suppliers to assure that all parts and components that we use in the manufacture of our products are of the finest quality and reliability. To establish better partnerships with our suppliers, and to provide the assurance that we do get 100% quality, 100% on-time delivery, and 100% correct quantities, we have instituted the Supplier Certification Process at Miller Electric.

"On behalf of all of the employees of Miller Electric, we are proud to present this plaque to the Osceola employees of Furnas Electric. You are our first supplier to achieve the status of a certified parts supplier.

"We thank you for your tremendous support, enthusiasm, and energy that you have devoted to this effort. We're confident that it will continue, and we look forward to always pointing with pride to the fine association between our companies."

The message on the plaque reads:

Presented to the Furnas Electric Company in recognition of your outstanding effort and total commitment to the Miller Electric Manufacturing Company Supplier Certification Process. We salute your efforts towards:

100% Quality
100% On-Time Delivery
100% Correct Quantities

As partners in Supplier Certification, we look forward to continued improvements and success.

WHAT IS SUPPLIER CERTIFICATION?

In October 1989, the Purchasing and Quality Assurance Departments began to develop and design the Miller Supplier Certification Process. Supplier Certification is one of the support systems of the overall Total Miller Quality (TMQ) program along with MEIP, SPC, and Business Teams. With over 50% of the sales dollars spent on purchased materials from outside suppliers, management recognizes the impact suppliers have on our product. There is a need for a process to work with our suppliers to assure that they are supplying a total quality part, in the quantity we need, when we need it.

Supplier Certification is a process whereby Miller Electric and its suppliers agree to work as partners to consistently provide a part that has 100% Quality, 100% On-Time Delivery, and 100% Correct Quantities.

Furnas is the first company to achieve the status of a certified parts supplier. A second supplier will be certified shortly, and three more are in process.

A successful certification process relies upon Just-In-Time delivery of zero defect material. Both Miller and its supplier can expect the following benefits:

Higher quality product	satisfied customer, increased business, fewer returns and warranty claims.

Commitment of companies	partnership, trust, cooperation, long term relationship.
Quality parts	elimination of scrap, returns, repairs, and rejects.
Frequent deliveries	set-up reduction, inventory reduction, fewer obsolete parts, less damage to inventory.
Smaller lot sizes	flexibility to schedule changes, meeting the customer's needs.
Reduction in total cost	more competitive product, increased sales.
Greater job satisfaction	fewer rejects, less rework, pride.

Supplier Certification is a very important process because to build the highest quality welders in the industry, we need suppliers who can help us achieve that goal. It is a total team effort. The support and participation of suppliers, teams, and employees are vital to the success of the process.

DYNACHEM ELECTRONIC MATERIALS
Tustin, California

Dynachem Quality Leadership Newsletter
"Improvements Through Involvement"

SUPPLIER CERTIFICATION SYMPOSIUM

As the last of the attendees departed the conference hall, it was becoming apparent that our first "Supplier Certification Symposium" had been a complete and total success. The certification team members that were able to attend and address the group were overwhelmed with the acceptance of their presentations. The March 12 symposium was attended by more than 200 people representing 150 of our worldwide suppliers. The day-long presentation was organized to introduce our evolving supplier certification process.

In support of our mission and vision statements, the process of supplier certification works to ensure Dynachem purchases goods and services from the best possible suppliers. Supplier certification is a process of making choices — choices to work with only the best suppliers providing quality products and services.

The supplier certification process has two primary goals. The first goal is to satisfy our customers. Everything we do as a company must be geared toward providing our customers with products and services that meet their requirements every time. The second goal is to eliminate waste. Waste is anything other than the absolute minimum resources of materials, machines and manpower required to add value to our products.

The supplier certification process was developed by a truly interdisciplinary team. The team included members from not only supporting organizations but from across the nation. The certification structure that has evolved through weekly team conference calls is unique to our business requirements. The team's success stems from their ability to focus and plan during their conference calls while following up on action items between calls.

Our certification program stratifies our suppliers into four classifications:

- **Certified.**
- **Qualified.**
- **Restricted.**
- **New.**

A certified supplier is our supplier of choice, one that has successfully completed the certification program. A certified supplier has received a rating of 90 or more during the evaluation.

Qualified suppliers have completed the evaluation process and received a rating of at least 70. Qualified suppliers will be used without restriction, provided there is no certified supplier for the same product or service.

A restricted supplier is one that has been evaluated and received a rating of 69 or lower. Restricted suppliers are only used when no certified or qualified suppliers offer the needed product or service.

The new supplier classification has been developed for those suppliers that have not been evaluated using the certification process.

The program certifies suppliers in four categories:

- **Production.**
- **Non-Production.**
- **Warehousing.**
- **Transportation.**

It further defines providers of materials or services. The system has established requirements for each category with implementation, selection and measurement criteria worksheets. Consistent throughout the four categories is our requirement that all suppliers must make a commitment that they are willing to work with us to complete the certification process.

In the four months since the symposium was held, nineteen (19) suppliers have been working their way through the 21-step process. To date, the team has reviewed and agreed to certify seven (7) valued suppliers. This is quite an accomplishment! Our congratulations goes out to both the newly certified suppliers and the team that has made the process work!

CONCLUSION

In this, our third edition of **Supplier Certification**, we have accomplished the task of developing a handbook for those who want to know more about this area. Supply Base Management will continue to gain respectability over the next few years. We certainly hope that by our fourth edition that we will be able to report on companies who have achieved World Class status as suppliers and customers. The examples we have provided in this edition from our clients and from seminar attendees show the remarkable progress made to date. We applaud those companies' commitment to Supplier Certification. And now, as we have said many times before, it is important to do something.

Put the book down
and
start the process!

BIBLIOGRAPHY

Peter L. Grieco, Jr., **WORLD CLASS:** *Measuring Its Achievement*, PT Publications, Inc., Palm Beach Gardens, FL.

Peter L. Grieco, Jr., Michael W. Gozzo, **MADE IN AMERICA:** *The Total Business Concept*, PT Publications, Inc., Palm Beach Gardens, FL.

Peter L. Grieco, Jr., Michael W. Gozzo, Jerry W. Claunch, **JUST-IN-TIME PURCHASING:** *In Pursuit of Excellence,* PT Publications, Inc., Palm Beach Gardens, FL.

H. Thomas Johnson, Robert S. Kaplan, **RELEVANCE LOST:** *The Rise and Fall of Management Accounting*, Harvard Business School Press, Boston, MA.

Tom Peters, **THRIVING ON CHAOS:** *Handbook for a Management Revolution*, Knopf, New York, NY.

Armand V. Feigenbaum, **TOTAL QUALITY CONTROL,** McGraw-Hill Book Co., New York, NY.

PRODUCTION AND INVENTORY MANAGEMENT REVIEW and APICS NEWS, Raymond G. Feldman, Editor; Richard D'Alessandro, Publisher; Hollywood, FL.

Lamar Lee, Jr., Donald W. Dobler, **PURCHASING AND MATERIALS MANAGEMENT:** *Text and Cases*, McGraw-Hill Book Co., New York.

PURCHASING MAGAZINE, James P. Morgan, Editor, John F. O'Connor, Publisher, Cahners Publishing Co., Newton, MA.

W. Edwards Deming, **QUALITY, PRODUCTIVITY AND COM-PETITIVE POSITION**, MIT Center for Advanced Engineering Study, Cambridge, MA.

HARVARD BUSINESS REVIEW, Theodore Levitt, Editor; James A. McGowan, Publisher; Boston, MA.

Thomas J. Peters, Robert H. Waterman, **IN SEARCH OF EXCEL-LENCE**, Warner Books, Inc., New York, NY.

Philip B. Crosby, **QUALITY IS FREE**, New American Library, New York, NY.

FORTUNE, Marshall Loeb, Editor, James B. Hayes, Publisher, New York, NY.

TRAFFIC MANAGEMENT, Francis J. Quinn, Editor; Ron Bondlow, Publisher; Cahners Publishing Co., Newton, MA.

MODERN MATERIALS HANDLING, Ray Kulwiec, Editor; William G. Sbordon, Publisher; Cahners Publishing Co., Newton, MA.

Peter L. Grieco, Jr., Paul G. Hine, **THE WORLD OF NEGOTIA-TIONS:** *Never Being a Loser*, PT Publications, Inc., Palm Beach Gardens, FL.

Jerry W. Claunch, Philip D. Stang, **SET-UP REDUCTION:** *Saving Dollars with Common Sense*, PT Publications, Inc., Palm Beach Gardens, FL.

Peter L. Grieco, Jr., Michael W. Gozzo, C.J. (Chip) Long, **BEHIND BARS:** *Bar Coding Principles and Applications*, PT Publications, Inc., Palm Beach Gardens, FL.

CREDITS

Waukesha — Mike Termini

Morton International, Dynachem — LeAnn Zunich

Pepsi-Cola General Bottlers — Bob Wagnon

JI Case — Jim Barbieri

Quantum

Aerojet Ordnance Company

Archive

Loran — Rob Loranger

Kraft-General Foods — Lori White and Ken Hollon

ANSWERS TO QUIZ ON PAGE 218

1. **Assignable Cause** — Special causes of variablity that can be identified and eliminated.

2. **Average** — Sum of values divided by number of values.

3. **C-Chart** — Control chart for plotting data based on total number of nonconformances in a sample.

4. **Capability** — Ability of process to make part to specification dimension. Generally measured by specified dimension to determine the spread of dimension being produced by that process.

5. **Common Cuase** — Variation inherent to a process that collectively influence the natural process fluctuations.

6. **Cp** — Index showing potential process capability by comparing total process spread to the total allowable specifications.

7. **Cpk** — Index showing actual process capability relative to the nearest specification limit.

8. **Loss Function** — Describing monetary loss due to variation — deviation from normal greater than the loss.

9. **Mean** — Measure of central tendency for a group of data values, the x values in a group of measurements, determine by adding all data values divided by the total of the number of data values.

10. **Pareto Chart** — Measures phenomenon whereby a small number of concerns are usually responsible for most quality problems.

11. **Population** — Entire group of objects about which information is wanted.

12. **$\overline{X}$ and R Chart** — Variable control chart including $\overline{X}$ tracks, process average, and R tracks. Range of process variability.

INDEX